One need not be a chamber to be haunted.
Emily Dickinson

Other Cabinet of Curiosities Books
By Troy Taylor

Cabinet of Curiosities 1
The History of the Supernatural in 20 Objects

Cabinet of Curiosities 2
America's Unexplained in 20 Objects

Cabinet of Curiosities 3
The Haunted History of America's Prisons, Hospitals, and Asylums in 20 Objects

CABINET OF CURIOSITIES 4

20 KEYS TO HAUNTED HOTEL ROOMS

TROY TAYLOR

© Copyright 2019 by Troy Taylor
and American Hauntings Ink
All Rights Reserved, including the right to copy or reproduce this book, or portions thereof, in any form, without express permission from the author and publisher.

Original Cover Artwork Designed by
© Copyright 2019 by April Slaughter & Troy Taylor

This Book is Published By:
American Hauntings Ink
Jacksonville, Illinois | 217.791.7859
Visit us on the Internet at
http://www.americanhauntingsink.com

First Edition – November 2019
ISBN: 978-1-7324079-6-1

Printed in the United States of America

TABLE OF CONTENTS

INTRODUCTION – 5

1. THE CECIL HOTEL – 12
2. THE CONGRESS HOTEL – 21
3. THE MENGER HOTEL – 65
4. THE CRESCENT HOTEL – 84
5. THE BOURBON ORLEANS HOTEL – 101
6. THE PFISTER HOTEL – 112
7. THE SEELBACH HOTEL – 120
8. THE ST. JAMES HOTEL – 133
9. THE HAWTHORNE HOTEL – 139
10. THE HOLLYWOOD ROOSEVELT – 150
11. THE SKIRVIN HOTEL – 164
12. THE REVERE HOTEL BOSTON COMMON – 170
13. THE BULLOCK HOTEL – 184
14. THE HOTEL CHELSEA – 201
15. THE MONTE VISTA HOTEL – 212
16. THE BILTMORE HOTEL – 219
17. THE COPPER QUEEN HOTEL – 234
18. THE ORIGINAL SPRINGS HOTEL – 247
19. HOTEL DEL CORONADO – 263
20. THE STANLEY HOTEL – 271

BIBLIOGRAPHY – 281

INTRODUCTION

I didn't give much credence to the ghost stories when I made the reservation at the Ruebel Hotel in Grafton, Illinois. I'd lived in nearby Alton for many years and had heard about the strange events that allegedly occurred when the building was being revitalized. I'd also heard about the ghost of the little girl that had been nicknamed "Abigail," who made frequent appearances for guests. But, as I said, I didn't think much of the stories. Small hotels across the country have long been known for their "ghosts" because, let's face it, having a resident spirit is a great way to book a few extra rooms.

But I'd always liked the Ruebel. I'd made many trips to Grafton over the years and I thought it might make a fun place for my partner, Lisa, and I to stay on our way home from an event in Southwestern Illinois. I'd eaten at the hotel plenty of times – as well as in the other restaurants and pubs in Grafton – but I'd never spent the night there. This was going to be the night.

It was also going to be the night when I would discover that the ghost stories of the Ruebel Hotel were true.

At the western edge of Illinois – where the waters of the Mississippi and Illinois Rivers meet – is the small town of Grafton. The town had gotten its start at the swampy meeting of the rivers in the 1830s, but it didn't truly come into its own until a flood in 1844 ushered in the steamboat era. The riverboats were joined by the railroad in the 1880s and during its peak, three separate lines came into town, making it a rough and often rollicking place. In addition to the railroad and the river men who came to town, many respectable travelers passed through Grafton and the town needed a decent place to stay the night.

In 1884, a former riverboat captain named Michael Ruebel opened what was then the largest hotel in all of Jersey County – the Ruebel Hotel. It had 32 rooms and a bathhouse in the back and mostly played host to riverboat travelers looking for a meal and a nice bed.

The hotel also boasted the finest saloon in town, at a time when there were 26 saloons operating in Grafton, including one called the "Bloody Bucket." The town was a rowdy place, but with a population of mainly Irish and German railroad and quarry workers, who were used to brawling and drinking contests, such a large number of taverns was a necessity. Because of its reputation on the river, the hotel was also frequently visited by river travelers and steamboat operators, further adding to the colorful atmosphere.

The Ruebel thrived until 1912, when it was badly damaged by fire. It was quickly rebuilt. However, this time a restaurant added on the first floor and a dance hall on the second floor. A new bar was installed, which was taken from a building on the grounds of the 1904 World's Fair in St. Louis. During World War II, the dance hall was turned into quarters for 30 Coast Guard men, who were stationed in Grafton to provide protection for the river traffic.

As time went on, the rest of the world passed Grafton by. After two World Wars, the Great Depression, floods, the end of the steamboat era, and the closing of the local rail lines, the town slowly faded away. And the Ruebel Hotel died along with it. By the 1980s, the building had become an abandoned derelict, its heyday long forgotten. Then, following the devastating Mississippi River flood of 1993, life began to return to Grafton. New businesses opened, new homes were built, and the town began to grow. The Ruebel was purchased by the Lorton family – who now own Grafton's Aeries Winery – and they set to work having the hotel restored. It reopened in the spring of 1997.

And that's when the stories started.

The contractors who did the restoration work on the hotel started them. They claimed that while the remodeling was being completed that their tools would vanish and turn up in other places, where they knew they hadn't left them. They said that lights turned on and off, doors mysteriously slammed closed, and their power tools developed a habit of turning on by themselves. It was unnerving, but it didn't send anyone running from the building in terror.

That would come later.

After the hotel opened for business, some of the staff members – and dozens of guests – began to claim that the building was haunted. It wasn't hard for most people to believe. Hotels, especially older ones, are ripe for a haunting. Literally hundreds of people pass through a hotel in any given year and are bound to leave a little piece of themselves behind. With a hotel like the Ruebel, which was more than 100 years old when it reopened, there have been tens of thousands of people who stayed within its walls.

Guests and staff spoke of doors locking and unlocking, objects disappearing, towels being tossed onto the floor, sheets and blankets being pulled from beds, and much more. Once in the middle of the night, a couple from the Chicago area woke up to see the television in their room turning on and off, followed by the slamming of their bathroom door. They cut their stay short and drove home immediately.

Who is the ghost that haunts the hotel? According to three overnight guests who met her face-to-face, she is a little blond-haired girl in a nightgown who roams the upstairs hallway and sometimes sits on the staircase that leads to the second floor. They reported the encounter to the staff, who started calling the spirit "Abigail." She has been seen in the hotel many times since it was reopened, but more commonly, she is heard. Guests say that they have often awakened at night to hear the sound of a child crying in the hallway outside of their rooms. When they checked to see what was going on, there was never anyone there. No one knows who "Abigail" might have been in life, but she is a sad little spirit in death.

Or, as I believed, so the story went... Having a resident ghost seemed to be a great way to drum up business and to get the hotel listed in places as a haunted spot. Hotels like the Ruebel all over the country do the same thing and when you write about this kind of stuff for a living, you know how it all works for struggling small business owners.

We didn't come to the Ruebel looking for a ghost. We just wanted to soak up the atmosphere of the old hotel and enjoy the town, which we did.

The ghost just turned out to be a bonus.

After dinner and drinks at some local establishments, we retired for the night. Things were quiet and I expected a good night's sleep. I didn't expect to be awakened around 3:00 a.m. to a baby crying out in the hallway. It was loud and right outside the door. Luckily, it didn't last long, and I assumed that the other guests, who had a small child with them, had been able to calm the baby down and had gone back to bed.

I probably wouldn't have thought any more about the incident if Lisa hadn't mentioned it at breakfast the next morning. I asked how she had slept, and she told me that she'd been awakened around 3:00 a.m. by a crying child in the corridor outside the room. It hadn't lasted long, she said, and then she went back to sleep.

I wish that I could remember the entire conversation that I had with the desk clerk when I turned in the room key that morning. It was just a chat, but somehow the conversation turned to the crying child in the night. I believe I asked if everything had been okay with the other guests and the clerk stared at me blankly.

"What do you mean?" she asked.

"I just wondered if anyone was bothered by the baby crying in the hall last night?" I replied. "I remember what it's like to have a little kid in a hotel and you never want to feel like you're bothering other people."

The clerk was just as confused as she had been by my first question. "There were no kids here last night. There were no other guests. You were the only people in the building. We locked up and left at midnight."

She was wrong, though. We weren't alone in the hotel. Abigail was there, too.

This installment of the ongoing Cabinet of Curiosities series is a book that is likely the closest thing that I have done with the series to a road trip – it's a visit to haunted hotels. I must tell you that it wasn't easy to pick only 20 of them across America. There are a lot of hotels out there with a reputation for being haunted. I had to sort through all of them – leaving out the small inns and bed and breakfasts – to put together a list of what I'd call my favorites.

Once again, I decided to tell these hauntings tales through a collection of objects – this time through room keys – that have been enclosed in the Cabinet of Curiosities that can be found within the pages of this book. During the Renaissance era, Cabinets of Curiosities were collections of marvels and unusual objects that were dedicated to things that, in those days, were not yet defined. Modern man would categorize the books, writings, and artifacts found in these cases as pieces of natural history, geology, archaeology, religious or historic relics, art, and sometimes outright bits of humbug like petrified mermaid carcasses and fish with fur. But no matter what the cabinets contained; they were collections of the unexplained. Even in those days, everyone loved a mystery. Man has always loved to question, to wonder, and to be baffled by things that he cannot understand. Cabinets of Curiosities were all the rage among those who could afford them and were eventually considered to be a precursor of the modern museum.

My own cabinet is a different sort. There are no fossils in it, no badly preserved bodies of mysterious animals – no, my cabinet is different, although it's just as puzzling as those from the past. My cabinet contains records and remnants of the supernatural – a curious collection of objects (both literal and figurative ones) that tell the story of the unexplained in our modern world. In this case, they tell the story of hotels that dot the landscape of America, leaving a haunting presence behind.

In the pages ahead, I'll be presenting a collection of 20 keys from 20 unique locations. Through the stories of these keys, the reader will enter the hotel rooms where death, tragedy, suicide, and misfortune occurred. As often as I can, I'll reveal the identities of the ghosts that are attached to those hotels and the reason that each was chosen to be on this list.

Some of the keys will unlock the doors of famous places like the Stanley Hotel, the Crescent Hotel, the Congress Plaza, and the Hotel Del Coronado, while others will take us inside of Route 66 icons, small town lodgings, and perhaps even places you've never heard of before.

But every key will tell a story and, in this book, the 20 that I have chosen will offer a chilling look at how the locations that they unlock have affected the haunted history of America. Each represents one of the most haunted places where you can stay overnight across the country.

I hope this new collection will inspire you to get on the road and check out some of these places for yourself. You never know what might happen behind the locked door of your haunted hotel room – perhaps you'll end up a story in a future book!

Good luck sleeping tonight,
Troy Taylor
Fall 2019

1. THE CECIL HOTEL
LOS ANGELES, CALIFORNIA

You've seen it on television, and you may have heard some of the stories, but there is little that can prepare you for the real-life tales of horror, death, murder, suicide, and spirits that haunt the Cecil Hotel in downtown Los Angeles. The City of Angels is supposed to be a place of sunshine, palm trees, movie stars, and sandy beaches.

But strange stories lurk here, often in places where you might least expect them.

The Cecil Hotel has a long history in the city, dating back to the 1920s. In recent years, the hotel has been renamed to Stay on Main, but the old original signs remain in place, as if the owners know that no amount of rebranding will ever erase the place's sordid and bloody past.

In 1924, hotel entrepreneur William Banks Hanner commissioned the construction of the Cecil Hotel. He envisioned a lavish, 600-room building with stained-glass windows, upscale rooms, expensive décor, and a gleaming marble lobby. Hanner hoped the rich design and spectacular amenities would attract tourists and business travelers alike. In 1927, the Cecil opened its doors, and it soon became a hot spot in downtown L.A.

But the good times of the Roaring '20s didn't last for long. In October 1929, the stock market crashed, signaling the start of the Great Depression. Cities across the country were impacted by the economic collapse, including Los Angeles. While the Cecil held onto its glamorous appeal through the 1940s, the bright lights of the surrounding neighborhood dimmed. Thousands of the homeless moved into the area, and Main Street, where the hotel stands, became L.A.'s Skid Row. Travelers and businessmen began looking for other, safer places to stay when they came to town.

In the years that followed, the hotel fell on hard times, turning into a sleazy spot that invited crime, drug use, prostitution, and violence. It was during these years that the darkest moments in the Cecil Hotel's history took place.

The first of many suicides to occur at the Cecil took place in 1927. Leaving behind a note in which he wrote that he had spent $40,000 in the last six months in a vain attempt to buy happiness, Percy Ormond Cook, shot himself in his room at the Cecil on January 22. According to the note, Cook had been a successful real estate developer in Providence, Rhode Island, but after being separated from his wife and son for several months, he decided the only way to escape his loneliness and despair was suicide. He wrote a letter to his wife, informing her of his plans, and then spent a week working up the courage to pull the trigger.

"Money cannot buy happiness," Cook wrote in his farewell message. "I have tried it and I find that it cannot be done. I have lost my wife, my son and my home, and I am doing the only thing left for me to do."

The next suicide took place in 1931. A Manhattan Beach man named W.K. Norton, 46, disappeared from his home on Saturday,

November 14, and checked into the Cecil under the assumed name of James Willys from Chicago. His body was discovered by a maid in his hotel room on November 19. He had apparently swallowed several capsules containing poison to end his life. The police found more of them in his vest pocket. Other items in his clothing revealed him to be Norton.

A little less than a year later, 25-year-old Benjamin Dodich checked into the Cecil with a gun in his suitcase. When the maid entered his room to clean it on September 17, 1932, she discovered his body. He had shot himself in the right temple only a few hours after he had checked in. Detective Lieutenant Baggot of the Central Homicide Squad could offer no reason for the suicide.

On July 27, 1934, former Army Medical Sergeant Louis D. Borden, 53, was also discovered dead in his room at the Cecil. He cut his own throat with a straight razor. He left behind a series of farewell notes, each detailing his poor health, which was the main reason why he decided to end his life. In one brief note, he asked that Mrs. Edna Hasoner of Edmonds, Washington, be the "sole beneficiary of the little I leave."

Grace E. Magro, 25, became the first person to fall to her death from one of the hotel's upper floors on March 14, 1937. When she jumped – or fell, her cause of death was never determined – from the ninth floor, telephone wires were ripped from poles during her descent and became entangled about her body. Police officers stated that M.W. Madison, a 26-year-old sailor from the *U.S.S. Virginia*, who had been sharing a bed with Grace, was sleeping at the time of the occurrence and could give no explanation as to how or why she would have gone out the window.

Leaving no note to explain his action, Marine fireman Roy Thompson, 38, took what police called a "suicide leap" from the 14th floor of the Cecil on Sunday, January 9, 1938. Registered at the hotel for several weeks, Thompson jumped from the window of his room. His body was found atop a skylight on a next-door building by a hotel employee, who called the police.

On Sunday, May 28, 1938, a 39-year-old Navy officer named Erwin C. Neblett checked into the hotel, took a large dose of poison, and then died soon after at an emergency hospital. He left a note behind that simply stated that he was "disgusted with life."

A schoolteacher named Dorothy Sceiger, 45, was discovered in her room at the Cecil after swallowing poison on January 10, 1940. Still alive, she was rushed to the Georgia Street Receiving Hospital, but she succumbed to the poison a short time later.

In 1947, Robert Smith, 35, jumped to his death from a window on the hotel's seventh floor. In 1954, 55-year-old Helen Gurnee also jumped from the seventh floor to her death. In 1962, Julia Moore, 50, jumped from an eighth-floor window to perish on the sidewalk below.

On Friday, October 12, 1962, Pauline Otton, 27, plummeted to her death from the ninth floor of the Cecil, killing an elderly man strolling on the sidewalk below. Pauline had been discussing marital problems with her estranged husband, Dewey, in the hotel room, and when he left for dinner, she jumped from the window. At first, detectives thought Pauline, and George Gianinni, 65, might have leapt from the window together, but they found that the man had his hands in his pockets and that he was still wearing his shoes, which investigators believed would have been knocked off if he'd fallen nine stories.

In 1975, an unidentified woman jumped from the twelfth floor of the building. She registered as "Alison Lowell" when she checked into the hotel, and authorities were never able to discover her real identity.

The most recent suicide associated with the Cecil occurred in 2015 when an unidentified man was found dead in front of the building. His body was in horrible condition, so it was presumed that he fell to his death, though no official cause of death was determined.

In addition to the hotel's inordinate number of suicides, the Cecil is also infamous for its history of violence, murder, and grisly deaths.

One of the most chilling incidents occurred on September 5, 1944, when 19-year-old Dorothy Purcell threw her baby boy to his death from an upper-floor window at the Cecil. Dorothy had been staying at the hotel for several days with Ben Levine, 38, a shoe salesman. She woke early that morning and realized that she was about to give birth. Not wanting to wake up her bed companion, she went to the hotel restroom on the same floor and delivered the baby alone. After giving birth, Purcell claimed she believed that the baby was stillborn, and threw him out of the window. The newborn's body landed on the roof of the building next door. Purcell was charged with murder and tried for the crime. In January 1945, she was found not guilty by reason of insanity.

Violence occurred again on June 4, 1964, when a hotel staff member found "Pigeon Goldie" Osgood dead in her room. Osgood, a retired telephone operator, was a resident at the hotel and was known locally for her daily trips to the park to feed the pigeons, hence the nickname. The hotel room had been ransacked. Next to Goldie on the bed was the Dodgers baseball cap she always wore, and a paper bag filled with bird seed. Investigators who were called to the scene determined that she had been raped, stabbed, and beaten to death.

A few hours after the murder, police arrested Jacques Ehlinger, 29, while he was walking through Pershing Square, where Osgood went to feed the birds, wearing bloodstained clothing. He admitted that he knew Goldie and had been near the hotel at the time the murder occurred but denied any connection to her murder. He was arrested but soon cleared of the charges.

As the police looked closer at the circumstances of Goldie's death, they realized that it had a remarkable resemblance to another recent murder. On May 16, 1964, Viva Brown was also murdered in a nearby hotel. The two slayings were linked after Goldie's autopsy report showed that she had been killed and assaulted in an almost exact manner as Viva Brown.

But to this day, both murders remain unsolved.

The most notorious murder linked to the Cecil Hotel didn't actually occur there, but the connection came from the fact that it was a favorite hangout of a young woman named Elizabeth Short.

On January 15, 1947, Beth's murder became the first major crime to galvanize the city of Los Angeles after World War II. Her body was discovered in the Leimert Park neighborhood of the city and the case became highly publicized due to the graphic nature of the crime, which included her corpse having been mutilated and bisected at the waist.

Beth spent her early life in Medford, Massachusetts and Florida before relocating to California, where her father lived, seeking fame in the Hollywood film industry. She acquired the nickname of the "Black Dahlia" after her death, thanks to her nightly prowls through the bars of Hollywood while dressed all in black. After the discovery of her body, the Los Angeles Police Department began an extensive investigation that produced over 150 suspects but yielded no arrests. To this day, Beth's murder remains unsolved.

It should come as no surprise that some witnesses still claim to occasionally spot Beth at the hotel bar, alone, and sipping a drink.

The Cecil was also the home for two different serial killers in the 1980s and 1990s. In the mid-1980s, Richard Ramirez, who became known as the "Night Stalker," preyed on Los Angeles women, breaking into their homes and brutally raping and killing them. He used a wide variety of weapons, including handguns, knives, a machete, a tire iron, and a hammer. Ramirez, who was an avowed Satanist, never expressed any remorse for his crimes. The judge who upheld Ramirez's 13 death sentences remarked that his deeds exhibited "cruelty, callousness, and viciousness beyond any human understanding".

Before his capture, Ramirez often stayed at the Cecil and sometimes tossed his bloodstained clothing in the hotel's dumpster.

In 1991, Austrian serial killer and journalist Johann Unterweger became a long-term resident of the Cecil Hotel when he was assigned to write an article about prostitution in America. Unterweger had already been convicted of murder in Austria in 1974, but was released after 15 years in prison after convincing the authorities that he was reformed. In L.A., he went back to his old habits and murdered three of the sex workers that he was writing about. He was arrested in 1992, convicted of murder, and sentenced to life in prison without the possibility of paroles in 1994. On the night of his sentencing, Unterweger hanged himself in his cell.

One of the strangest occurrences to take place at the Cecil Hotel involved Elisa Lam, a 21-year-old Canadian college student who checked into the hotel on January 28, 2013. She was scheduled to leave L.A. and travel to Santa Cruz on January 31, but when her parents didn't hear from her, they called the police.

A little over two weeks after Elisa Lam's apparent disappearance, guests at the hotel began complaining of low water pressure. On the morning of February 19, staff members went to check the hotel's four rooftop water tanks and found Elisa's naked body floating in one of the tanks.

Investigators struggled to make sense of Elisa's final hours and her mysterious death. The hotel's roof is off limits to guests. The doors are kept locked and only staff members have keys and passcodes. Any attempt to force open the doors would have triggered an alarm. The water tanks are also nearly impossible to access and, presuming that Elisa was alone, also challenging to close from inside.

And then there was the elevator surveillance video recorded at the hotel.

The hotel video showed Elisa in one of its elevators, on the date of her disappearance, behaving erratically. In the pixelated footage, she can be seen stepping into the elevator and pushing all the floor buttons. She steps in and out of the elevator, poking her head out sideways toward the hotel's hallways. She peers out of the elevator another few times before stepping out of the elevator entirely. The last minutes of the video show Elisa standing by the left side of the door, moving her hands in random gestures, and pressing herself into the corner of the elevator car. She appears to be speaking to someone, but she is alone in the video. Investigators released the clip as part of their investigation. It soon went viral, with many viewers finding it unsettling to watch.

The Los Angeles coroner's office ruled that Elisa's death was the result of accidental drowning, with bipolar disorder contributing to the cause of death. After she had checked into the hotel, she had been staying in a hostel-like room with other young people. After a number of complaints from others in the dorm situation, she was moved out of the room by hotel staff. It is believed that she was not taking her medication properly or had missed several doses, leading to her strange behavior and death.

Still, many questions remain, fueling speculation and internet conspiracy theories. Some point to Elisa's mental state. Others suspect foul play. While others -- especially those focused on the eerie elevator footage -- believe paranormal forces were at work.

This comes as no surprise, based on the myriad of accounts that state that the Cecil Hotel is one of the most haunted places in the city. Its long history of suicide, death, violence, and murder make it a likely place to find restless, lingering spirits.

One incident with a ghost even made the local news in 2014. A Riverside boy named Koston Alderete noticed a window from the outside of the Cecil. He claims that he got a creepy feeling, like the window was staring at him, so he took a photo of it. When he viewed the picture, Alderete could see a transparent figure standing on the ledge of the window as if about to jump, or as if they were standing on a balcony that no longer existed.

Other accounts of hauntings at the hotel are less documented but are told and re-told in newspaper stories, on podcasts, and even paranormal television shows – shows that often show up at the Cecil, looking for spirits.

The hotel is plagued by shadow figures. Staff members are afraid to go into the basement because of the shadows that seem to chase them. Some guests have claimed to see shadow figures in their rooms, out of the corner of their eye.

Guests are sometimes tormented while they sleep. There are accounts of bedsheets being tugged at, being sat on by an unseen person, as well as multiple accounts of guests dreaming of a strange figure in the room, and, once they wake up, they see a figure before it quickly disappears. One spirit has a penchant for hugging people while they are sleeping; however, the spirit then escalates to forced tickling. One guest recalled the spirit holding down her foot so she could not move, and then tickling her until it felt like it would scratch her skin off. Guests have entered their rooms to see someone sleeping in their bed, but when they go to remove the blanket, it collapses with no one underneath it.

The bathrooms are just as haunted as the bedrooms are. There are accounts of faucets and showers being turned on when no one is using them, and then when people go to check, they are turned off before they arrive. Once the person begins to leave, the faucet turns back on, as if someone is playing a trick. Some guests hear a person singing or humming, sometimes in the shower when the room is empty.

Guests can hear shrieking coming from the rooms where people died and sounds coming from rooms that should be vacant. Doors and windows can be heard opening, especially the roof access door that Elisa Lam used to get to the water tanks. Hotel staff members have recounted cleaning a room in its entirety, and, after looking away, they turn back to find the room in shambles. Possibly most terrifying of all, at night, you can hear screams coming from outside as if someone is falling from the top of the building.

If you are a traveler in search of a haunted hotel, then the Cecil Hotel – or Stay on Main, as it is called these days – may be just the place for you. If you are hoping to get a good night's sleep, though, it's probably not something you should count on.

2. CONGRESS PLAZA HOTEL
CHICAGO, ILLINOIS

Built in 1893 to accommodate the scores of tourists arriving in Chicago for the World's Fair, the Congress Hotel was regarded as the most elegant establishment of its kind in the city. The ballrooms and restaurants inside of the hotel were the finest in Chicago and attracted both travelers and city-dwellers to its doors. History has left quite a mark on this old hotel in the way of both triumph and tragedy – and has left a myriad of ghosts behind.

The World's Columbian Exposition, the formal name of the fair, attracted people from all over the nation and beyond to Chicago. It was grand and amazing event and like nothing that America had ever seen before. The magnificent halls, looming pavilions, fabulous attractions, and amazing wonders of the fair were the stuff that dreams were made from. There is a reason that the "White City," as the fairgrounds were known, inspired Chicago writer L. Frank Baum to change the color of the city to emerald when he transported it to the Land of Oz.

Countless people came to the fair by train, steamship, and road, all hoping to get a glimpse of the gleaming city by the lake and to walk the fairgrounds, where marvels, sensations, and curiosities waited to be discovered. Ordinary folks mortgaged their farms and dipped into their lifesavings to make the journey. For the tourists who came from all over the country – and from countries around the world – Chicago offered every sort of accommodation possible. Visitors with healthy bank accounts could stay at a luxury hotel downtown, while those on smaller budgets were happy to settle for a well-kept boardinghouse. The demand was so great for decent lodging, especially on the South Side, within walking distance of the fairgrounds, that anyone with a clean room to spare could pick up a few extra dollars by renting out a room to a desperate tourist. A landlord with even a few empty apartments could make a nice profit in a very short amount of time.

But a wealthy businessmen and hotel developer like R.H. Southgate, aware of the deluge of people that was coming, was able to plan ahead and open a brand-new hotel just in time for the fair. He hired Clinton Warren, a former employee of Burnham and Root -- the firm that had constructed the magnificent buildings and pavilions of the White City -- to build his hotel as an adjunct to the Auditorium Theatre. The theater was already located at the northwest corner of South Michigan Avenue and Congress Street. Southgate also brought in the designers of the Auditorium to serve as consultants so that the two structures would be harmonious.

What is now the North Tower of the Congress Plaza Hotel opened as the Auditorium Annex in 1893. It originally had 500 rooms. The facades of the hotel and the theater matched and there was even an underground passageway – known as "Peacock Alley" – that connected the two. The passageway earned an international reputation. Diplomats. Opera stars, writers, artists, socialites, sportsmen, dignitaries, politicians, and celebrities of every kind passed through Peacock Alley, making it a legend. Believe it or not, it's still there but has been bricked off for years.

After the fair, the hotel began to expand. In 1898, a squarish, four-story block of rooms was attached to the south side of the North Tower along Michigan Avenue. The South Tower was added between 1902 and 1907 to serve as apartments. One part of the new construction was the Gold Room, a massive ballroom that was the first venue of this type to be air-conditioned in the city.

One floor above the Gold Room was the Florentine Room, a slightly smaller room decorated with reproductions of Italian paintings on the ceiling. This room became a favorite of politicians. It was in this room that Theodore Roosevelt made the startling announcement that he was leaving the Republican Party, under which he had served as president from 1901-1909. Six weeks later, Roosevelt was back in the Florentine Room and it served as his headquarters during a bid for presidency as the nominee of the Progressive Party, which, after a remark made by Roosevelt to reporters in the room, became known as the Bull Moose Party. The Florentine Room eventually became a popular spot for women's suffrage meetings, as well as dances, skating parties, and banquets.

Along with the Elizabethan Room and the Pompeian Room, two other event rooms, the Congress Plaza --as it was rebranded by new owners – soon became the favorite hotel for Chicago society. By then, the place boasted more than 1,000 guest rooms.

Each passing decade seemed to add to the hotel's history. It was often referred to as Chicago's "Home of Presidents." Several of them – including Grover Cleveland, William McKinley, Theodore Roosevelt, William Howard Taft, Woodrow Wilson, Warren Harding, Calvin Coolidge, Franklin D. Roosevelt, and Richard Nixon – either stayed there, attended political events there, or made a public address at one of its events. The hotel's Presidential Suite was where the phrase the "smoke-filled room" was born and became a place where political hopefuls discussed their colorful campaigns.

In the 1930s, the Elizabethan Room became known all over the country when it was turned into a dance club with a revolving bandstand. In 1935 and 1936, the nightspot was branded the Joseph Urban Room and NBC radio broadcasts from the Congress, featuring bandleader Benny Goodman, introduced much of the nation to swing music.

The hotel played host to guests that included Lillian Russell, "Diamond Jim" Brady, "Buffalo Bill" Cody, Thomas Edison, Jean Harlow, Wallace Beery, Eleanor Roosevelt, Jack Dempsey, the Vanderbilts, Astors, Rockefellers, Palmers, Rothschilds, and many more.

During World War II, the U.S. War Department took over the hotel and used one portion of it for federal offices and as army officers' quarters, but it was returned to private hands when the war ended. The hotel has been through several ownerships since then, each putting their own stamp on this historic landmark. Today, the hotel has 871 rooms and suites and continues to draw travelers from around the country.

And many of them come here not just for a nice place to stay along South Michigan Avenue but because of the hotel's unusual history. It hasn't always been happy travelers, society parties, and swing music – the Congress Plaza definitely has a dark side. Over the years, the hotel has been linked to mobsters, murders, bizarre occurrences, suicides, unusual deaths, and, of course, many stories of ghosts.

In the late nineteenth century, the Congress – still known then as the Auditorium Annex – was the venue of choice for Chicago's rich and sometimes infamous. But haven for society folks or not, the hotel was already becoming a hotbed for scandal.

On March 21, 1899, prominent State Street merchant John T. Shayne was shot in the café of the Auditorium Annex. The wealthy hatter and furrier had been having lunch with two female acquaintances and his fiancée, who he planned to marry in April. The man who shot him, Harry Hammond, was a merchant tailor who owned his own company on Wabash Avenue. The two men had been friends for many years, so one might wonder what caused one of them to try and kill the other.

Shayne's fiancée was Martha Hammond – Harry's recently divorced wife.

Shayne and his party had entered the restaurant around 1:30 p.m. With John and Martha were two friends, Mrs. James Davis and Miss A. Howard, and they were seated at a table in the middle of the room. They had been in the restaurant only about 15 minutes when Howard came in through the Michigan Avenue entrance. He stopped just inside the door and looked around until his eyes fell on their table. He then walked directly toward them. Miss Howard, facing the door, saw Hammond approaching and she whispered across the table to Martha.

"Hush," Martha whispered back. "Say nothing and don't see him."

Shayne was talking to Mrs. Davis at the time and didn't hear the exchange.

Hammond rushed up to the table and, without a word, produced a handgun from his coat. He pointed at Shayne's head, steadying his right hand with his left, and fired.

At the sound of the shot, Martha sprang to her feet and screamed, "He will shoot me! He will shoot me, too!" Then she ran, still screaming, across the restaurant, followed by her friends, who were also wailing in terror.

Hammond's initial bullet missed Shayne and struck the back of his chair. He tried to scramble to his feet but slipped and fell on his hands and knees. He shuffled forward under the table and was almost out of sight when Hammond fired again, striking Shayne in the back. He let out a cry of pain but continued to crawl beneath the table. Hammond grabbed the tablecloth in his hands and whipped it free, exposing the cowering man. He fired a third time, striking Shayne in the right thigh.

Then Hammond stood up, tucked his gun into his pocket, and walked slowly toward the door. He never said a word, before or after the shooting.

Meanwhile, the restaurant guests were in a panic. There were more than 50 men, women, and children in the room when the first shot rang out and there was a mad rush for the door that led into the hotel's lobby. Among the guests was Edith Ogden Harrison, wife of Chicago's mayor. She was one of the first to reach the entrance and cried out for the manager, "There's a crazy man, a lunatic; he is shooting!" A rush of people followed her into the lobby and some of the men sought refuge in the tunnel that led to the Auditorium Theater. They did not stop running until halfway through the passage.

Paul Gores and W.A. Dunning, the clerks on duty at the time, rushed to the entrance of the dining room when they heard the shots and tried to allay the panic of the guests. Following the frightened diners, Harry Hammond walked coolly from the entrance. He was met by Paul Gores.

"He did it! Arrest him!" several men cried out.

Hammond replied, "You know me, Paul. It's all right."

"Yes, I know you," Gores said and grabbed Hammond by the arm. "What did you fire for?"

"I shot him," Hammond muttered and gestured back toward the restaurant.

Another man stepped forward. "He shot John T. Shayne," he said and took Hammond by the other arm. They took Hammond toward the hotel office, trying to get him out of sight of the flustered guests. As they walked toward the office door, Hammond reached into his coat and pulled out the revolver. When he did, the crowd of excited men on the scene understandably backed away.

"Here is the gun," he said and handed it over to his captors. They took him into the office to await the arrival of the hotel detective, who would summon the police. Hammond refused to explain why he had shot Shayne.

"It will all come out in the end," he said.

Not everyone had fled from the restaurant. While Hammond was being taken into custody, several men were rushing to Shayne's assistance. He was still lying under the table, bleeding from his wounds. They pulled him from beneath the table and he carefully got to his feet. "I can walk," Shayne told them, but then he sank to the floor. The men managed to get him into a chair, and they carried him out of the dining room.

"The man who shot me was Harry Hammond!" he called out as he was loaded into the elevator and taken upstairs to room 1202. He was examined by the hotel doctor and the two bullet wounds were discovered. He sent for a surgeon, who agreed to come as soon as possible. Martha Hammond and her friends, as soon as they recovered their wits in the housekeeper's room, joined Shayne in the suite. By then, he had been given an anesthetic to prepare him for surgery. She refused to speak to anyone about the shooting.

Her former husband was also refusing to talk. He quietly submitted to arrest by detectives and was taken to the Harrison Street police station. He wasn't booked – his charges would depend on whether or not Shayne survived – but was locked in a cell. He told officers that he would not speak until his attorney, George W. Miller, arrived. Even then, he would not speak with the bevy of reporters who crowded into the station, all hoping for a scoop on the motive behind the attack.

When he finally revealed the reason that he tried to kill Shayne, it caused a sensation in the city. "I know what I have done, "Hammond said, "I know it too well. I know that this man posed as my friend. I know that I went into the Annex and saw him sitting alongside Mrs. Hammond. I knew that Mrs. Hammond was to become Mrs. Shayne next month. I know that the man I shot down despoiled my happiness, broke up my home, and destroyed my piece of mind."

Shayne had stolen his wife and Hammond wanted to punish him for it.

While Shayne was in surgery, his attorney spoke on his behalf. John Goodrich simply stated, "The shooting was deliberate. Hammond came into the room and fired the shots with the utmost deliberation. I do not know what his object was. I cannot tell what was in his mind that provoked the attack unless it was insane jealousy, but there can be no doubt as to premeditation."

Goodrich didn't know it at the time, but he had just offered Hammond his defense.

However, he went on to add that the relationship between Shayne and Martha Hammond had been open and discussed with Hammond prior to plans for the wedding being made. The Hammonds were already divorced, he claimed – which would turn out to be untrue – when Shayne began courting her. Shayne's wife had died several years before and before her death, the two couples had been friends. After

Martha sued her husband for divorce, obtaining custody of their four-year-old son, she had started seeing John Shayne.

"Hammond never had any provocation, before or after the divorce, to justify the shooting," Goodrich added. "It was a cowardly act and one that showed Hammond's character."

But the lawyer was going to find out that a jury didn't agree with him.

John Shayne was in serious condition after the shooting, perhaps more from infection caused by the probing of the surgeon in a hotel room than from the bullets themselves. Fearing that he was near death, he and his attorney drew up a will, leaving his entire estate of about $200,000 to his son, Roy, a student at Cornell University.

Somehow, though, he survived. He and Martha were married, and he was recovered enough by the fall of 1899 to see his assailant go on trial for attempted murder. The trial began in early November and lasted only a few days. Hammond's lawyers insisted that he had been temporarily insane at the time of the shooting. It was a difficult case to make but it likely didn't really matter. On November 11, 1899, the jury – which only deliberated for two hours – found Harry Hammond "not guilty."

Only one of the jurors went on record with the press when the trial was over. He told a reporter, "It was a question whether a rich man could go into the home of a poor man and steal his wife, and I would have stayed there a hundred years before I would vote to convict Harry Hammond."

John Shayne, the jury believed, had deserved it.

Ten years later, Shayne would be dead. He died on August 20, 1909, at the Kenilworth Insane Asylum, where Martha had placed him two years before.

Shayne's sanity was called into question in September 1906, when he was called before a judge to prove his mental fitness. Even though family and friends tried to keep the proceedings secret, the newspapers learned of the story. Some believed that the shooting at the Auditorium Annex was to blame for his insanity, but friends insisted that it was stress caused by overwork. Shayne testified on his own behalf and while records don't exist of what he said, the judge found him mentally unfit and turned his business over to a conservator and placed Shayne in Martha's custody. A year later, unable to care for him herself, he was placed in the asylum where he died.

It was a strange end to a story of jealously, violence, and madness.

Although the gangland "one-way ride" didn't become a slang term in the Chicago underworld until the 1920s, the first such ride took place in 1904 – and it left from the Auditorium Annex Hotel.

A "one-way ride" occurred when a victim was taken by car to a remote location where they were killed, and then their body was dumped there. The moniker for this kind of execution was reportedly first used by North Side gangster Earl "Hymie" Weiss, who was the last man seen in the company of Steve Wisniewski, a criminal who had recently hijacked one of his Weiss's beer shipments in July 1921. When Weiss returned from his jaunt, he explained the other man's disappearance by saying he, "took Stevie for a one-way ride."

The "one-way ride" was used countless times during the Prohibition era, but the city's first "one-way ride" took place on November 18, 1904, when a dashing ladies' man named John William "Billy" Bate left the Auditorium Annex in an automobile with his killer at his side.

His killer was a mysterious man known only as "Mr. Dove." Around 8:00 p.m. he had asked a desk clerk to telephone a garage on Wabash Avenue – the Dan Canary Garage – and request a car and driver. The call was placed, and Dove asked for a vehicle that would accommodate two passengers. After some bargaining, he agreed to pay the driver $5 per hour.

At the garage, Billy Bate was passing the time with some other drivers playing a game of coin toss. Bate agreed to take the car request and he asked the night manager if Dove was "all right." Edwin Archer, who had taken the call but later remembered nothing more about it than that the customer argued about the price, told Bate, "I don't know, and I don't care. Get your money and pick him up."

Just after 9:00 p.m., Billy arrived at the Auditorium Annex to pick up his two passengers. Only one was waiting for him – Mr. Dove.

Witnesses later described Dove as a wealthy-looking man who was attired in evening clothes and a derby hat. A bystander later stated that Mr. Dove left the hotel with a small valise and climbed into the car.

By 9:15, they were traveling south on Michigan Avenue. Billy was driving a mint green Pope-Toledo touring car and was wearing a chauffer's cap, goggles, and driving gloves. It was the last time that Billy was seen alive – and the last time that "Mr. Dove" was seen at all.

On the morning of November 19, a farmer named Peter Freehauf found the touring car parked along an abandoned road near his home in south suburban Lemont. Billy Bate was slumped over the steering wheel and he had been shot twice in the back of the head with a .22-caliber pistol.

Billy's death seemed a mystery to police until they uncovered the existence of the mysterious Mr. Dove, as well as Billy's string of jilted girlfriends.

Officers questioned everyone who lived in the rural area and found a farmhand, on his way home from a date the night before, had seen Billy's car around midnight. It had been parked on Archer Avenue, about three miles from Lemont. He had seen three people in the car – and one of them was a woman.

Peter Freehauf, who first telephoned the police that morning, was not surprised to find a body in the car. He and his wife had heard someone pounding on their door during the early morning hours, followed by two gunshots in rapid succession. The couple huddled in terror, refusing to open the door. They didn't go out until dawn, when they found Billy's corpse.

After speaking to the staff at the Auditorium Annex, they started searching for Mr. Dove. They were able to trace some of his movements. He had continued to Joliet by train, wagon, or some other method, pausing at a boarding house to purchase a bottle of benzine (a harsh cleaning solution) to get some of the blood out of his clothes. A kitchen helper at the house described Dove as a nervous chain-smoker who smelled of women's perfume. They noted that his teeth were very small and white and that he had a soft voice "like a woman." He apparently confessed to having a girlfriend in Pittsburgh, which the police found interesting since Bate claimed to have a fiancée there.

They entertained the idea that the chauffer had been murdered by a woman posing as a man but then eventually concluded that Dove was a man, albeit an effeminate one.

Mr. Dove boarded a train in Joliet the next day and was never seen again.

The police pulled five love letters from Billy's vest pocket and the next day, the *Chicago American* printed allegations that Bate was keeping company with a wealthy society matron and had left a trail of broken hearts and spurned lovers that extended from New York to Chicago. One of the more poignant letters was from a woman named "Rose" who wrote:

> *I understand you have won the love of Bertha, and I presume that you have no further use for me. I hope that your future love will be successful. Of course, it is pretty hard on me, but I will let the matter drop and say no more. With love, Rose*

Investigators scoured the countryside looking for clues to the identity of the woman who was seen in Billy's car. They even searched for a body; in case she had been murdered, too. Detectives feared that she might have been picked up outside Chicago, murdered, and then dumped before Billy was killed. The nearby canal and the roadside ditches were searched, but no trace of her was ever found. If a woman had been murdered during this drama, the killer had caused her corpse to vanish without a trace.

The Bate murder mystery -- although mostly forgotten today -- was the subject of newspaper stories and gossip for many weeks to come. It soon stalled out, though, and went cold. We will never know for sure what happened that night but Billy Bate earned his place in Chicago criminal history as the victim of the city's first "one-way ride."

And the Congress Hotel gained infamy as the place where it began.

In 1908, Chicago – and in particular, the Auditorium Annex Hotel – attracted the attention of infamous anti-liquor crusader Carrie Nation. On the night of July 13, she startled patrons when she barged into the Pompeian Room with her trusty hatchet and proclaimed that she was going to "clean out the darkest spot in the house." Dressed all in black, she stood in the center of the floor with her right hand raised above her head and loudly denounced the patrons of the lounge. She criticized the men she saw with women at the tables and accused them of being "women's downfall." She grilled the management, declaring they were running a saloon under the guise of being a hotel. She railed about cigarettes, alcohol, and the low necklines on the gowns the female patrons were wearing.

Quick work on the part of hotel detectives prevented her from doing any violence with her hatchet. They gently removed her from the barroom as she was offering a female a scathing rebuke over her drink, dress, and choice of companions. She was returned to her room on the nineteenth floor – but she didn't stay there for long.

Once the detectives were out of site, she took the elevator back to the lobby and then burst into the barroom from the street door. "I bring a message from God to this den!" she shouted as she entered the room. She began singing a hymn until she passed the table where a young couple were sipping cocktails. "It is a shame for you, my dear girl, to be in a place like this. A man should be ashamed for bringing you here," she said loudly and then took a long look at the woman's dress. "Shame, shame, shame, for going out that way," Carrie sniffed. "You should put on more clothes."

By this time, someone had again summoned the hotel detectives. Everyone in the place was on their feet, watching the show. Carrie waved her arms around and shouted," This is such a hell-hole for women to be in!"

As she was being led gently – yet forcibly – from the room, she decided to take a last shot at the drinkers in the form of verse: "Touch not, taste not the old demon rum; It will ruin your life and that of your son. Turn in your footsteps, the straight path trod; It is a safe road and will lead you to God."

After Carrie had been rushed out of the room, grinning customers followed her to the door and watched as she was loaded into the elevator. "Get out of that filthy place, men," she cried out, "think of your wives and mothers."

The elevator door closed, and she was gone. The crowd in the Pompeian Room got a good laugh at Carrie Nation's expense that night, never dreaming that in just 12 more years, a prohibition against liquor would be the law of the land.

During the 1920s, the Congress Plaza was a favorite place for Chicago gangsters. There are many claims that it was once owned by Al Capone, but this isn't true. Capone didn't own the Congress Plaza and in fact, didn't even have a suite there. Many have mixed up the Congress with the now-vanished hotels where Capone once lived – the Metropole and the Lexington. However, Capone did hold a weekly card game at the Congress Plaza and many of the men who worked for him lived there. In fact, Jake Guzik, one of the men closest to Capone, kept a suite at the Congress. According to telephone records, lengthy calls took place between Guzik's suite at the hotel and Capone's house in Florida during the first week-and-a-half of February 1929. The conversations stopped on February 11. Then, a single call was placed to Capone in Florida three days later.

That call came on February 14 – St. Valentine's Day – just hours before seven gangland rivals of Capone were gunned down in a garage on North Clark Street.

Capone's men lived at the Congress Plaza and so did many of his rivals. The Congress was a sort of "neutral" zone where men who normally would have shot one another lived on different floors in the South Tower. It was a strange situation, but it worked.

One of Capone's most fearsome enemies, Vincent "The Schemer" Drucci, one of the top men in the mob once run by North Side mobster Dean O'Banion, also had a suite at the Congress. On August 10, 1926, he and his friend and fellow mobster Hymie Weiss were walking down the street toward the Congress when a carload of Capone's killers opened fire on them in the street. Both men survived the shootout, which the newspapers dubbed the "Battle of Michigan Avenue." It proved that you could shoot your enemies on the way to the Congress Plaza – you just couldn't do it when they were inside.

Drucci and Weiss may have missed their appointment with the Grim Reaper that morning, but far too many guests of the Congress Plaza weren't so lucky.

On April 8, 1900, a Spanish-American War veteran, Captain Louis Ostheim, was found dead in his room in the Auditorium Annex. He had been killed by what appeared to be a self-inflicted gunshot to his head, but a coroner's inquest ruled that it was not suicide. He had – as one of the newspapers of the time said – "met death in a dream."

Louis apparently had everything to live for. He was in Chicago, having returned from the Philippines just five weeks before, to be married. After his death, a marriage license and two engraved gold rings were found in his room. On Monday, April 9, a wedding was supposed to take place between Louis and his fiancée, Eva Woods, at the Chicago home of her uncle, Walter H. Pfister. A honeymoon trip had already been planned to Philadelphia, to see Louis's family, and then on to Savannah, where Louis, as part of the First U.S. Artillery, was stationed.

Louis had arrived in Chicago on April 2, and had checked into the Auditorium Annex. His luggage was delivered to his room and he settled into a quiet life at the hotel. The staff spoke highly of him and noted that he was a very pleasant guest. A clerk noted that he was reserved in his manner, looked well after his overseas service, and seemed to be in excellent health.

But as would soon be learned – appearances can be deceiving.

Louis was last seen by the hotel staff on Saturday night, around 8:00 p.m., when he asked desk clerk Arthur O'Connell for the key to his room. He made a passing remark about the fine springtime weather before he went upstairs.

When a chambermaid went to his room on Sunday morning, she found the door bolted from the inside. This was not unusual, so she went to work on other rooms on the floor. Later, she returned to the Captain's room and found the door was still locked with the deadbolt. She reported this to the desk clerk, who suggested that perhaps Captain Ostheim was very tired and wanted some extra sleep. He would, he assured her, check on the room later that day.

Finally, at nearly 8:00 p.m. on Sunday evening, staff members attempted to rouse Louis from his sleep. When he did not answer the door, they had to force it open, removing one of the wooden panels. One of the clerks inserted his arm, twisted the lock, and opened the door.

They found Louis lying on the bed. He had been dead for hours. There was a bullet hole in his right temple and a shiny, new revolver was found next to him, tangled up in the twisted bed covers that had been nearly torn away from the bed itself. It appeared that he had killed himself, but a search of the room revealed no suicide note or clues. All that was found was an envelope addressed to his sister, Clara, in Philadelphia, that had no letter inside, the marriage license, the two rings, $500 in cash, and a check for $210.

For some reason --- which might have something to do with the fact that Walter Pfister and his niece, Eva, were well-known in the city's society circles – Louis's death was initially covered up by the hotel staff. No effort was made to contact the police. In fact, it seemed as though the hotel's management tried to keep the police from hearing about it at all. The coroner was not contacted. Instead, they notified an undertaker, who took charge of the remains. The police heard about the death in the newspaper and then contacted the coroner. The six jury members who took part in the coroner's inquest were workmen from the new Montgomery Ward building that was being constructed near the hotel. They returned a verdict of "accidental death."

But was it really? Most reporters didn't think so, especially in light of the evidence provided by Walter Pfister.

He admitted that Louis Ostheim was actually not in "excellent health." His return from war had been a traumatic one and that he had been suffering from "temporary insanity," caused by the conditions that he experienced overseas. Pfister said that Louis had been complaining of ill health and that one of the symptoms of his stress were terrible dreams and insomnia.

He had seen Louis on Saturday night around 11:30 p.m., before he retired to his hotel room. Louis told him that he had been suffering from nightmares and depressing dreams since his return to the States and that, in his sleep, he often relived the battles and fought with imaginary enemies. Pfister was certain that Captain Ostheim's death had been an accident. He had purchased the revolver because he was carrying a lot of cash, not so that he could shoot himself, and it must have gone off when he was in the middle of a dream, fighting some foe from his nightmares.

The coroner decided to accept the verdict and convinced the jurors to go along with it. He was willing to say that it had been an accident. Louis Ostheim was just about to be married and it seemed impossible that he would have taken his own life. Obviously, the understanding of post-traumatic stress was still many decades in the future.

This was the first case of what the newspapers called "self-destruction" at the hotel, but it would certainly not be the last.

On Saturday, March 12, 1904, a group of guests were horrified to see Elevator Conductor A.J. Berinston as he plunged past them to his death from the fourth floor of the Auditorium Annex. The tragedy occurred during the promenade hour, just before dinner, as groups of "handsomely gowned women and prominent men" were crowded around the elevator bank, waiting impatiently for Berinston's car, which had become stuck in the shaft. Suddenly, the conductor's body flashed by them and struck at the bottom of the shaft with a sickening sound. Several women standing nearby screamed in horror.

In those days, the Auditorium Annex had an open elevator shaft and a cage-like car that, due to a miscalculation on Berinston's part, had come to a stop several feet above the fourth floor. When he attempted to lower it, the elevator refused to move by control lever, so he opened the door and climbed out to see if he could get it to move. Looking beneath the car, he discovered the cause for the halt, and then attempted to jump back into the car.

But he slipped.

Missing the edge of the car, he fell feet-first into the shaft. He tumbled more than four stories into the basement and hit the concrete floor, breaking his back and smashing his skull. An ambulance was called to the scene from the Harrison Street police station and it raced him to the Samaritan Hospital. When it arrived, Berinston was dead.

Oddly, in the wake of the accident, the newspapers would use more space talking about the way it affected the "wealthy and prominent" witnesses than how it ended the life of a young man who had just been doing his job.

In 1908, the Auditorium Annex became the scene of another sorted love triangle but, in this case, one of its members ended up dead.

In June 1907, Charles Brockett, formerly of Davenport, Iowa, met a young woman named Ruby at the White City amusement park. It was raining and Ruby had dropped her umbrella on the pavement. Brockett picked it up and gave it to her. Ruby thanked him and added, "You look as if you were in trouble."

"Yes," Brockett smiled, "And you seem to be in the same boat."

It would have been a romantic meeting between two restless souls if Ruby hadn't already been married to a man named William Pishzak. Their marriage was a stormy one, made unsettled by frequent arguments and cruelty, especially after the birth of their son, John.

Soon after the meeting, Ruby packed up her trunks and separated from her husband, leaving her child in the care of William's mother. She moved into a boarding house on Vernon Avenue -- where Charles Brockett became a frequent visitor -- and broke off all contact with her husband. William spent two months searching for her and finally found her in August 1907, after she filed divorce papers.

At that point, he had no idea that his wife was seeing another man. He followed her one day to the Douglas Presbyterian Church, where he saw her with Brockett. He made repeated visits to the boarding house, pleading with her to come home, but his calls usually ended in an argument. Eventually, William wore her down and Ruby agreed to come home and reconcile with him – or so he thought.

On January 3, William returned to the boarding house to see his wife. When he arrived, he found Brockett outside, hiding behind a tree. The two men began to argue, but before things could turn violent, Ruby came outside and broke the news to Brockett that she was going home with her husband. Brockett left, but it was at this point that he began to make his plan – a plan that he believed Ruby would go along with.

After the tragedy, several letters were found in Brockett's pockets that revealed what he intended to do. It was his intention to try and persuade Ruby to enter into a suicide pact with him. A letter addressed to his sister and brother read:

Dear Sadie and DeWitt – Put Ruby and I side by side. We choose to die together. Our acts are one of love.

Had Ruby planned to go along with it? Possibly, but when she changed her mind, it seems that Brockett came up with another idea. Or at least a fallback plan if suicide didn't work out.

On the morning of January 4, he placed a telephone call to William Pishzak and asked him to meet with Ruby and himself at the Auditorium Annex Hotel. "Is this you, Will?" Brockett asked. "I want to meet you and talk this whole matter over. I intend to do the right thing and no longer place any obstacle in the way of your wife returning to you. I have told her so."

Although Pishzak never suspected that the meeting might be his last on earth, he wanted nothing to do with the man who believed had ruined his home. He was convinced that Ruby planned to return to him and no interest in meeting Brockett.

It turned out to be one of the best decisions of his life.

As for Ruby, though, she might not have been thinking as clearly. She left the rooming house where she had been staying around 10:00 a.m. Where she spent most of the day is unknown, but she was seen leaving the Hillman Department Store at 5:30 p.m. – with Charles Brockett. They walked together to the Auditorium Annex and then were seen pacing back and forth together outside for several minutes. Witnesses later told the police that the woman seemed to be resistant to whatever the man was saying to her. She tried to leave once or twice, but Brockett pulled her back. Finally, Ruby turned abruptly and started away.

That was when Brockett pulled out a gun and fired a single shot. Ruby sank to the ground without a sound, a bullet hole in her cheek. Then, he turned the gun on himself and fired a second shot into his chest. He died on the scene.

Ruby was rushed to the hospital in critical condition. When the police contacted her husband, he immediately arrived at her side. He now realized how close he had also come to death. Pishzak was convinced that Brockett had intended for all three of them to die. This, he realized, was the reason for the telephone call.

Charles Brockett died that day outside the Auditorium Annex but Ruby survived. She spent several weeks in the hospital but was eventually released and went home with her husband. Apparently, the newspapers speculated, the couple's brush with death had convinced them to "forgive and forget."

But not for long. By November, Ruby had moved out again and this time, William sued her for divorce. She had revealed a secret about her relationship with Charles Brockett that he couldn't live with. What was it? We will never know but perhaps she had not been as resistant to the idea of the suicide pact as her husband originally thought.

The hotel had chalked up one more scandal – and another death.

Later that same year, another suicide occurred at the hotel and, once again, wealthy relatives attempted to dismiss the incident as an "accident." But the facts in the death of John Alden Hossack seem to suggest it wasn't simply an accidental fall from an eighth-floor window.

On April 2, 1908, John Alden Hossack of Odell, Illinois, arrived in Chicago to consult with physicians about what was called a "threatened nervous breakdown." Hossack was the grandson of famed abolitionist John Hossack, who was charged in Chicago courtrooms more than 50 years before for his role in the Underground Railroad. John Alden was only 26-years-old and in poor mental health. His mother, his sister, Frances, and his fiancée, Anne McWilliams, had traveled with him to the city from Odell.

On Saturday, April 4, they consulted with several nerve specialists and all of them agreed that "an outdoor life in the west" would be beneficial to the young man. It was decided that he should leave immediately for Lincoln, Nebraska, where a friend had a ranch where he could stay. There were not a lot of other options when it came to treatment for mental health in 1908.

According to the other members of his party, John was very encouraged by what the doctors told him, and he talked cheerfully throughout the rest of the evening. After looking over railroad schedules and guides, they all retired early. They were intent on having an early breakfast and getting John to the train on time.

At just after 7:00 a.m. on April 5, Helene Nelson, the hotel housekeeper, heard a loud sound at the bottom of the building's airshaft. She notified the clerk and he and a few others rushed to the scene. They found John Hossack's body lying crumpled at the bottom of the shaft. He had fallen – or jumped – from the window of his room on the eighth floor, plunging to his death in the air shaft. He had been killed by the fall.

John W. Scott of the Carson, Pirie & Scott Company, and friend of the Hossack family, was called and immediately came to the hotel to assist the family. He was also instrumental in assisting the police and the coroner in reaching their findings about John's death.

Not surprisingly, no one was able to determine whether John deliberately jumped from the window or accidentally fell, "perhaps becoming dizzy while looking out," a report suggested.

John McWilliams was the president of the bank in Odell where John worked. His uncle, F.N. Hossack, was the head cashier. McWilliams told a reporter, "The boy had been suffering from extreme nervousness for some time but had persisted in keeping up his work at the bank until it became imperative that he seek relief."

But, McWilliams added, "We do not feel that he committed suicide. Owing to his extreme nervous state, it seems quite reasonable to believe that, being in a strange place, he was impelled to jump from his window as the result of a dream or a nightmare."

I wouldn't say that it was "quite reasonable" to believe that but whatever happened, the hotel had claimed another victim of "self-destruction."

On June 8, 1908, another case of "self-destruction" occurred at the Auditorium Annex and this time, there was no question that it was intentional suicide. Roy Gormely, a grain broker from Detroit, checked into the hotel on June 4. He was in Chicago for business – or so he told the desk clerks. It's possible that he had come to the city for a week of drinking instead. Gormely, 38, had recently separated from his wife because of a love affair with another woman. A telephone call between Gormely and this mystery woman may have been the thing that finally sent him over the edge.

During his stay at the Auditorium Annex, Roy spent most of his time drinking in the Pompeian Room. Before the orchestra quit playing on Sunday night, June 7, he had insisted that they play "The Dead March from Saul." The bandleader told him that he didn't have the music but jokingly said that he would bring it with him on Monday night.

Gormely just shook his head. "It will be too late then. I want to be here to listen."

He made the musicians drink with him and paid for another round of drinks for the band on Monday night.

On Monday afternoon, shortly after 3:00 p.m., a telephone call from Detroit was put through to Gormely's room. The hotel operator later told the police that it had been a woman on the line. No one knows what the conversation was about, but it didn't last long. Five minutes later, hotel detective Frank Repetto heard the sound of a gunshot on the eighth floor and he rushed to Gormely's room. The door was unlocked, and he pushed inside to find Gormely lying across the bed. He was dead with a bloody bullet hole in his chest. The revolver had tumbled onto the floor. He had taken a seat on the edge of the bed to pull the trigger. He was fully dressed and still wearing his shoes.

There was no note to explain the suicide, only a scrap of paper that had an enigmatic message scrawled on it. In pencil, it read: "…is according to Hoyle… The Million Dollar Kid."

Repetto searched the room and found the dead man's suitcase. He was surprised to find it empty. Gormely had no cash on him – he'd apparently spent it all in the barroom buying drinks – but he did find a check from a Detroit bank for $130 in Gormely's pocket.

Repetto was still in the room when the telephone rang. It was the same woman from Detroit, and she had again asked to be connected to Gormely's room. Repetto picked up the receiver.

"Is that you, Roy?" the woman asked.

Repetto wasn't sure what to say and, in the silence, the woman repeated the question.

"No, this isn't Roy," he finally said.

"Well, I want Roy Gormely."

The detective sighed, "I regret to inform you that Mr. Gormely is dead. He shot himself in his room this afternoon."

The woman gasped. "My god, is that so?" She immediately hung up the telephone. She didn't call back.

On Saturday, May 21, a Congress Hotel guest named James Keany joined the list of suicides connected to the hotel. Keany was a clerk for the New York Life Insurance Company and had mysteriously arrived in Chicago on May 15. He checked into the hotel under the assumed name of "J. Austin, Philadelphia." He was only identified by tailor's markings on the inside of his trousers. Detectives were able to trace the labels back to a shop in New York.

Once his identity was learned, his brother, Thomas, an attorney, told police that his brother had been missing for more than a week. Nothing had been heard from him until May 19, when a friend, Charles Cheney, received a letter from James, explaining that he was in Chicago. It also contained some money and a pawn ticket. He asked Cheney to redeem a ring from a pawn shop, using the money that he'd sent. There was no mention of personal affairs or that he was contemplating suicide.

At some point on Saturday morning, Keany had left the Congress and walked to Lake Michigan. There, overlooking the water, he had shot himself in the head with a small, pearl-handled revolver. His body was discovered a short time later by two boys who were playing near the water. They summoned a police officer, who found a key to his hotel room at the Congress.

A search of the room revealed only a suitcase, clothing, two sets of pajamas, a Chicago street guide, and a pair of scissors. Keany had carefully removed all the laundry marks from his clothing and had even cut the buttons which contained the name of the maker off his clothes. He had overlooked the markings in his trousers.

He left no suicide note behind, leaving a mystery in his wake.

In the summer of 1916, Morse Davis, a mining engineer and promoter connected with the Royal Financial company of Vancouver, British Columbia, died at the Congress after drinking cyanide of potassium. His wife, Mary, was found seriously ill from a concoction of the same poison – an overdose that she claimed was an accident.

On the morning of Wednesday, August 9, the hotel switchboard operator received a flash from room 312, which was occupied by the Davises. An incoherent woman was mumbling over the wire. Knowing something was wrong, she immediately contacted hotel detective James Rooney and sent him to the suite. Rooney found the door unlocked and burst inside to find Mr. Davis lying on the bed. Mrs. Davis was staggering around the room, unable to speak. He called Dr. P.B. Welch, the hotel physician. The doctor quickly determined that Morse was dead. Marie was moved to another room and the timely application of a stomach pump saved her life.

As soon as she was able to speak, she told the hotel staff that she and her husband had taken the poison by mistake. "We thought we were taking salts," she claimed.

Mary said that the couple had eaten a salad the night before which had disagreed with them. They feared that it was food poisoning and decided to take some Epsom salts to settle their stomachs. They had taken poison by mistake.

Probably because it was his job to believe the guests, James Rooney went along with her explanation. "I'm sure there was no suicide pact," he told a reporter. "If there had been one, the couple would have doubtless left a note. Mrs. Davis's desperate efforts to summon aid disprove any plan of suicide."

The detective had found an empty glass sitting on the floor next to the bed. In the bathroom, there was a glass bottle half filled with crystal cyanide of potassium, sitting on a shelf next to a box of Epsom salts. He believed that either Mr. or Mrs. Davis had made a mistake and grabbed the poison instead of the salts – but I have been unable to find any reason why the poison would have been in someone's bathroom by mistake.

And I'm not the only one who was skeptical about their story.

Although, honestly, Detectives John Russell and Edward Halpin from the South Clark Street station weren't just skeptical – they didn't believe the story at all. They said that the bottle with the poison in it was sitting on the floor next to the empty glass.

"It looks like a suicide pact," Russell said. "I can't see how anyone could have confused cyanide of potassium in a bottle with salts in a box."

As more was discovered about the financial situation of Morse Davis, suicide began to look even more likely. Davis had come to Chicago to try and sell off the American rights to an explosive that he had invented. He had invested heavily in Canadian real estate but had lost everything, thanks to the decline in land values caused by the start of World War I. A few years earlier, he had, as part of a syndicate, also bought up large tracts of land in Wisconsin. Unable to pay his share, the deal had continued without him. At the time of his death, Davis had only $1.60 in his pockets. He was to have settled his hotel bill of $40 that morning and had told the cashier that he would do so. Whether or not he actually had the money remains unknown.

Mary recovered from her near fatal poisoning but was left adrift without her husband. With no place left to go, she applied for aid from the sisters of St. Mary's Mission house, which adjoined the Cathedral of Sts. Peter and Paul at Peoria Street and Washington Boulevard. She was told that she could remain there until she found employment.

Then, on Sunday night, August 20, she startled the sisters by screaming and running to a third-floor window, where she cried that she was going to leap out and kill herself. She was restrained and the police were called. They took her to a psychiatric hospital, where she ranted and raved to the attendants that her late husband had been about to receive some money from his investments and that she had been cheated out of her share.

Sadly, Morse Davis had been nearly penniless at the time of his death. There were no investments – and no money. Mary Davis died under the delusion that the wealthy life she had lived with her husband had not come crashing to an end.

On June 18, 1920, another suicide attempt occurred at the Congress, this time in the Pompeian Room of the hotel. In this incident, the young woman who swallowed poison didn't die, but her story was just so bizarre that I had to include it anyway. The question is – was it suicide? Was it some sort of stunt for attention? And who was this strange woman?

According to the hotel staff, the young woman arrived at the Pompeian Room for a party around 9:00 p.m. with two men, Harry Davis, an insurance broker, and I.E. Friedman, a friend of Davis from New York. They were seated at a table and at about 10:30 p.m., the woman swallowed several poison tablets. She was rushed to a hotel room that belonged to Mr. and Mrs. D.H. Naylor of Minneapolis – who were seated at the same table -- and the hotel physician administered first aid. Her situation was so serious that she was rushed to the American Hospital on Irving Park Avenue, where the doctor in charge, Dr. J.I. Mandel, told reporters that he did not expect her to live through the night.

Early the next morning, I.E. Friedman quickly checked out of the hotel and returned to New York. No one seemed to be able to find Harry Davis and the girl was known at the hotel only as "Miss Johnson." She was wearing expensive evening clothes and diamonds when she arrived at the party.

When she arrived at the hospital, the young woman was still conscious. Dr. Max Thorek drained her stomach. He told reporters that the girl had taken the pills under the belief that it was headache medicine. "We are diagnosing the contents of her stomach," he said, "to determine the nature of the poison. I do not believe that she tried to kill herself. She begged us to save her life."

But then he added a sentence to his statement that would define the entire incident: "She evades all my questions."

The initial newspaper stories about the "mystery woman," as reporters called her, started bringing an assortment of characters out of the woodwork.

The first was Ernest Schaefer, a soldier who had recently returned from France, where he had been gassed during the war. He believed that the girl was his wife, whose maiden name was Bessie Johnson.

Schaefer was under treatment at a nearby psychiatric hospital and heard about the case in the newspaper. He and his wife had an argument on Tuesday night, and she had left him. When he arrived at the hospital, Dr. Mandel refused to let him see her. In the end, it didn't matter, she wasn't Bessie Schaefer – well, probably not, anyway.

Miraculously, the "mystery woman" made it through the night and began to recover. Doctors determined that she had swallowed several bichloride of mercury tablets at the party, believing them to be headache pills. Even after she regained her wits, she still refused to reveal her identity.

There were more people who managed to identify her, though.

On Friday, June 20, a middle-aged woman, holding a young girl by the hand, arrived at the American Hospital and asked to see the "mystery girl." She believed her to be her daughter, Alma Johnson, 19, an actress from Evanston. She told nurses that Alma had recently appeared at the Winter Garden in New York as a dancer.

Mrs. Johnson was escorted to the room and as she entered, a glad cry came from the patient, who was sitting up in bed. "Mama, when are they going to let me out of here?" she asked.

The two of them spoke for a few minutes and then Mrs. Johnson left the room, disappointed. No matter what the patient had said, she was not her daughter. Why she called the older woman "Mama" was anyone's guess.

Later that afternoon, Morris Leonard, an attorney with an office on West Randolph Street, contacted the hospital. He was in New York at the time but believed he could identify the patient. She was Alfa Johnson – whose real name was Alfa Lanee, the daughter of Charles J. Lanee of Evanston – and she'd recently asked him to file suit against a man. He refused to give the man's name or any details. However, when the hospital staff tried to find the Lanee family, they discovered that they apparently did not exist.

But there was a reason for the confusion – maybe. On Saturday, another family came forward and claimed the "mystery girl" as their own. Carl Johnson and his wife, Hazel, of Evanston, are positive that the girl at the hospital was Alfa Johnson – who used the stage name of Alfa Lanee. They believed that their daughter tried to kill herself because of an affair with a wealthy New Yorker known to them only by the initials "H.D." She had talked about him frequently.

Mystery solved. Well, not so fast.

The patient told reporters that she was certainly not Alfa Johnson. She also denied taking poison because of a love affair. "My real name is Alfa, all right, but it is not Johnson," she stated. "I remember a woman and a child coming in to see me, but she was not my mother. I know my mother too well to make a mistake. If I was delirious, I might have called her my mother, but not otherwise."

She also told reporters that she didn't know any rich man from New York that she would have loved to the point of committing suicide over. "I am not in love with anyone," she sniffed. "I do not know in whose room I went to rest after taking the tablets. I only know that a woman aided me."

It was obvious, especially to the jaded reporters, that she was enjoying the attention and the mystery about her identity. Her room was filled with flowers and nurses said they had arrived all morning, but the girl would not tell them where they came from – or where she had purchased the tablets that nearly caused her death.

"When I get out of her, I'm going to go away," she explained. "My life is not ruined or anything like that. I took the tablets by mistake and that's all there is to that. I didn't love any man and I never would think of committing suicide. It's ridiculous. I have told no one my real name and I'm not going to. It's nobody's business but mine what I am, where I came from, or what I'm going to do."

And with that, her story came to an end. Who she was, and why she needed to remain a mystery, remains, well, just that – a mystery.

The next victim of "self-destruction" at the Congress Hotel wasn't so lucky. On Friday, August 11, 1922, a wealthy Los Angeles widow named Eva M. Gleason, was found unconscious in her room by a member of the housekeeping staff. She died a short time later.

The motive for the suicide was unknown, but it was rumored that the widow, 37-years-old and very attractive, was despondent over a love affair.

Hotel physician, Dr. Joseph M. Blake – always making sure the hotel, which frowned on wealthy guests being found dead in their rooms, was protected – stated that he believed Mrs. Gleason took a large dose of sleeping pills by mistake. "She had complained of nervousness on Thursday," he told reporters, "and I gave her a harmless sleep-producing prescription. Probably it did not produce the desired effect, and she took more of the powerful drug."

It's true, she took more of it – the entire bottle.

On Wednesday evening, July 28, 1926, Mrs. Harriet Harrison shocked dozens of guests when she plunged six stories to her death in the hotel's elevator shaft.

Mrs. Harrison and her husband, George, had checked into the hotel the previous afternoon as they prepared to depart for a European trip. They planned to leave on the evening of July 28 for Montreal, where they would sail for England, and remain on the Continent until September.

But the trip came to an end before it even got started.

At the time of his wife's death, Harrison was out of the hotel, taking care of some business. He was a photographer and was regarded as one of the wealthiest residents of Galesburg, Illinois. He and his wife were active in the community and highly regarded. He didn't learn of Mrs. Harrison's death until he returned to the hotel several hours later.

Her tragic death had been an accident. She had entered the elevator in the lobby to go up to her room on the seventh floor. At the sixth floor, the elevator operator had stopped the car to take on another passenger, Mrs. Mary Corum. As Mrs. Corum stepped into the car, Mrs. Harrison, thinking that she had come to her floor, stepped out. She realized her mistake in a moment and, whirling about, fell through the still half-open door of the shaft, missed the car completely, and plunged headfirst to the bottom.

As guests gathered around the open door in the lobby, they heard her scream and saw her flash past before also hearing the thud of her body as it hit the concrete floor at the bottom of the shaft.

Glenna Davidson was the next young woman to commit suicide at the Congress Hotel. On Saturday, March 17, 1928, she swallowed poison in her room. She was discovered by a maid and treated by the hotel physician, but her condition was serious enough to send her to the county hospital. She told the police that she was 23-years-old and married but would not reveal where her husband or family were. When she registered at the hotel, she had only disclosed an address of Indianapolis, Indiana.

She died later that night; her story shrouded in mystery.

On May 28, 1930, Calvin Fletcher Combs, described as a "globetrotter and copy writer," shot and killed himself in his room at the Congress Hotel. The 33-year-old man was a native of Buenos Aires.

According to news articles, Combs had arrived in New York on March 17, armed with letters of introduction from the foreign representatives of a dozen or more U.S. corporations. But he didn't find New York to his liking, so he traveled west to Chicago and checked in at the Congress on May 26.

When the police investigated the scene of his suicide, they found numerous letters from advertising agencies that had replied unfavorably to his inquiries for employment. This led Captain John Prendergast and Deputy Coroner Ray Conerty to believe that his failure to find work had prompted his suicide.

On June 9, 1930, Miss Georgiana McClurg, 50, joined Combs in death. She was found unconscious in her room at the Congress after ingesting an overdose of sleeping pills. She was rushed to the county hospital but died a few days later, on June 13. She left behind no clues to explain her suicide.

On Saturday, May 23, 1930, showgirl Jean Farrell died in Grant hospital under mysterious circumstances. She had fallen ill while at the Congress in the company of Colonel Anthony Lorensen of the Illinois National Guard, who rented a suite at the hotel, and Barney Franklin, who also lived there. Franklin described himself as a "stock and bond broker" but was, in reality, a mobster who had once owned the Moulin

Rouge and the Kit Kat Club, both of which had been shut down by Prohibition agents.

A postmortem examination of Jean's body revealed no natural cause of death. Her roommate, Barbara Bossie, who shared an apartment with her on Sheridan Road, told police that Jean had become very ill after drinking heavily at a party at the Congress on Wednesday night. Unable to sleep that evening, she had taken six sleeping pills. The corner believed that she might have ingested poisoned bootleg liquor, which had already led to many deaths in the city during Prohibition.

An inquest into her death was held on Friday, May 23, but only the deputy coroner appeared as a witness. Colonel Lorensen, Franklin, and Miss Bossie all failed to show up. The inquest was delayed until June 5 but was eventually cancelled. Her cause of death – conveniently – remained a mystery.

The year 1931 saw the suicides of two financial men at the Congress Hotel, both of whom had lost a fortune in the stock market crash of 1929. On June 11, Bruce Ramsey, 50, the assistant vice president of the First National Bank of St. Louis, jumped from a window on the fifth floor of the hotel. He had the bad luck of landing on a court that was only three stories below and survived – but not for long. He died the next day at the Illinois Central Hospital.

On November 10, Curtis G. Dunham, 27, an investment broker who lost over $2 million in the market crash, killed himself by leaping from the hotel's twelfth floor to the sidewalk below. This was not Dunham's first suicide attempt. A nurse, Miss Mildred McClellan, had been hired to watch over him after he had tried to jump from the window two days before. According to her statement to the police, Dunham had awakened around 3:00 a.m. and started talking irrationally about "gangsters who wanted to get him." When he started for the window, Mildred tried to stop him, but he flung her against a dresser and jumped out the window.

There is no record as to whether detectives asked her why he had not been moved to a lower floor.

Loss of a racetrack bet by which he tried to recoup his losses after the market crash led to the suicide of Hoyt P. Smith, 54, a gambler and stock speculator at the Congress Hotel on August 31, 1932. He shot himself in his room, just as his brother, Arthur, arrived at his room.

Smith left behind several notes in his room. One of them referred to a race at the Hawthorne track on August 10. "If Siskin had not been pulled," it read in part, "I might not have to do what I am doing." Siskin, Smith's "lucky" horse, had been a favorite in the race but had been beaten by two other horses. Siskin was described by sports writers as the "victim of a bungling ride by jockey A. Richard." The note scrawled in pencil, referred to the jockey when it said, "Tell Sunny goodbye. He rode me to death. If he had given me a chance, I might have recovered."

Another note left his personal effects to his brother and a third listed his debts, including $2,000 that he owed to the Congress Hotel.

In a note to his brother, he wrote:

Dear brother, when you receive this I hope to be in the other world, and I certainly hope I can make a good job of it. Just can't stand it any longer. Bills coming in everyday and a hotel bill so large that I know I can't go much further here. Have not been able to eat and sleep for three days.

Sorry that I am not able to leave anything toward paying funeral expenses, but I think Bill Schmitt [owner of an undertaking parlor on Irving Park Boulevard] will stand you until you get some money. He no doubt won a nice bet when his Charleigh beat my horse Siskin.

Smith was credited with being the only man to ever break the bank at the casino in Havana, Cuba, but all those wins were just not enough to offset the losses caused by the stock market crash. He hung on as long as he could but, in the end, saw death as the only way out.

On August 10, 1935, Harry J. Meyer, the 33-year-old son of Irving Meyer, a successful Division Street restaurant owner, registered at the Congress and left instructions to be called at 2:30 p.m. on Sunday afternoon. Unable to arouse him, a bellboy entered the room and found Meyer dead. He had ingested a large quantity of poison.

He left a note next to his body on the bed expressing regret over the failure of his life.

On April 22, 1938, former hotel and club manager Frederick Marshall Crosby, shot and killed himself in his room at the Congress Hotel. Crosby was well-known in Chicago but had seen a run of bad luck after several businesses in which he was involved were closed due to the Depression. In poor health and unable to find work, he committed suicide.

In 1939, with a debt of more than $2 million, the owners of the Congress Hotel filed for bankruptcy. A receiver was named to handle the bills and outstanding debts, and the hotel continued to operate until it could be sold at public auction. The hotel limped through this difficult period, but it was certainly not the worst thing that happened at the Congress that year.

On Thursday night, August 3, Adela Langer, a Czechoslovakian refugee, jumped to her death from the top floor of the hotel. As if this was not bad enough, she took her two sons, Karl, age 6, and Jan, age 4, with her when she went. It was an unspeakable tragedy that played out before the startled eyes of pedestrians along Michigan Avenue.

Adele and her husband, Karel, had fled from Prague earlier that year, one step ahead of the Nazis. At home, Karel had been the owner of the Hynek Marpeles textile mill, which had been valued at more than $1.5 million before the war and the German invasion. The Langers were Jewish and knew that they would be forced to surrender the mill to the government if they didn't sell it first. Langer sold the firm – the largest textile and cloth mill in the country – for pennies on the dollar.

"I practically gave it away to my oldest employees," he later said," because I felt Hitler would seize it and force me to give it away. We left our homeland for the sake of the children. We hoped to find opportunities to give them a better life."

Unfortunately, their lives would be cut short far too soon.

The Langer family came to the United States in July 1939 on a six-month visitor's visa, but they also had a visa to Bolivia so that they could not be sent back to Czechoslovakia when their time in America expired. They came to Chicago to be near two aunts of Adele's and rented a basement apartment on Humboldt Boulevard.

With only $7,500 that he had managed to salvage from his business, Langer hoped to establish a business in Canada and had written to some friends in Ontario, asking them to help him find work and a home. The family had been waiting patiently in Chicago until word arrived from across the northern border.

Perhaps it was the waiting that weighed on Adele's mind. Or perhaps she was depressed over losing the family business and fleeing from her home to the United States. Regardless of the reason, she had become despondent in Chicago. She often talked of committing suicide – and taking her babies with her.

The children were also unhappy. They were upset and confused about the overseas journey and didn't like living in the cramped basement apartment. They were both sent to a boy's camp to learn English but were unhappy with that, too. Adele tried hard to keep them occupied but felt that she was failing miserably. On the afternoon of August 3, she told her husband that she was taking the boys to the beach. She dressed them in their swimming suits and Langer gave her $20 to take with her for lunch and treats for the boys.

When Adele took the boys between 1:00 p.m., when she left the Langer apartment, and 5:00 p.m., when she arrived at the Congress Hotel, is unknown. It's very possible that she did take Karl and Jan to the beach for one last outing, but there's no way to know for sure.

When she arrived at the Congress, she asked the desk clerk for a "light and airy" room. She didn't particularly ask for one that was high above the street, but for $8, she engaged a room that turned out to be on the top floor. Adele and the children were seen once more in the lobby about an hour later but the rest of the time, they remained in the room.

We only know what happened next from the witness reports on the street.

The bodies landed on the sidewalk along Michigan Avenue, just south of Congress Street. The boys, when found, were still dressed in their swimsuits. The police believed that they may have been asleep when hurled out the window, or when carried out by their mother. They probably never knew what happened to them – we can only hope.

None of the witnesses were sure about who fell first – the mother or the children. However, the bodies fell in a small circle in front of the hotel. Several women screamed in terror at the sight. A police officer named William Gonoude ran to the scene and believing the boys might still be alive, scooped them up, got them into a car, and took them to St. Luke's Hospital, where they were officially pronounced dead.

When the identities of the victims were discovered, police officers tracked down Karel Langer at his home on Humboldt Boulevard. He immediately fell apart when he heard the news through an interpreter, attorney Otto Oplatka. He began to cry and shake and after threatening to end his own life after learning his family's fate, the police kept him on suicide watch in a cell overnight.

Karel Langer survived his ordeal, but who could blame him if he was unable to go on? He lost his home, his business, and his entire family in one cruel summer.

On February 3, 1946, one guest was killed, dozens more were injured, and more than 2,000 people had to be evacuated from the hotel because of four mysterious fires that caused Fire Marshal Anthony J. Mullaney to place 15 guards in corridors to watch out for the unknown arsonist.

The first fire was discovered around 1:00 a.m., burning in a passage between the hotel kitchen and the Glass Hat cocktail lounge. The second was found a little more than three hours later, burning in a locked, unoccupied room on the sixth floor. Both fires were easily put out by hotel staff members with fire extinguishers – but the other fires were much more serious.

The third fire broke out on the fifth floor around 6:30 a.m. near the room of Frank J. Van Hoesen, a secretary for a paint and wallpaper company in Brighton, New York. The flames swept toward the room where he had been sleeping and Van Hoesen tried to climb out of a window in the bathroom and onto a fire escape. He never made it. His partially clothed body was discovered by firefighters in the bathtub beneath the window. He died after being overcome by the smoke.

The fire burned out 24 rooms on the fifth and sixth floors and another 16 rooms became temporarily unusable due to smoke and water damage. Deputy Fire Marshal John Haberkorn estimated the loss to the hotel was about $25,000.

The fourth fire, which put an additional 95 rooms out of use and caused another $25,000 in damage, was discovered at noon in a room on the twelfth floor about a half-hour after the last occupant, Alfred Robbyn of New York, checked out.

Guests were not alerted to the first two fires but when the 6:30 a.m. fire – which killed Frank Van Hoesen – started, calls began to be made to room phones. If no one answered, bellhops were sent to awaken guests by pounding on their doors. More than 1,000 people in bedroom slippers and with coats thrown over their nightclothes were herded into the lobby, where they were served coffee by the staff.

Firefighters rescued three people from high window ledges at the rear of the hotel with ladders. Scores of people who thought they were trapped on upper floors descended by fire escapes, and some tied sheets into ropes to drop from windows to the roofs of extensions of lower floors.

Two firemen were injured in the third and fourth blazes, along with several dozen guests, who were treated in the newly remodeled lobby. Many suffered from minor burns and shock. One man, Irving Pollack of San Francisco, who had a room on the sixth floor was rushed to St. Luke's Hospital after having a heart attack.

Firefighters were unable to trace the cause of any of the fires. "It looks suspicious," Marshal Mullaney told reporters. "Two fires could be a coincidence, but not three or four."

After Mullaney assigned firefighters to guard the hotel against further outbreaks, Chief of Detectives Walter G. Storms order the police bomb and arson squad to start an investigation. A uniformed police squad of one sergeant and 15 patrolmen joined the guard duty at the hotel. Based on how quickly the fire spread on the twelfth floor, some of the investigators believed that a flammable liquid had been used to start the fire. Others believed that the flames were spread by a strong breeze off the lake, blowing into the corridor from broken windows.

No matter how the fires spread, the question remained: who started them? The police and fire department believed that an arsonist was at work. They questioned guests and grilled every staff member, but the culprit was never found.

After all these years, the killer of Frank Van Hoesen has never been found.

On Saturday, October 10, 1948, another "mystery woman" was found near death in her Congress Hotel room. The woman, around 35-years-old, had checked in under a false name five days before. It was later discovered that she was an heiress to a wealthy family in Peoria named Francis Page. Her brother, Timothy, manager of the Peoria Cordage Company, later said that his sister had an operation in July and had been prescribed sleeping pills. He never imagined that she would use them to take her own life.

House detectives gained entrance to her locked room through a window transom after the hotel operator reported that the telephone had been removed from its cradle. The woman was found in a coma on the bed. An empty bottle of sleeping pills was next to her.

She was taken to St. Luke's Hospital while police officers searched the room. They found a bottle of whiskey, expensive-looking clothes, $1,000 in traveler's checks, and a scrawled, almost undecipherable note. All that could be read of the note was:

Last incident of an incident in politics, October 1937. Abby Bildens's, father, kidnapped me to New York. He was director of the National Bank of Northampton, Mass. Cremate me.

She died before the police could learn what happened to her in 1937 and why she had committed suicide.

Tragedy struck the Congress Hotel again on August 25, 1950, when William Seng, 41, the hotel's credit manager, was shot and fatally wounded by a guest, John Raymond, 25, of St. Louis, who then shot himself.

It happened because of an unpaid $104 bill.

The shooting occurred when Seng and Dominic Talarico, the hotel's head of service, went to Raymond's room to ask him about the unpaid bill. Raymond had been at the hotel since August 16, racking up overnight and room service charges.

When they knocked at his door, Raymond admitted the two men and asked them to wait while he got his wallet from the other room. He stepped into the bathroom and quickly returned carrying an automatic pistol. He ordered the two men to stand against the wall but as Seng moved toward him instead, Raymond fired. The bullet slammed into Seng's chest, but he didn't collapse until he made it into the hallway. Talarico fled the room and as he made it into the corridor, he heard Raymond moan loudly behind him.

"Oh, why did I shoot him?" he cried.

The utterance was followed by a second shot. When the police arrived, they found Raymond facedown in the hotel room.

William Seng died a short time later, leaving behind a wife and three children.

The police found a Missouri driver's license in John Raymond's wallet, as well as $6, a draft card, a copy of his discharge from the Marines, and his sister's address in Evanston. When contacted, his sister, Mrs. Frances Robb, told police that Raymond was an accountant for a construction company in St. Louis. He had been given a medical discharge from the Marines and when she had seen him last, he seemed "despondent." She had no explanation for why he would have shot the hotel staff members, or himself, but knew that he had recently been dealing with financial difficulties.

Perhaps it was that one last bill that finally sent him over the edge, putting William Seng in the wrong place at a very wrong time.

Fire claimed another life at the Congress Hotel on Saturday, March 4, 1961. The fire was discovered about 10:15 a.m. when a doorman happened to look up and see smoke billowing from windows on the tenth floor. Before he could alert the other staff, a call came into the switchboard and a woman began shouting, "Fire! Fire!" but hung up before she told anyone which floor she was on.

Managers, clerks, busboys, bellhops, and porters immediately ran to the hotel's South Wing to knock on doors and alert the guests. While they were being dispatched to the rooms, the hotel's five telephone operators rang all the rooms on the upper floors of the South Wing to warn guests of the danger. Other employees manned the seven elevators to help take guests from the upper five floors of the South Wing to lower levels.

About 750 of the hotel's rooms were occupied when the fire occurred, including 12 of the 17 rooms in the South Wing's upper floors. The fire did more than $100,000 in damage and many of the 40 burned rooms had been newly decorated as part of a $5 million remodeling program started the previous year.

Most of the guests got out unscathed, except for two. Dorothy Speer, 22, was trapped on the ninth floor of the building, where she called for help for more than 30 minutes. Hundreds of guests watched from windows below as firemen tried to raise a ladder and lower a rope to her. Finally, firefighter James Cross slid a makeshift scaffold out a window diagonally across from her and led the young woman to safety. She was treated for burns and shock at Mercy Hospital.

Harry Williams, 49, of Iowa and owner of the Colonial and Pacific Frigidways company, was not so lucky. He perished in the blaze. Firefighters were hampered by a gas leak on the top floor, which prevented them for getting to his room in time to save his life.

On December 16, 1961, John Koplin, president of Anderson Tires, Inc., was found dead from a gunshot wound in his apartment at the Congress. A hotel maid had found him slumped in a chair at his desk with a .38-caliber revolver in his hand. He had shot himself in the left temple.

Police officials said that Koplin left a note behind, asking the hotel to notify his company of his death. Joseph B. Phillips, manager of the tire company, said that Koplin had been in ill health.

It was the only explanation that he could offer for his suicide.

On February 28, 1968, a prominent attorney from Rockford, Illinois, was brutally slain in his room at the Congress Hotel. Frederick Haye, 57, was the president of the Winnebago County Bar Association and a graduate of the John Marshall law school in Chicago. What happened on that terrible night in 1968 remains a mystery but it ended with one man dead and another one in prison.

According to Thomas Keegan, Haye's law partner, Haye had left Rockford at 4:45 p.m. on a bus that was bound for O'Hare Airport. He transferred at O'Hare and took an airport limousine into the city, eventually winding up at the Congress, where he checked into a room. Haye's wife, Eleanor, said that he called home at about 9:00 p.m. that night from a supper club in the "Rush Street area" on the Near North Side. He told her that he planned to eat there and then go for an after-dinner drink at another club.

Apparently, he didn't leave the second club alone.

On the way back to the hotel, Haye stopped at a liquor store, where he bought a bottle of whiskey. It was later found in his room, along with three drinking glasses – two of which had fingerprints on them that did not belong to Haye. The clerk at the liquor store was the last person – aside from the killer, or killers – who recalled seeing Haye that evening.

The following morning, a hotel maid named Bessie Davis discovered Haye's naked body in his room. His hands and feet had been tied with his socks and he had been strangled with the sleeve of his shirt. According to Police Commander James Riordan, Haye's wallet was empty except for his identification cards. He was reported to have been carrying $1,000 in traveler's checks in preparation for a vacation that he was taking the next week.

Riordan said that Haye's clothes had been hung in the closest, but neither of the twin beds in the room had been slept in. There was no sign of a struggle nor were there any signs that the door to the room had been forced open. Whoever had killed the attorney, he had apparently been invited into the room.

The murder was quickly solved. On March 4, detectives arrested Ronald D. Coffey, 21, for Haye's murder. Coffey, an unemployed laborer, led police to Joseph Henry Norman, 32, a petty criminal who had met Coffey in county jail. The two of them put together a scheme that involved luring men back to a hotel room and robbing them.

Police were still on the lookout for Norman when he killed again. This time, his victim was Charles R. Meader, from Springfield, a state auditor for the department of revenue. He was discovered dead – naked, tied up with socks, and strangled with his necktie – at the Sherman House Hotel on May 17. Norman was arrested at the Greyhound terminal the following day. Hotel employees identified him as the man seen going up to Meader's room with him. Norman's fingerprints matched those found in Meader's room, as well as those found on the drinking glass in Haye's room at the Congress.

In court, Norman pled guilty to the two murders. He was sentenced to a term of 18 to 30 years on March 26, 1969. Ronald Coffey, however, was freed after Norman told the judge that he had not taken part in the murders. The state decided there was insufficient evidence to charge him with the robberies and he was released after spending nearly a year behind bars.

On November 12, 1970, an electrician named David Meenan, 23, was working in the hotel's boiler room, using an electric grinder to remove old bricks from around a boiler. It should have been an ordinary day at work, but David didn't have all the information he needed. He struck a hidden water line behind the bricks and was electrocuted.

He was rushed to Michael Reese Hospital but was dead when he arrived.

As you can see, the Congress Hotel has seen more than its share of tragedies over the years but, even so, these stories are certainly not all the deaths and strange events that have occurred there. As time went on, the staff got a lot better at keeping things out of the newspapers. Even so, there were scores of natural deaths, suicide attempts, suicides that were hushed up, rapes, beatings, robberies, and brushes with violence. In 1933, the Congress saw its liquor license restored when Prohibition came to an end. During the "dry" years, the hotel had been fined numerous times for providing guests with alcohol, usually by bellhops who promised they could get adventure-seekers "anything they wanted."

It became the hotel of choice during the Century of Progress fair, which brought an increase in out-of-town thieves and burglars. There were numerous instances of rooms being robbed and guests being beaten during the early 1930s. In April 1932, New York Syndicate gangsters Meyer Lansky and Charles "Lucky" Luciano were picked up by Chicago police as they were leaving the Congress with Outfit man Paul "The Waiter" Ricca. On another night, six former members of the Capone gang, including Tony Accardo, were arrested on charges of disorderly conduct at the Congress. They had been meeting to try and assist Jake "The Factor" Barber as he tried to free his kidnapped son. A friendly judge let them off with a warning but it's no surprise that mobsters continued to gather and live at the Congress – the hotel had opened the Eastman Casino (which changed its name to the Congress Casino in 1937) there in the middle 1930s. Where there was gambling, there were always gangsters. The Congress even played a role in the arrest of Leo Brothers, the St. Louis gunman who was tried and sent to prison for the murder of "Al Capone's favorite reporter," Jake Lingle.

It's not surprising that decades of death, violence, and suicide that the Congress has earned a reputation for being haunted. In fact, I consider it to be not only the most haunted hotel in Chicago, but one of the most haunted in the entire country.

There are numerous ghosts associated with the place, although some are more far-fetched than others. Rumor has it that Franklin D. Roosevelt, Theodore Roosevelt, Thomas Edison and Frank Lloyd Wright all haunt the place. These rumors have no basis in fact – or actual experiences – but they make for good stories. The true encounters in the building are much more unnerving, though. Staff members are not shy about admitting that there are certain floors and rooms that they prefer to avoid at night.

Guests of the hotel have told of lights, and especially televisions turning on and off by themselves. This activity is usually attributed to the ghost of "The Judge," one of the last elderly people to live in the hotel full time. In his declining years, the Judge would entertain himself by wheeling around in his wheelchair with a remote control, confusing people by turning their televisions off and on from the hallway outside. For whatever reason, his ghost is said to have remained behind, still repeating the activity that amused him so much during life.

There have been several reports of a little boy and girl running up and down the hallways. The boy is far more commonly seen than the girl. He has been seen all over, including in the kitchen and in guest's rooms in the middle of the night. He is most active on the 12th floor of the north wing, which is commonly said to be the spookiest floor of the hotel.

There are a couple of different theories about the boy's identity and, in truth, it could be more than one ghost. Perhaps the most common suggestion about who this boy might be is that he is Karl Langer, the six-year-old who fell to this death with his mother and brother in 1939. Adele Langer was distraught over the loss of her home and husband's business in Czechoslovakia at the start of World War II and often spoke of killing herself and taking her babies with her. On August 3, she did just that, plunging to her death from the twelfth floor with her two boys, Karl, 6, and Jan, 4. They landed on the sidewalk along Michigan Avenue in front of startled onlookers – but at least one of them – likely Karl – has never left the hotel.

There are also some who believe that the boy and girl are Donald and Zudel Stoddard, two children who were killed in the 1903 Iroquois Theatre Fire. The story goes that their mother spent a frantic day searching for them before returning to the Auditorium Hotel – as it was known then – where she learned that their bodies had been discovered in the theater's ruins. Some believe that the two spectral children are the spirits of her children, still looking for their mother.

In a 2006, several staff members reported that there had been calls from guests on the seventh floor of the south wing saying that a vagrant with an artificial leg was lying in the hallway. Security arrived but found no trace of the man. The ghost -- sometimes known as "Peg Leg Johnny" -- is thought to be that of a peg-legged hobo who is believed to have died in the hotel in the 1920s. If that's true, though, I've never been able to find any record of it. Since then, he's been seen all over the building, including in the ballroom known as the Gold Room.

And if he does haunt the Gold Room, he doesn't do so alone. There are several ghosts reported there, including a bride and groom who have been reportedly seen on the balcony. Security guards also claim that they have heard a phantom orchestra playing in this room. However, when they open the doors to the ballroom, it's always found to be dark, silent, and empty. Much of the activity on this floor isn't in the ballroom, it's around it. It has been reported that the ovens in the nearby kitchens will turn themselves on, despite the fact that they aren't connected to anything anymore.

As spooky as the Gold Room can be, it is the Florentine Room that the staff seems to regard as the scariest. At least three security guards have reported hearing old-fashioned music coming from the room in the middle of the night. Some attribute this to music played in the room when it was used for roller skating parties years ago. Others have heard the piano in the room play of its own accord. Still others have reported seeing phantom dancers, and many have reported the feeling of a hand on their shoulder.

One of the most chilling stories of the hotel involves a group of U.S. Marines who were scared out of their wits in the middle of the night by a "shadow figure" in their room. They rushed down to the lobby in their underwear and refused to go back into the room for their luggage. Veterans and others connected to the military have also encountered this shadow man in the hotel and one security guard claimed to encounter him on the roof one night.

With his connection to the military, it's thought that perhaps this is the ghosts of Louis Ostheim, the soldier who returned home from the Philippines with post-traumatic stress disorder and shot himself in his room at the Auditorium Hotel on the eve of his wedding. His friends believed that he awakened and shot himself in the midst of a nightmare. Perhaps the terror that he felt that night left a presence behind at the hotel.

Whoever these ghosts might be, there is no question that they have become an indelible part of the history of the Congress Hotel.

Sightings and first-hand encounters continue to this day and so anyone hoping for a paranormal adventure has a very good chance of finding it if they choose this hotel for their Chicago vacation.

3. MENGER HOTEL
SAN ANTONIO, TEXAS

Firmly entrenched on the National Register of Historic Places, the Menger Hotel is one of the oldest and most famous hotels in the state of Texas. It may come as no surprise to readers that it's also known as one of the most haunted. And why shouldn't it be? Not only does it have a storied history of its own, but it's located adjacent to what may be the most famous place in the state – the Alamo.

As if the hotel doesn't have enough ghosts of its own, the wandering spirits of the fateful battle just may have taken up residence there, as well.

My first visit to the Alamo came far too late in life. It was a place that I had always wanted to see. I'd been told to expect disappointment over the size and location of the Alamo. It's a very small place, I was warned, right in the middle of downtown San Antonio, right next to a hotel. I shouldn't go there expecting too much. But my visit to the Alamo and the Menger Hotel was anything but disappointing.

I found myself overwhelmed by the place. The quiet stillness of the old mission makes it easy to believe that the heroes of yesterday have left a chilling impression behind at a place many consider to be the most haunted in Texas.

And the Menger? We'll come back to that in a moment.

The beginnings of the Alamo were humble ones. In the early 1500s, all the land that would later make up the state of Texas belonged to Spain. For the next two centuries, this vast frontier was molded and shaped by famous explorers like Alvarez De Pineda, Francisco Vásquez de Coronado, and others. But whatever accomplishments that were made by these men, they were overshadowed by the demands of the Catholic Church in the region. During the late 1690s, Spanish priests were enlisted to help colonize the Texas Territory in the name of the King of Spain. The key to this monumental endeavor was the conversion of the Native Americans living in the region to Catholicism. It was believed that this was an act of benevolence that would not only save the Indians' souls, but would also ease their eventual assimilation into European culture.

Almost from the start, this ill-conceived and poorly-executed campaign met with failure. Hampered by repeated Indian attacks and food shortages, the priests, largely Franciscan, were forced to abandon their plans for the region. Unable to admit defeat, the Church returned in the 1700s and established a series of frontier missions along a line that stretched from the present-day town of Guerrero all the way to the Rio Grande. In 1718, a group of monks constructed the Alamo in a cotton grove in San Antonio de Béxar.

Life at the mission could be brutal. Disease and starvation were rampant. In 1739, a smallpox epidemic ravished the mission and the surrounding countryside. It was in a remote location and a site almost abandoned by Spain because there were no gold deposits nearby. Even so, the Alamo survived, and over the next several decades, it slowly expanded into a fortress-like mission, changing in both size and complexity. A small military garrison was stationed at the mission, and in 1789, an eight-foot stone wall was erected around the chapel and its 16 outer buildings. The barrier served as protection from Indian attacks for the town's 275 men, women, and children.

In December 1802, a full company of Spanish soldiers was posted at the Alamo in the hope that the increased military presence would dissuade the French or the Americans from planning any sort of invasion into the Texas region. But as it turned out, invasion by foreign countries was the least of Spain's worries. Between 1805 and 1821, a series of uprisings turned Mexico into a hotbed of rebellion. For 16 years, the inhabitants fought and died for their freedom until Spain finally relinquished its hold over Mexico in 1821.

By 1824, Mexico had developed into an independent nation and had established a democratic constitution. Around that time, American settlers began to be courted to try and get them to immigrate to Mexican Texas (then part of the Mexican State of Coahuila y Tejas) and establish settlements, colonies, businesses, farms, and plantations. The Mexican government believed that this would accelerate civilization in that part of Mexico. The American colonists were offered large tracts of land and guaranteed protection and assistance by the Mexican government.

This practice continued without problems until the Texians, as they were called, revolted when Antonio López de Santa Anna became President of Mexico in 1835. Upon coming into power, Santa Anna rescinded the democratic constitution of 1824, dismantled the state legislatures, and proclaimed himself as dictator of Mexico.

Large groups of Americans flooded into Texas to assist in the revolt, hoping to help the Texians and the Tejanos -- former Mexicans living in the region -- achieve independence. Though most of them were untrained for military operations and could count their time in Texas by weeks rather than years, they were a dedicated group. Together, they moved to capture Mexican military outposts and garrisons in the area. After a major conflict on December 10, 1835, in which the new Texas Army defeated the Mexican garrison at San Antonio de Béxar, they were able to drive out any remaining Mexican military from the region.

After taking San Antonio, the spirited Texians declared their independence from Mexico, established a provisional government, and elected Davis Burnet as president. A capitol for the fledgling Republic of Texas was founded at Washington-on-the-Brazos. The Americans and Texian colonists who had volunteered to help drive out the Mexicans believed that the revolution was over, and the Republic of Texas was in place. Most of them returned to their homes and families, leaving a skeleton army to maintain the new republic's independence.

Santa Anna, a man not to be crossed, did not agree. He saw the "revolution" as nothing more than an insurrection, and one that needed to be put down immediately. With a strong show of force and a violent, unforgiving hand, he believed the Texians would suffer the consequences of their rebellious actions and not dare to rise up again.

President Santa Anna gathered an army more than 6,000 strong. Within days of being informed of the loss of San Antonio de Béxar, he assumed the title of general and personally led his vast army on a march into Texas. Once in Texas, he split his army, sending 900 men with General José de Urrea to San Patricio. Santa Anna continued the march to San Antonio himself, as he wanted to be the one to personally put down the Texians and retake the settlement.

After the Texians had overtaken San Antonio and evicted the Mexican military, protection from Mexican retaliatory attacks became their primary goal. Two forts blocked the entrances into Texas from the interior of Mexico: the Alamo in San Antonio de Béxar and Presidio La Bahía in Goliad. Both forts would remain frontier outposts for the protection of the new republic. Colonel James W. Fannin was put in command of the fort in Goliad and Colonel James Neill was assigned to command the Alamo.

Colonel Neill worked hard to strengthen the former mission. The walls were thick and high, but they were simple masonry. The buildings were not strategically designed for protection. His principal efforts were directed toward placing the 24 artillery pieces scattered around the mission inside the fort's walls for the greatest effect. There was also a severe shortage of supplies. The fort was seriously undermanned and low on both ammunition and horses. Neill complained to General Sam Houston that his men were underfed and exhausted. A message he sent to the provisional government stated: "Unless we are reinforced and victualed (provided with food and supplies), we must become an easy prey to the enemy, in case of an attack."

Soon after, on January 19, Colonel James Bowie arrived with a small company of men. He was impressed with the work already done and he worked well with Colonel Neill. Complaints again went out stressing the lack of horses. There weren't even enough horses to send out scouts to watch for signs of the approaching Mexican Army. Again, a meager number of reinforcements were sent to the Alamo. Colonel William Travis arrived on February 3, with a small contingent of cavalry. Five days later, David Crockett, the famous frontiersman and former U.S. congressmen, arrived with a small group of American volunteers. Sadly, they were still significantly low on supplies and ammunition. The number of soldiers positioned at one of the two forts protecting the whole of the Republic of Texas had risen to only 150 men.

At noon on February 23, 1836, Santa Anna and the forward part of his army reached the crossroads just outside of San Antonio. Guards that had been positioned south of town came riding in hard with the news that what looked like the entire Mexican Army was moving in. With Neill absent as the result of a family emergency, Travis and Bowie began giving orders. Some men were sent to collect what food stores they could find, and others worked to drive their few head of cattle inside the fort. Most of the Mexicans living in San Antonio were hostile to the Texians, but there were a few people living outside the walls of the Alamo who were invited inside for protection.

Two hours later, after a brief respite, Santa Anna marched his men into the village and sent word to Travis, demanding immediate and unconditional surrender. Travis answered with a cannon shot. Santa Anna initiated a bombardment of the fort and gave orders that it continue around the clock. Travis sent off an express message to Colonel Fannin in Goliad, 90 miles to the southeast, where Fannin had a contingent of 300 soldiers. Travis described the situation at the Alamo as extremely serious and requested immediate assistance.

The 13-day siege of the Alamo had begun.

On February 24, Travis sent an appeal to the provisional government for supplies and reinforcements. He and Bowie knew that without them, they had no chance of withstanding the attack.

As Colonel Travis was composing his message, Bowie became ill. He was believed to have fallen victim to what was then known as "hasty consumption" (rapidly active tuberculosis). Bowie remained in his bed for the rest of the siege, except for the noon officers' meeting, when he would crawl from his bed to attend, and then crawl back to bed.

On February 26, a light skirmish between the fort's defenders and Mexican cavalry erupted, but it amounted to nothing. A storm had blown in and the temperature dropped to 39-degrees. Santa Anna brought up more reinforcements and posted more guards around the Alamo, but the Texians were able to sneak out for wood and food and return safely. While they were out, they burned a few houses. The bombardment of the Alamo continued.

Early in the day on February 28, Colonel Fannin and 200 men with four pieces of artillery left Goliad for the Alamo, leaving 100 men to guard the Presidio La Bahía. After marching only 200 yards, though, a wagon carrying supplies broke down. They decided to return to the Precidio La Bahia and Fort Defiance in Goliad. They would not be reinforcing the soldiers at the Alamo.

Meanwhile, the bombardment of the Alamo continued. No help was coming.

On March 1, Captain John Smith slipped into the Alamo, bringing 32 Texians with him. That brought the number of men inside the walls to 188. Outside, Santa Anna's troops numbered 5,000. The defenders were holding their own, but the walls of the fort were weakening. The Mexican troops were rested and well-fed while the Texians were starving and exhausted.

By the tenth day of the siege, March 3, Santa Anna's men had erected a fourth battery to the north of the fort, within musket range. Travis sent off another desperate request for reinforcements and supplies. This was to be his last appeal to the president. By then, he had ceased expecting any help to come from Colonel Fanning.

The final day came on March 6 when, just after midnight, Santa Anna pulled his entire force into town and surrounded the fort. His troops had been supplied with scaling ladders and they waited quietly for the word to attack. At 5:00 a.m., they received their orders. The troops moved forward and the ladders were placed against the wall, ready to scale. But the Texians were ready and met them with heavy fire, driving the Mexicans back. They made a second attempt with the same results, followed by a third and a fourth. Each time, they were repulsed by the Texians. For Santa Anna, the fifth try finally met with success.

The Mexican troops flooded up and over the wall and into the Alamo. Completely overwhelmed, the Texians had no chance -- but they kept fighting. Travis was one of the first to be killed. The beleaguered Texians fought until nearly all lay dead in the dirt inside the Alamo. Santa Anna had given orders that the wounded were to be killed. The Mexicans then moved through the fort, looking for anyone who might be hiding. During this search, the men came upon Colonel Bowie, still in his sickbed. Knowing he was one of the commanders of the fort, they butchered him.

After 12 days of bombardment, the Alamo was taken by the Mexican Army in just 90 minutes. By 8:00 a.m., every fighting man who had defended the Alamo lay dead.

After the dead Texians had been collected and brought into the center of the courtyard, the bodies were looted for valuables. The bodies were then stripped of their clothing and stacked like cordwood and set on fire. Witnesses related that the corpses smoldered for three days.

Despite the savagery of the attack, several people survived the day. Santa Anna distinguished between those who had fought against him and others who had not. The survivors were all released without harm. They included the wife of a slain officer and her infant daughter; Travis' black servant, and two Mexican women from San Antonio, cousins of Travis' widow. Each of the survivors were given a blanket and two dollars and sent on their way.

The Mexican Army stood victorious but at a tremendous cost. Records vary, but best estimates put the number of dead at nearly 500, with almost as many wounded.

The heroic defenders of the Alamo were wiped out to the last man.

And the battle that Santa Anna thought would frighten the rebels into submission became an inspiration to the people of Texas. Their battle cry for freedom became, "Remember the Alamo!" After the battles that followed, Santa Anna was defeated, and the Republic of Texas was born.

The Alamo was already 93-years-old at the time of the famous battle. The first stones for the Spanish mission were laid in 1744. There were several hundred burials in what is now known as Alamo Plaza. In 1793, the Catholic Church moved the religious artifacts to a nearby mission and turned the property over to the town. It officially became the Alamo, the Spanish word for cottonwood, when it was used as a barracks for Spanish soldiers in 1803. The building was vacant and abandoned between 1825 till 1835, when General Martin Perfecto de Cos of the Mexican Army made it into a military fort. It changed hands between the Mexicans and the Texans three more times, including the Battle of the Alamo in 1836. After that time, a variety of purposes were found for the structure until it was purchased by the state of Texas and opened to the public as a state shrine.

After so many different uses by so many different people, it is not unexpected that the old mission chapel and surrounding property is considered quite haunted. However, the primary reason that the Alamo is so haunted can be linked to the battle that occurred there in 1836, when hundreds of people died violent deaths over a period of just over two hours. Added to that, the bodies of the Texians were stripped, desecrated and burned, with no proper burial. Even the bodies of the Mexican soldiers were mishandled in ways that would have been considered improper in their religion and their culture. They were either burned, thrown into the San Antonio River, or left to rot as carrion for wild animals and vultures.

The land within and surrounding the old mission is essentially a cemetery. After the bodies were burned, their ashes and charred bits of bone and teeth were raked out and mixed in with the soil. Is it any wonder that spirits of the past are still believed to linger at the Alamo?

There is no record of any hauntings or ghost sightings before the battle in 1836, but one of the most prominent paranormal legends stems from just a few weeks afterwards. General Santa Anna and the bulk of his forces stayed on at San Antonio de Béxar for a few weeks before leaving to chase down General Sam Houston and the Republic of Texas Army, leaving a garrison of men at the Alamo under General Juan de Andrade's command.

Shortly before leaving, Santa Anna ordered General de Andrade to demolish the Alamo, leaving nothing standing. General Andrade then instructed Colonel Jose Juan Sanchez-Navarro to get the job done. Colonel Sanchez-Navarro took his men to the site of the Alamo. After 12 days of constant bombardment, the place was not much more than rubble. The only recognizable structure still standing was the mission chapel. The colonel ordered the men to begin demolishing the church and the men complied, although there was some grumbling among the ranks about it possibly being sacrilege to tear down a former Catholic church.

According to legend, as the men began to work, six ghostly forms emerged from the chapel walls. The soldiers immediately stopped what they were doing and backed away, crossing themselves and muttering "diablos!" (devils) under their breath. The forms, often described as monks, slowly advanced on the soldiers, waving flaming swords and warning the men in inhuman voices, "Do not touch the walls of the Alamo!" Colonel Sanchez-Navarro and his men ran screaming from the chapel, back to their encampment.

When Sanchez-Navarro told General de Andrade what they had witnessed, the general was furious and chastised the colonel for his cowardice. Taking matters into his own hands, de Andrade collected a detail of men and marched them to the Alamo to get the work done. As added protection, he took along a small cannon and instructed the gunner to aim it directly at the front doors of the chapel. But before they could blast the doors, the six ghostly monks again took shape and issued their warning. The general's horse took fright and reared, throwing de Andrade to the ground. Before following his men in retreat, he turned to look at the building again and saw giant flames blast up from the ground. The smoke curled and twisted into the shape of a huge man. The menacing figure held balls of fire in each hand and hurled them at de Andrade.

General de Andrade affected a hasty retreat and the phantom protectors of the Alamo won out, but this part of the legend is not borne out by fact. Apparently, de Andrade was not frightened away for good, since he must have returned to complete his orders. According to official records and archeological investigations, much of what remained of the mission was demolished, including many of the fort's walls.

In the 1890s, the Alamo chapel and some of the old barracks were used as a police station and local jail. Soon after moving into the old buildings, the prisoners and guards began complaining about a variety of unexplainable experiences. They reported that a ghostly sentry walked from east to west on the roof of the police station, formerly the old barracks. This and other events were described so frequently and fervently that stories about the hauntings were picked up by the newspapers.

The *San Antonio Express News* published two articles, in 1894 and again in 1897, about the ghostly goings-on. The articles described several types of "manifestations" that were witnessed within the walls of the police station and jail. These were mysterious man-shaped shadows moving about the rooms and corridors, and strange moaning sounds that could not be explained. According to the newspaper reports, these were frequent and so frightening that many of the guards refused to patrol the area after dark.

As the stories of the hauntings became more well-known, complaints were brought to the San Antonio City Council, where councilmen took the position that making the prisoners sleep in a building with ghosts roaming around and moaning amounted to "cruel and unusual punishment," and that it was unsafe for the public because of the guards refusal to walk their patrols after sunset. Shortly after the second article was published, the city moved the police station from the Alamo to a building that was not haunted.

Many of the same types of incidents that were reported in the 1890s are said to continue to happen today, except that now, the ghosts of the Alamo no longer seem to distinguish between night and day – they prefer to conduct their hauntings around the clock.

For decades, visitors, park rangers and passersby have described seeing a mysterious sentry walking his patrol. There have also been countless reports of unexplained noises: men screaming in pain, battle cries, and voices and whispers seeming to emanate from the walls of the chapel. People walking past the Alamo at night have seen distorted and disheveled human shapes emerging from the exterior walls.

A commonly seen apparition is that of a man dressed in clothing of the early 1800s, walking across the courtyard. Although visitors have described seeing this man many times over the years, the story was validated for Alamo officials by one of their own park rangers. The ranger noticed a man dressed in period costume walking toward the library. The ranger decided to follow him and see what he was up to. To his surprise, the stranger faded away to nothing as he approached the chapel.

Another commonly witnessed ghost is that of a blond boy who has been seen wandering the buildings and courtyard but is most often seen in the gift shop. He apparently likes to interact with children and has been known to carry on conversations with them. He has told several children that he was present during the battle and believes that he died there. He seems to selectively appear to specific people, with children waving goodbye to him while their parents see no one.

The basement of the mission, which is now used mostly for storage, has also been the scene of supernatural manifestations. Staff members have often felt that someone is sneaking up on them while they are working. When they turn to see who might be approaching, a shadowy apparition is glimpsed as he quickly steps backward through the wall and disappears. Employees are – not surprisingly – often reluctant to enter the basement for fear of encountering this mysterious phantom.

The Alamo is a sacred place, there is no doubt about that. It is also a haunted one. If the horror of war can leave psychic scars on a battlefield, a landscape or a building, then the eerie atmosphere that still surrounds the Alamo can be easily explained.

Dating back to the days that followed the battle, common, everyday people began having experiences at the old mission that they could not explain. Without a doubt, some of the stories that have survived can be dismissed as folklore or the products of overactive imaginations, but what do we make of the other encounters? The ones that cannot be explained away by logic and rational thinking?

For the countless ghost hunters, tourists, and park rangers who have found themselves frightened, unnerved, and even exhilarated by a brush with the lingering spirits of the Alamo, there is no question that the place is haunted.

And for those with a taste for spirits who are looking for a place to spend the night, there is no need to walk any further than directly next door, where the Menger Hotel awaits with open doors.

The Menger Hotel opened on February 1, 1859, in Alamo Plaza. It was built by William and Mary Menger on the site of the couple's popular brewery, which is believed to have been the first brewery in Texas.

Menger, a German immigrant, arrived in San Antonio in the early 1840s and went into the beer business a few years later. In 1857, he and his wife decided to build a hotel to accommodate the many customers who frequented the brewery. A year later, they hired local architect John M. Fries to design a two-story cut-stone building, which featured an abundance of classical detail. It was unlike anything else in town. At that point, most overnight accommodations in San Antonio were boarding houses. The Menger opened in 1859 and became an immediate success.

The hotel did so well that the Mengers immediately made plans to build an addition between the hotel and the brewery. Construction on the 40-room annex was started in August and completed the following year. The hotel featured a tunnel opening from the basement, through which Menger led groups of selected guests on tours of the brewery.

The Menger continued to operate – mostly successfully-- even through the years of the Civil War and the turmoil of Reconstruction. As the prospect of war gained momentum in South Texas, soldiers flooded into San Antonio. The men stationed there created a need for rooms and the Mengers provided lodging for soldiers and officers. After the war began, it was a struggle to maintain business, so the Mengers decided to use the building to aid the war effort. The guest rooms were closed during the war, but the dining room remained open to feed locals and military personnel. They also offered space for medical care of wounded soldiers. Once the war ended, the hotel resumed operations.

Unfortunately, just a few years after the war ended, William Menger died in 1871, leaving Mary and their son, Louis, to run the hotel and brewery. Mary ran an advertisement in the San Antonio newspaper to announce that she would carry on the business and that her husband's death "would cause no change in affairs" within the hotel or brewery.

She also made plans to enlarge the hotel again to better accommodate the guests she was serving. She bought a parcel of neighboring property – more land where the men of the Alamo died, and their bones were scattered – in order to add more rooms to the hotel. Over the course of the next year, she hosted more than 2,000 guests in her hotel, making it the best-known overnight lodging in the Southwest. Writers praised the cuisine offered in the hotel's Colonial Dining Room, which included such specialties as wild game, mango ice cream, and snapper soup made from turtles caught in the San Antonio River.

On February 19, 1877, the first railroad line arrived in San Antonio, which contributed to the further growth of the hotel. This brought thousands of additional guests to the Menger. This led to more changes when Mary began installing bathrooms, proper water closets, and bells to the building. In 1879, she had gas installed, becoming one of the first establishments in town to offer gas lighting.

By this time, Mary felt she was getting too old to care for the Menger in the way that it needed. Since Louis was not interested in taking over the family business, the decision was made to sell the hotel to its original contractor, Major J.H. Kampmann. The sale went through on November 7, 1881. He purchased the Menger and all its furnishings for $127,000, which would be around $3 million in today's currency.

Almost immediately, Major Kampmann began making changes to the hotel's structure. He studied the criticisms raised by the local newspapers about what the Menger was lacking and began remodeling it. Soon, there was the addition of more rooms in an east wing, a relocation of the kitchen, another lobby, and a dining room that would accommodate 160 people. He made it possible for water to be piped to every room, added a laundry, and installed private bathrooms, a luxury offered in very few hotels at the time.

Major Kampmann, much like William Menger, wanted to provide an establishment that allowed travelers to enjoy a hotel that delivered the best. In addition to being known as the most famous hotel in the Southwest, it was now the most elegant. By 1885, it also boasted a bar room, billiard hall, and a barbershop.

Major Kampmann eventually retired, turning over ownership of the hotel to his son, Herman. He died in Colorado Springs in 1885, when he was 66-years-old. He left the Menger in capable hands. Herman was an avid businessman who became one of the wealthiest people in San Antonio. His father had made many changes to the hotel, but Herman felt there could be more. One of his first additions was a new saloon, which was a replica of the taproom in the House of Lords Club in London. This bar would come to be a huge success among both the local citizens, as well as famous celebrities. The Menger Bar, as it is known, gave off an elegant appeal with its "ornate mahogany tables and chairs... large mirrors... fine crystal and sterling silver." There was a solid cherry bar, cherry-paneled ceiling, French mirrors, and gold-plated spittoons and it became one of the marvels of San Antonio. The beer was chilled by the Alamo Madre ditch, which passed through the hotel's courtyard, mint juleps were served in silver tumblers, and hot rum toddies became the bar's popular cool weather drink.

The hotel's bar became closely connected to Theodore Roosevelt, who first visited the Menger in 1892 while in Texas for a javelina hunt. He returned to recruit the Rough Riders in the bar in 1898 and attended a banquet there in 1905.

A few years later, Herman added a fourth floor to the Blum Street side of the hotel. The always growing demand for rooms became the hotel's most urgent need. Herman also continued to introduce the newest technologies, like a steam elevator, electric lights, and artesian wells. He also added a reading room to the hotel. History notes that "many early writers and chroniclers of life in the Southwest" came to the Menger and wrote and worked in this room. In 1897, Herman remodeled the kitchen again and installed new furnishings and fixtures in the dining room.

As the business continued to thrive, Herman found it difficult to operate alone, so he turned the day-to-day management decisions to J.W. McClean and J.H. Mudge. Tragically, Herman died in a buggy accident in 1902. The hotel's ownership passed to his family and they tried to continue his desire for changes and updates. In 1909, they hired architect Alfred Giles to alter the hotel's main façade by adding Renaissance Revival details in stuccoed brick, pressed metal, and cast iron. He also designed the interior rotunda and created a patterned tile floor in the lobby. In 1912, the dining room was renovated once more, and 30 guest rooms were added with an addition on the south side.

The Menger Hotel remains the center of San Antonio social affairs and served as a meeting place for visiting celebrities – for a little while longer, at least. The early glory days were coming to an end with the start of World War I and the Great Depression. By that time, it was so neglected that it was removed from guidebooks. The Depression years led to the hotel's abandonment. There was simply not enough money to make the necessary repairs and renovations. By the 1930s, there was talk of tearing the place down to build a parking lot.

If this had occurred, it would have been a tragic loss to the city. The hotel had been the center of many important events and hosted many famous guests – some before and others after the decline, like Presidents Ulysses S. Grant, Benjamin Harrison, Theodore Roosevelt, Woodrow Wilson, William H. Taft. William McKinley, Harry Truman, Lyndon Johnson, Richard Nixon, Ronald Reagan, George H.W. Bush, Bill Clinton, and George W. Bush; military figures like Sam Houston and Robert E. Lee; and scores of celebrities and popular figures like Oscar Wilde, Babe Ruth, Mae West, and many others.

World War II kept public focus away from the destruction of the Menger, until 1944, when it was purchased by William Lewis Moody, Jr. Moody had arrived in Texas with a law degree from the University of Virginia and had founded the National Hotel Corporation in 1928. In June 1944, the corporation took over the hotel. Moody had plans to remake the place from top to bottom with new plumbing, electrical fixtures, new decorations, and a complete restoration of the Spanish patio gardens. In addition, he wanted to have the floor coverings replaced with carpeting, completely renovate the guestrooms and public rooms, and have the kitchen newly equipped. Moody also had the paintings restored by local artist Ernst Raba, the antique furniture refinished and refurnished, and lastly, the Colonial Dining room was totally restored.

In 1948, the lobby that J.H. Kampmann had constructed in 1881, along with several guestrooms above it, was torn down and replaced with a new lobby and three floors of air-conditioned guestrooms. In 1951, a new wing was added and two years later, the hotel gained a swimming pool. In 1976, the hotel was added to the National Register of Historic Places and over the years since, it has been remodeled several additional times.

In addition to its significance as a historic landmark, it still offers unmatched amenities that include the famous Colonial Dining Room, the Menger Bar, and 316 guest rooms and suites. Many rooms overlook the Alamo next door, reminding guests of the turbulent events that led to the creation of San Antonio as we know it today.

And perhaps serving as a reminder of one of the reasons that the Menger Hotel is believed to be such a haunted place.

32 ghosts.

That's how many spirits are said to still be making the Menger Hotel their ethereal home. Regardless, it seems that they don't mid sharing the space with the living. All of them go about their business, only mildly unnerving the staff and guests.

With the hotel being adjacent to the Alamo, many of the spectral visitors are believed to be some of the many people who died during the battle. Often, heavy footsteps and kicking are heard, tromping up and down the hallways. Old military boots are sometimes seen by the guests and hotel workers. One morning, a guest emerged from his shower to see a man dressed in a buckskin jacket, gray pants, and military boots having a heated conversation with an unseen presence. The specter demanded, "Are you gonna stay or are you gonna go?" three times before he vanished. Had he been one of the Texian defenders of the Alamo, trying to convince another man to stay and fight?

But not all the spirits can be connected to the battle. One of the most famous resident haunts is former President Theodore Roosevelt. It was at the Menger, in the saloon, where he recruited hard-living cowboys to his detachment of Rough Riders. Reportedly, Roosevelt sat at the bar and when the cowboys came in, he offered them a free drink – or more than one – as he worked his recruiting strategy on an unsuspecting cowpoke. Many sobered up the next morning to find themselves on their way to military training and a boat to Cuba. Over the years, Roosevelt has reportedly been seen still having a drink in the barroom off the main lobby.

The most often encountered ghost of the Menger, though, is Sallie White. Long ago, Sallie was a chambermaid who worked at the hotel. One night, after an argument with her husband, she decided to stay the night instead of going home. The next day, her husband turned up and threatened to kill her, believing that she was seeing another man. On March 28, 1876, he attacked her and left her for dead. She died of her injuries two days later. The hotel owners paid for her funeral costs and, perhaps, in exchange for this kindness, Sallie continues to perform her duties at the Menger. She has been seen numerous times wearing a long gray skirt, with a bandana around her head, a common uniform during her era. Usually appearing at night, Sallie is usually spotted walking the hotel corridors with an armload of clean towels for guests.

Another apparition that is often reported is that of Captain Richard King, the founder of what was once one of the largest ranches in the world – the King Ranch of South Texas.

Born in New York City to a poor Irish family in 1824, King was indentured as an apprentice to a jeweler in Manhattan at the age of nine. In 1835, he stowed away aboard a ship bound for Mobile, Alabama. He was discovered, but was adopted into the crew and trained in navigation, becoming a steamboat pilot at age 16. During the Texas Revolution, King's friend, Mifflin Kenedy, convinced him to join the war effort along the Rio Grande and the two men later founded a steamboat company that largely controlled the river for decades.

With immense profits from his steamship business, King began speculating in land, beginning with lots in Brownsville and Cameron County. In 1852, he traveled to Corpus Christi and became fascinated with the grasslands between the Nueces River and the Rio Grande. He started buying up land titles along Santa Gertrudis Creek, eventually acquiring two ranches that formed the center of the King Ranch. In time, it spread over 614,000 acres of South Texas.

During the Civil War, King sold cattle to the Confederacy and was active in the Cotton Road trade route that allowed the Confederates to sell their cotton through Mexico. King profited from the cotton caravans that stopped at the King Ranch for supplies and made money from the steamboats operating under Mexican registry that transported cotton south of the border and returned to Texas with military supplies.

When the Union Army invaded Texas to stop the Cotton Road trade, King helped to shift the route to Laredo. Around Christmas 1863, Union soldiers attacked King Ranch. King was warned in advance and fled the ranch house, leaving his family under the care of ranch hand Francisco Alvarado. When the troops opened fire on the house, Alvarado was killed while trying to warn them that only women and children were inside. Union soldiers searched the property for King, vandalized the house, and took the ranch hands as prisoners. This left King trapped in Matamoros, Mexico, for the remainder of the war. On July 14, 1865, he was given amnesty and allowed to return to Texas.

In the years after the war, King became a frequent visitor to the Menger Hotel. In fact, he even rented a personal suite for himself. In 1885, in obvious poor health, he moved to San Antonio to be closer to his doctor and took up residence in the hotel. When he learned of his impending death, he wrote a will that would dispose of his great wealth at the Menger and summoned his friends there for a final goodbye. He died at the Menger of stomach cancer on April 14, 1885. Captain King's funeral was held in the hotel parlor the following day.

He checked into the Menger Hotel in 1885 and never checked out.

Today, his suite is known as the "King Ranch Room" and it's there that the rancher is often encountered. He is often seen entering his old room, going right through the wall where the door was once located before it was remodeled.

Another phantom of the Menger is an old woman who is sometimes spotted in the original lobby of the hotel. She wears an old-fashioned blue dress, small, wire-framed spectacles, and has a tasseled hat on her head. She is always seen sitting quietly, patiently knitting. On many occasions, new or unknowing staff members have stopped to ask her if she needs anything, only to receive an unfriendly "No" in reply. A moment later, she disappears.

Other spirits have been known to "help" in the kitchen, moving pots and pans, closing doors, opening the refrigerators, and causing utensils to vanish or move about through the air. Placing something on a counter and leaving it unattended can often be tricky in the hotel's kitchen.

Beyond the recognizable ghosts and the military spirits of the Alamo, other guests are thought to be those of people who stayed at the hotel over the decades, along with some of the Rough Riders, who didn't return alive from the Spanish-American War.

Though the number of resident entities at the Menger is believed to be high, all of them are an ever-present reminder of days gone by. They are as much a part of the hotel as the guests and staff members of the present day – and a constant embodiment of the old adage that "the past is never truly past."

4. THE CRESCENT HOTEL
EUREKA SPRINGS, ARKANSAS

Located in the rather isolated resort town of Eureka Springs, Arkansas, stands the gothic Crescent Hotel. Called by some the "Grand Old Lady of the Ozarks, the hotel has served as many things over the years and each incarnation has managed to contribute to the legion of phantoms that stalk the corridors of the building. If there is a single place in the Ozark Mountain region that can be called "most haunted," it is undoubtedly this intimidating old hotel.

The Crescent Hotel is one of my favorites in this book. I have stayed there many times over the years and have always enjoyed my stays in Eureka Springs. It's a unique town that changed from a health resort to a mid-twentieth century epicenter of religious dinner theaters. The influx of bible-waving tourists inspired the fading motor lodges and funky campgrounds that still exist today. But among the kitschy spots are thriving mom and pop stores, great restaurants, and the worn elegance of yesterday.

Up on the hill, looking down on all of it, is the Crescent Hotel.

I will confess before this chapter begins that I have never encountered a ghost at the hotel. It's a wonderful place, filled with history and lore and I'll certainly admit that its colorful past certainly makes the place ripe for a haunting. However, its spirits have eluded me.

But as with many other locations that I have visited over the years, I have spoken with scores of others who do claim to have come face-to-face with guests and residents of the hotel's past. There are far too many stories for them to have all been part of someone's imagination.

They leave me with little doubt that the Crescent Hotel is a very haunted place.

The Crescent Hotel was built on the ridge of West Mountain between 1884 and 1886 and may have gained its first ghost when a workman fell from the roof during the construction. His body landed in the second-floor area where Room 218 is now located. It's no coincidence that many believe it to be one of the most haunted rooms in the hotel.

The Crescent was designed by Isaac L. Taylor, a well-known Missouri architect who was famous for several buildings in St. Louis and who would go on to greater fame for his designs during the 1904 World's Fair. The financing for the hotel came from a syndicate of wealthy individuals and businessmen, including Powell Clayton, the governor of Arkansas from 1868 to 1870, and later the U.S. Ambassador to Mexico. Clayton formed the Eureka Improvement Company to seek investors and to acquire land, hoping to take advantage of the "boom time" of the period. Many of the other investors included officials with the Frisco Railroad, like Richard Kerens. Other members of the board included Logan Roots, an Arkansas congressman and Dr. C.F. Ellis, a homeopathic physician who was a promoter of the area's healing waters.

The construction of the hotel, and development in the area, was vitally important at that time because of the national attention that had come to Eureka Springs -- and other locations in Arkansas -- for the "healing waters" that were bubbling from the earth nearby. During the late 1800s, people traveled from all over the country to take in the waters and to hopefully ease and cure their many ailments. In addition, spring water was also bottled and shipped out, further enhancing the small town's reputation.

In the 1880s, railroad companies were making a fortune by putting together excursion trips by train to resorts, parks, and attractions across the country. The Frisco Railroad had built a spur from Seligman, Missouri, to Eureka Springs to accommodate the tourists who wanted to visit the area. It was in the railroad's best interest to develop a fine hotel in which their passengers could stay. This provided the incentive for officials for the company to invest not only their own money, but also railroad funds. As the Crescent neared completion, liveried footmen would meet guests at the railroad depot and transport them by coach to the portico of the new hotel.

The hotel was completed at the cost of $294,000, which adds up to more than $8 million today, if that gives the reader any indication of the hotel's intended luxury. The building itself combined several architectural styles to create a unique – and sometimes foreboding – setting. It was equipped with numerous towers, overhanging balconies, and granite walls that are more than eighteen inches thick. Although the five-story interior has been altered many times over the years, the lobby is still fitted with a massive stone fireplace that dominates the room. At one time, more than 500 people could be seated in the dining room. The original construction included electric bells, Edison lamps, a hydraulic elevator, rooms with bathrooms and modern plumbing fixtures, and was heated with steam. Downstairs, in the south wing, were two Brunswick regulated bowling alleys and a billiards room. Off the south end of the hotel, at the opposite end from the ballroom, was the solarium. The lawn outside was decorated with gazebos, winding boardwalks, and flower gardens and guests were offered tennis courts, croquet, and other outdoor recreations.

The hotel officially opened on May 1, 1886, with an open house held about two weeks later. The Crescent hosted a banquet for 400 people, followed by music in the Grand Ballroom. The guest of honor was James G. Blaine, Republican presidential nominee, and he spoke at the dedication ceremony that was held immediately after the banquet.

The Crescent became almost immediately popular and attracted people from all over the region. It flourished initially as a summer destination, but when it was taken over in 1902 by the Frisco System Railroad, the company began running the place as a year-round resort. They leased it from a new owner, C.H. Smith of St. Louis, who bought the hotel for $30,000 from the Eureka Springs Improvement Company, when it was closed for the winter of 1901-1902.

The railroad leased the hotel for the next five years. Since the hotel had been in operation for a few years and needed a facelift, one condition of the lease was that the railroad had to spend a minimum of $50,000 on new furnishings and improvements.

The hotel, along with Eureka Springs itself, thrived for the next decade, but changes came when people began to realize that while the local hot springs were certainly wonderful, they held no curative powers. The springs soon lost the interest of the wealthier class, who had many other pursuits in that "Gilded Age" and business for the town dropped off. The loss of revenue convinced the railroad to abandon their attempt at running a hotel. They did not renew their lease after five years and the hotel was closed in the winter once again.

In 1908, to provide financial support during the off-season, the hotel became the Crescent College and Conservatory for Young Women in the fall, winter, and spring. It was an exclusive academy for wealthy young ladies. During the summer, it still catered to the tourist crowd, but the money it made was not enough to keep the aging monolith in business. The costs of operating, heating, and repairing the place were so overwhelming that they could not even be offset by the staggering tuition charged to the students.

The college was opened by A.S. Maddox and J.H. Phillips of the Eureka Springs Investment Company, with Maddox as the first president. He served in that role for just two years. He was followed by Richard Thompson, who remained as president until 1923, when the hotel was sold again.

Thompson first came to the school after he was offered a job by A.S. Maddox as a language teacher for $1,500 annually, including room and board. After taking over the presidency, he turned the

Conservatory into a junior college, and it was accredited. His wife, Mary, became a teacher at the college, even though she had little formal education. However, her grandfather had once served as Vice-President of the United States and her father was an ambassador to many countries while she was growing up. This allowed Mary to receive an unusual education and to learn several foreign languages.

While Richard was president of the college, the Thompsons had two children, a boy, Breckie, and a girl, Polly, who only lived for a few hours. At age four, Breckie contracted an intestinal illness that turned out to be fatal. After his death, Richard and Mary were shattered. Their marriage did not survive and after a hasty divorce, Mary left town. Richard did not remarry until 1957.

The college earned a fine reputation under Thompson's supervision. When he took over, it had been in debt, but he managed to work the school out of it. The students came from all over the country. It was a boarding school, although it did have some local young women who also attended. The school had a literary department and conservators in art, music, expression, domestic sciences, domestic arts, and business skills. Average enrollment for boarding students ranged from about 80-100 young women each season. Tuition began at $270 per year, but was raised to $375 after 1912 and this included courses, room, and board, but not laundry.

A uniform was required. A "Peter Thompson" dress – usually a long, navy dress with a sailor's collar with white stripes – was worn for fall and spring and a navy coat was added for winter. Warm woolen underwear was required and a long-sleeved woolen housedress with heavy stockings was suggested – the building was hard to heat in the winter. Each girl also brought along their own quilt, napkin-ring, Bible, walking shoes, umbrella, raincoat, rubber overshoes, laundry bags, and hot water bottle.

There was an assortment of rules for boarding students. For example, they could not make purchases from town without permission and correspondence with anyone in Eureka Springs was forbidden. At the start of the school year, they had to furnish the dean with a list of those whom they wanted to write. There were also, needless to say, no young men allowed on the property – but this didn't always stop them. The girls had a big basket that they would lower and pull up with a rope so that they could smuggle boys into the hotel. One night, after learning about the basket, President Thompson got into it and they began pulling him up to a third-floor window. But when they realized who was inside, they got nervous and dropped him. Luckily, he landed in some bushes, but he still ended up with a sprained ankle and some bruises.

In 1923, it was announced that the hotel would be sold, and that Richard Thompson would have to buy it to continue the school's occupancy there. He offered $50,000 but the owners wanted $100,000. Unable to raise the money, the school closed.

The following year, it was inexplicably sold for $40,000 to Albert Ingalls and W.T. Patterson, two local businessmen. Apparently, though, they found it just as difficult to operate the hotel year-around as everyone else did because in 1929, the college re-opened as a junior college during the off-season. It remained open until 1933, when the Great Depression finally shut it down for good.

Meanwhile, the hotel was still operating during the summer.

By the 1920s, the automobile was transforming Arkansas into a vacation state. One estimate even claimed that nearly a half-million people drove to the Ozarks for vacations in 1929, a staggering number for the time. Because of this, there were several businesses that leased the Crescent as a summer resort after the school ended its classes for the year.

After the 1929 season, though, the hotel was closed and went through a variety of owners and tenants. It served as the previously mentioned junior college for a time and was generally operated as a seasonal hotel, depending on the current owner. According to some accounts, an owner would sell the hotel to another, who would operate it for a season, and then sell it someone else. No one seemed to be able to get it to operate on a sound financial basis.

And then, a new owner stepped in and transformed the hotel into something else altogether. The next three years would be the darkest time in the Crescent's history, and there is no other period that has contributed as much to the hauntings of the building than the era of Norman Baker's "cancer clinic."

On July 31, 1937, the doors were closed at the Crescent Hotel and the building was sold to Norman Baker, who remodeled the building. The structure underwent a strange transformation, and thus began the most bizarre chapter in its history.

Norman Glenwood Baker was born in Muscatine, Iowa, in 1882. He made his first fortune in 1903 by inventing the Tangley Air Calliope, an organ that played with air pressure instead of steam. He made millions of dollars with his invention, but Baker was a born charlatan, who was never happy without his next scheme. He considered himself something of a medical expert, although he had no training. He wasn't a doctor, but he called himself one and he wasn't merely eccentric – he was mentally ill. He claimed to have discovered a number of "cures" for various ailments, but he was sure that organized medicine was conspiring to keep these "miracle medicines" from the market. He was also sure that these same "enemies" – namely, doctors from the American Medical Association -- were trying to kill him.

Baker opened his first "hospital" in Muscatine in 1929, but ran into legal problems over his "cure" for cancer. He was convicted of practicing medicine without a license in 1936, and all his medicines were condemned by the American Medical Association. Nevertheless, he purchased the Crescent Hotel with plans to turn the place into a hospital and "health resort" for cancer victims.

Baker's remodeling of the hotel reportedly cost almost $50,000, and he tragically destroyed much of the original decoration that remained on the structure. On the exterior of his "cancer clinic," the wood-turned balustrades, which had so enhanced the hotel, were removed and concrete porches were poured in their place. He painted the beams, columns, and woodwork in garish shades of red, orange, black, and yellow.

He was obsessed with the color lavender. He painted whole sections of his hospital lavender, even the venetian blinds. His obsession went beyond mere paint. He drove a lavender Cord automobile, wore white suits with lavender silk shirts and ties, and wrote on lavender stationary. Even the drinking glasses used by the patients had "Baker Hospital" etched on them in lavender. His private office had once been the Governor's Suite of the hotel and, of course, it was painted lavender.

Fearing that he might be attacked by his "enemies" from the American Medical Association, he kept two submachine-guns hanging on the wall within easy reach. He also installed bullet-proof glass around his desk. There were rumors of secret passageways, entrances, and exits in case of any incursions by the authorities – rumors that turned out to be true. Years later, a secret staircase was found in his suite that led up one floor to his girlfriend's room.

On the roof, he installed a calliope that could reportedly be heard for many miles away. The place certainly didn't look like a hospital, but it generally gave the locals plenty to talk about.

After the remodeling was completed, Baker moved his hospital staff and 144 patients from Iowa to Arkansas. He advertised the health resort by saying that no X-rays or operations were performed to save his patients' lives. The "cures" mostly consisted of drinking the natural spring water of the area and various home remedies, but you wouldn't know it from the brochure that he had printed and widely distributed. According to the advertising, the hospital could cure cancer and all sorts of other ailments. On the back cover was a solicitation – "isn't this book worth a dime?" – and Baker planned to send out 10 million of them to "save thousands from the grave." He conducted an ongoing battle against the so-called medical establishment and implored people to "help us battle for medical freedom."

Thanks to his calliope wealth, he purchased the second most powerful radio station in North America, XENT, which was located in Nuevo Laredo, Mexico. He advertised his clinic on the air and irritated the medical community even more.

Baker's bizarre behavior and egocentric nature turned many of the local citizenry against him. Perhaps this is the reason why the bizarre rumors about his clinic got started in the late 1930s.

While some of the cancer patients at the hospital succumbed to their illnesses, no reports exist to say that anyone was actually killed by Baker's treatments. Local rumor, however, had a different story to tell. The legends say that when remodeling was being done at the hotel in later years, dozens of human skeletons were discovered hidden within the walls. These stories claimed that Baker was no harmless eccentric, but a dangerous and terrible man who experimented on both the dead and the living. One of his "miracle cures" for brain tumors was to allegedly peel open the patient's scalp and then pour a mixture of spring water and ground watermelon seeds directly onto the brain. Dozens of the patients died and Baker was said to have hidden the bodies for weeks until they could be burned in the incinerator in the middle of night. As his publicity claimed that he could cure cancer in a matter of weeks, he had to keep the press from finding out that many of his patients died every month. It has been said that he would put the extreme and advanced cases into an "asylum," where they would die in terrible pain. That way, no one would know that they actually died of cancer.

Those were the stories that were sometimes told about Norman Baker (some still are), but it should be noted that no records or first-hand accounts exist to say there is any truth to these rumors. Most likely, they are simply tall tales that have been told to enhance the Crescent's spooky reputation over the years.

Or are they?

At least some of the stories about Norman Baker were given credence in early 2019. On February 5, while working to extend a parking area on the north end of the hotel, a landscape gardener discovered some strange, medical-looking bottles. They turned out to be almost identical to bottles that had once been on one of Baker's advertising posters. As more bottles were found, workers realized there was "something" floating in the liquid inside. They turned out to be the phony "tumors" that Baker used to show what his "miraculous" cures for cancer could offer. Work was stopped on the parking area until the police, a hazmat team, and archaeologists from the University of Fayetteville could be called. After the bottles were deemed to be safe, archaeologists carefully peeled back the layers of dirt at the site to expose more bottles. It turned out to be a dump site for the notorious doctor's fake medical specimens. Who knows how many people he literally fooled to death with the bottles, checking into the hospital in hopes that their cancer would be cured?

Federal authorities eventually caught up with Norman Baker. He was charged with using the mail to defraud the public about his false medical claims. He was convicted in 1940 and sentenced to four years in Leavenworth. He was released at age 58 on July 19, 1944.

After that, Baker moved to Florida and spent most of the rest of his life there or in Mexico. In the summer of 1958, he became ill and was advised to see a doctor in Detroit. But, since he didn't believe in doctors, he refused to go. He died on September 8, 1958. He was buried in Greenwood Cemetery in Muscatine, next to his sister. Only a handful of people attended his funeral.

His cause of death? Cancer of the liver.

The brooding old hotel closed after Baker's conviction and stayed that way until 1946, when new investors took it over and began trying to restore the place. The new owners were four Chicago businessmen: Herbert Shutter, John Constantine, Herbert Byfield, and Dwight Nichols. Nichols went on to become the resident manager for the next 25 years. He had seen the hotel after visiting Eureka Springs with his friend, Joe Parkhill. With help from Parkhill's Oklahoma oilman uncle, they bought the Basin Springs Hotel downtown in 1945. The following year, Nichols talked some Chicago friends into becoming partners with him at the Crescent.

They paid $45,000 for the building to Thelma Yount, Norman Baker's girlfriend. The place needed a lot of work. The hard years showed, and the hotel was described as "seedily elegant." They set aside $20,000 for renovations. There was a lot of lavender paint to cover and a lot of woodwork and furnishings to replace.

Nichols soon had the hotel back in operation, offering Ozark vacation packages from the end of April to the end of October each year. Most of the advertising was done in the Chicago area, which brought a new breed of tourists to the region. The packages included the hotel room, three meals a day, hayrides, trail rides, cookouts, dances, and float trips. Most of the travelers who came were women.

They took a train as far as Monet, Missouri, and then caught a bus to the Crescent.

Over the next 25 years, Nichols made scores of improvements to the hotel. A dance platform was added in the parking lot, lit by electric lights. A bar was added to the basement called the "Cedar Chest," located next to the bowling alley. Air conditioners were also added to all the rooms. In the lobby, a disc jockey worked each day for a Berryville radio station. He used the area every day for two hours broadcasting dance music on his radio show.

In 1967, a serious fire broke out during the off season. The hotel was not scheduled to open for another month, but Nichols and a maintenance man were both there. The priest at St. Elizabeth's Church noticed smoke and called the fire department. It destroyed the center tower, which was Nichols' office, the south penthouse, and the rooms on the east side of the top floor. It was believed to have been started – according to Dorothy Nichols, Dwight's wife – by squirrels at the top of the elevator shaft.

A $50,000 insurance policy allowed Nichols to repair the damage, put on a new roof, and replace the old elevator.

In December 1972, the heirs of Nichols' partners sold their interest in the hotel to Jim and Bob Boehm. Nichols stayed on as manager until 1976, when the hotel was sold again to the Crescent Heights Development Company of Wichita, Kansas for $198,000.

But they had no plans to operate it – they bought the hotel to tear it down. The limestone had already been committed to a stone company in Kansas. They had never even been inside of the place and had no interest in it. Luckily, plans changed. Lowana, the wife of one of the company owners, Bob Feagins, fell in love with the building and convinced her husband not to tear it down. Instead of demolition, $800,000 was committed to doing an extensive restoration of the building.

Over the next few years, a new kitchen was installed, the dining room was renovated, new air conditioning units were put into place, the lobby was given a complete facelift, rooms were remodeled, and a brand-new boiler was added. The entire hotel was updated and given a new lease on life.

The Feagins began offering Eureka Springs packages that included food, lodging, and entertainment for just $40. Guests attended the local Passion Play on one night of their stay and then watched old movies at the Crescent on the second. After the opening of the Pine Mountain Jamboree, the hillbilly music show – showing off the local atmosphere for big city tourists – replaced movie night.

In 1980, the hotel was sold to National Historic Registry Hotels, which owned five other hotels across the country, including the Basin Park in Eureka Springs. They hired a local management company to oversee the Crescent and Jerry Hope took over as manager.

Over the next few years, more renovation work took place, mostly consisting of new carpeting and paint – over 600 gallons were purchased – a replacement swimming pool, a new lobby bar, and a general update of the building.

In 1987, though, the hotel ran into trouble. First it was closed temporarily for failure to pay State and Local taxes, and then a year later, the hotel owners filed for Chapter 7 bankruptcy. They blamed it on the costs of recent renovations. The company's hotels were sold to the bank, who hired a succession of management companies to operate the hotels until 1992, when all were sold except for the Crescent. It remained under the bank's ownership until 1993.

At that point, it was sold to Gary and Carole Clawson of Florence, Oregon, who operated several restaurants and owned a theater that offered live shows in Eureka Springs. They were in town, took a tour of the Crescent, and bought it three days later. They hired a manager but were as hands-on as they could be from Oregon. Carole came quite often and took care of the hotel's books. They reluctantly sold the hotel in 1997.

It was purchased by Marty and Elise Roenigk, who also owned the Basin Park Hotel. They began a massive restoration of the hotel, bringing back and reviving elements of the building that had been lost or neglected over the years, like the center tower lost in the 1967 fire and the solarium. They also turned the old staff annex into honeymoon suites, built cottages, replaced the basement bar with a spa, and much more. After years of successes and failures, the hotel finally regained its lost glory and now stands as an elegant and breathtaking piece of Ozark history.

And it is also, according to numerous staff members and countless guests, a very haunted place.

The ghost stories about the Crescent Hotel first received national attention in the 1970s. Bob Feagins, the owner at the time, was interviewed about the hotel by a reporter for the *Christian Science Monitor*. However, the article ended up being sold to the *National Enquirer*, who turned Bob's passing mention about haunted happenings at the old hotel into the centerpiece of the story.

The article mentioned the hotel's storied past, including its time as Norman Baker's "cancer clinic," but focused on the present-day and Bob's two sightings of resident ghosts. Both occurrences had taken place in the off-season, he said, when the hotel was empty. As he told the reporter, "The first time, I glanced over toward the staircase in the hotel's main lobby and saw a man dressed in black and wearing a white shirt. He was as real as you and me, but very pale. He wore a mustache and a frock coat in the style of the late 1800s. My first thought was 'Who is he and how did he get in here?' but as I stared at him, he simply melted away – completely disappeared!"

The second encounter, Bob explained, was much more unnerving. "I woke up at 2:00 a.m. to find a strange man standing at the end of the bed looking down at me. The incredible thing was, he was glistening in the dark. He was an older man – with a beard and a mustache – and his body looked like a collection of silvery threads, dangling in thin air. All of the sudden he began to melt into the three-foot-thick stone wall near my bed and disappeared."

Architect Kyle Wentcroft, who had done some of the design work during the renovations on the hotel, also had an unforgettable encounter while staying at the Crescent in 1974. "Suddenly, I was awakened by the distinct impression of someone trying to push me off the bed." At first, he didn't see anyone, but then caught a glimpse of a figure that shouldn't have been in the room. He tried to catch up with it, but quickly found no one was there.

The reporter also spoke with the manager of the hotel's laundry, Glenda Camp, who said that a Swedish carpenter who was killed while helping to build the hotel appeared to her often. "He looks like he's in his 20's," she said, "with blond hair, a bushy blond beard, and blue eyes. There are times when I actually have to tell him to quit bothering me."

The word was out. This was the first time the ghostly occupants of the hotel were talked about beyond the stone walls of the Crescent, but it would not be the last. In fact, Glenda Camp's Swedish carpenter would become a staple of the hotel's eerie tales.

Staff members have long received frequent reports from guests about the strange happenings in their rooms and hallways. Room 424 had had many visitations, but the most famous haunted room is 218 – where Michael, the carpenter fell to his death. Guests and employees have experienced both strange sounds and sensations in the room. Lights and televisions turn on and off, the water runs by itself, doors slam shut, and some people claim to have been shaken awake at night. One guest was asleep in the bed when his shoulder was violently shaken back and forth. He awakened just in time to hear footsteps hurry across the floor – but there was no one in the room.

One night, a clerk heard footsteps and the toilet flushing in Room 218, which was right above his desk. Realizing that he had not rented the room that night, he went up to check and found that no one was in the room.

Another story of Room 218 involves the wife of one of the hotel's past owners. She stayed in this room and at some point, in the middle of the night, she was found in the hallway by the staff. She was screaming in terror and told the night manager that she had awakened to see blood spattered all over the walls of the room. The staff took a look and found no blood and nothing else out of the ordinary.

Another resident spirit is that of a distinguished-looking man with a mustache and beard and who dresses in old-fashioned, formal clothing. He seems to favor the lobby of the hotel and the nearby bar. People who claim they have talked to the man say that he never responds, he only sits quietly and then vanishes. In an interview, a staff member recounted one odd experience with the silent ghost, "During the summer, we had two auditors work for us because we're so busy.

One of these men left the front desk to get a drink of water in the bar, after it was closed. He told me that he saw some guy sitting on a barstool, staring straight ahead. He didn't say anything, and he didn't move. Our guy left to get his partner, who was still at the front desk. They came back and spoke to the man. They thought he was drunk."

When the man again did not respond, the two auditors decided to leave him alone and go back to work. As they looked back over their shoulders on the way out of the bar, they saw that the barstool was now empty. The man was nowhere in the room.

"One of them started searching for the man," the staff member added. "He looked around the lobby, which is about 25 to 30 yards across, everywhere in that area. The auditor who was looking around went over to the steps (a staircase ascends from the lobby). The fellow from the bar was on the second-floor landing, looking down at him. He went up but as he got to the second floor, he felt something push him back down again. That's when he got the manager and told him what had happened."

It may have been this same old man that hotel night auditor Gary Jeffries encountered one night. He reported seeing a figure on the second-floor landing of the lobby staircase. He left the desk to investigate, climbed the stairs, but saw nothing. As he turned to go back down, he was suddenly pushed by unseen hands from behind him. He tumbled down the staircase, but luckily, was unhurt. He did, however, refuse to work any longer at night.

But Michael the carpenter and the old man don't haunt the hotel alone.

There are many different phantoms encountered at the Crescent, from every era of its operation. They include the apparition of a young woman who wears the traditional uniform of the college that operated here in the early 1900s, and a little boy, perhaps 4-years-old, who appears in the hallways at night, often playing with a ball. He has been reported to sometimes pout and utter the words, "It's not fair!" He stomps his foot and disappears. Some believe this might be the lingering spirit of Breckie Thompson.

There is also a little girl who roams the corridors. No one knows who she might have been in life – perhaps the child of a guest? Legend has it that she died after a fall on the staircase, but no one knows for sure. She is often seen on the fourth floor, running in the hallway. She has also been known to appear next to the bed of a sleeping guest in the middle of the night.

The office of Dr. Ellis, the hotel physician, was once located in Room 212. He is sometimes seen going into his office without opening the door. On other occasions, the smell of his favorite cherry pipe tobacco is noticed around this part of the hotel.

It's likely that the era of Norman Baker's cancer "hospital" may have left the greatest ghostly impression on the hotel. In July 1978, a guest from Kansas City, Anne-Marie Taylor, who got a shock when she stepped out of her room and "saw – and I swear this is true – a nurse pushing a trolley like the ones that are used in hospitals to push patients down the hall." As she watched, the nurse pushed the gurney toward a wall and then vanished.

Before – and since – Taylor's encounter, scores of other guests have witnessed the same apparition and have seen it reenacted in the same way. The nurse is always reported wearing a 1930s-style uniform on the third floor and she is repeating a scene that happened often during the days of the "cancer clinic." Patients who died were removed from their rooms at night, when others were asleep, and taken to the morgue in the basement. That way, they had no idea that anyone else had succumbed to cancer and had not been healed by Baker's miraculous "cures."

Not everyone has seen the apparition – many have heard it instead. Even those who have seen the nurse can agree that the phantom gurney that she pushes has terribly squeaky wheels. Many third-floor guests have awakened to hear the squeak of those wheels in the corridor in the dead of night.

An apparition that is believed to be Norman Baker himself has been spotted around the old recreation room, near the foot of the stairs going to the first floor. Those who have seen him say that he looks lost, first going one way and then another. Could Baker be "trapped' in the hotel, perhaps paying for misdeeds that were committed many years ago?

A former cancer clinic patient – dubbed "Theodora" by staff over the years – is said to haunt Room 419. She is neat and organized and some say that she will pack your suitcase for you. If not, she simply appears as a full apparition and then vanishes.

Several years ago, an antique switchboard from the days of the hospital was finally removed because of all the problems it caused. A staff member explained, "In the summer we would get phone calls on the switchboard from the basement recreation room. There was no one on the other end because the room was unused and locked. We could check it out and find that the phone had been taken off the hook. There was only one way in or out of the place and the key was kept at the front desk."

This same staff member checked out the recreation room one night after receiving another of the strange calls. He found the phone on the hook, but he still maintains that he felt another presence in the room with him. "I just wanted to get out," he added.

He locked the door and went back upstairs, but within five minutes the switchboard buzzer went off again, indicating that a call was coming from the same room that he had just left.

This time, he decided not to go and check it out.

The Crescent Hotel is undoubtedly one of the most haunted places within these pages. The memories of the past seem to be stored here, replaying themselves over and over again to the fear and delight of the living. The past revisits the present, reminding us that history is never really forgotten.

5. BOURBON ORLEANS HOTEL
NEW ORLEANS, LOUISIANA

In the heart of New Orleans' French Quarter – just beyond Jackson Square and the St. Louis Cathedral – is the Bourbon Orleans Hotel. It is a place where the past truly collides with the present in both colorful and eccentric ways. The building, and the ground that it stands upon, has seen a wide variety of uses during its history, and it seems that every one of those moments in time has left behind an impression in the shape of ghosts and spirits.

There are many haunted hotels in New Orleans – a city that I believe is the most haunted in America – but for sheer variety, nothing rivals the many hauntings of the Bourbon Orleans.

The street on which this graceful hotel now stands was there when New Orleans was in its infancy. The avenue bore the name "Orleans" and it became the center of a growing settlement, the original city that we now know as the French Quarter. Populated first by the French, it became a mixing pot of cultures, attracting both the rich and the poor. The blend of French, African, and Spanish became known as Creole, a term used in many culinary, cultural, linguistic, and architectural variations, that sets the city apart from anywhere else in America. It was the Creole society that built the city and made it something that can never be imitated or replaced.

Entertainment was desperately sought in the hostile early days of the settlement. As the citizens struggled against floods, diseases, and early deaths, they looked for ways to distract from their hardships. Most of them, so far from home, craved music, opera, and dance from home. This led to the first small theater being built on St. Peter Street in 1792. The first performance, a comedic aria, introduced New Orleans to French opera.

When the poorly-constructed theater closed down 12 years later, theater manager Louis Tabary built a new theater, Theatre d'Orleans, one block away, just off Bourbon Street. It took years to complete, finally opening its doors to Creole society in 1815. The French-provincial building rivaled other small theaters that had opened before it, offering luxury that could only previously have been found in France.

But an arson fire reduced the theater to ash just one year after its debut.

The lot where the theater once stood was snapped up by New Orleans entrepreneur John Davis and he rebuilt the Theatre d'Orleans and added a grand ballroom, Salle d'Orleans, on the site that is now the Bourbon Orleans Hotel. Davis hired British-born American architect Henry Latrobe, who designed the U.S. Capitol in Washington, D.C., to build the new theater and ballroom with hopes of outshining the other theaters and concert halls that had opened in the city.

And it worked. Multiple dramatic corps traveled from France to New Orleans to perform at the new theater. It was a masterpiece of classic architecture that held breathtaking scenic arrangements, elevated and spacious seating, gallery boxes, and perfect acoustics. The theater offered a wide variety of entertainment, too. There were operas, plays, and musical exhibitions, making the Theatre d'Orleans the most important music venue in the city before the Civil War.

The circles of Creole society flocked to the theater. It seated 1,300 people and was almost always sold out for every performance. From music stands to orchestral chairs, from wardrobe to ticket windows, Davis spared nothing, often making personal sacrifices to ensure that the theater succeeded. New Orleans became known as the "Opera Capital of North America."

But Davis was not without competition. Many other theaters came and went during the decades of the Theatre d'Orleans' dominance in the city. Davis always tried to find an edge and wanted to offer something that other venues didn't. As a lover of gambling, he set up an elegant gaming parlor in the building. Up until that point, cards and gambling had been viewed as a socially unacceptable pleasure that was only found in riverfront dives and sporting houses. Davis gave it an air of sophistication, though, introducing faro and blackjack to the Creole men of society. He served fine wine and delicacies, and, soon, the wealthy were flocking to his gambling parlor to indulge in games of chance.

The Theatre d'Orleans enjoyed its golden era during the 1840s. The gaming parlor and ballroom were frequented by the city's finest residents and by worldly patrons who loved drama, dancing, and dice.

But all good things must come to an end. By the end of the 1850s, the theater was already deteriorating when John Davis passed away. His death dealt a blow to the entire city. He was one of New Orleans' leading citizens and his funeral was the largest the city had ever experienced.

Then, in 1866, the Theatre d'Orleans burned to the ground – but thankfully, the ballroom was untouched by the fire. This created another chapter in the history of the Bourbon Orleans Hotel.

The Salle d'Orleans, Davis's ballroom, had been the scene of music and dancing in the city since 1819. Within the walls, theatergoers gathered after the show next door to marvel at the ballroom's brilliant lighting, elaborate mirrors, and its imported carpets, chairs, and chandeliers. This gilded entertainment palace became an icon, known not only for hosting the city's most glamourous social events, but for its perfect location in the center of the French Quarter.

During the era of its construction, Creole society held balls at the high social season of autumn and winter. They celebrated special events such as engagements or weddings, and regularly scheduled masquerade balls, as well.

The Salle d'Orleans was the pride of the city. Joining the ballroom with the adjacent theater allowed dances to drift from one room to the other as the orchestra played and filled the halls with music. Nights at the ballroom were said to be the most impressive galas held on American soil.

Some of the greatest events in the city's history were held at the Salle D'Orleans. Perhaps the most famous was a night held in honor of the Marquis de Lafayette, the French aristocrat and military officer who served alongside George Washington during the American Revolution. Lafayette visited New Orleans in 1825, and a party was held in his honor in the ballroom with more than 800 of the city's most prominent citizens in attendance.

There are also stories that say that Andrew Jackson announced his candidacy for president within the walls of the Salle d'Orleans. Jackson was considered the hero of the city after the Battle of New Orleans in 1815 and it's been said that he accepted the nomination of his party while in New Orleans. He won the election in 1828 and served as the seventh U.S. President for nearly a decade.

That same year, a fire burned the Louisiana Capitol Building and forced the State Legislature to find an alternate site to conduct business. The ballroom provided them assembly space, allowing state officials a place to meet until a new capitol could be built.

This was not the last time the ballroom was used as a political meeting space. From 1852 to 1881, the First District Court was in session at the Salle d'Orleans. While housing the criminal court of Orleans Parish, numerous cases were heard during the day while dancing and music echoed off the walls at night.

It was during a slightly earlier era that Mardi Gras began to be celebrated at the Salle d'Orleans. The development of Carnival began when the city was first founded, but it wasn't until 1838 that the first parade occurred in the French Quarter. Masqueraders celebrated on foot, in carriages, and on horseback, throwing trinkets to the crowd. In

1857, the first Mardi Gras – as we know it today – began when mule-drawn floats built by the Mystick Krewe of Comus introduced the torch-lit processions and thematic parades that we think of today.

Generally, the grand finale of the iconic Mardi Gras parades ended with a ball at the Salle d'Orleans. At this masked galas, mock royalty was presented and honored, while attendees danced and drank the night away.

However, Mardi Gras parties were not the best-known of the grand balls to be held at the Salle D'Orleans. In the first half of the nineteenth century, the ballroom became better known for what were called the "Quadroon Balls."

New Orleans has always been a wild mixture of cultures and races. Three centuries of the kind of chaos created by this society gumbo makes the city what it is today. Almost since the beginning, African American culture has been a more powerful driving force in New Orleans than in perhaps any other American city. The first Africans to come to Louisiana came as slaves in 1719. Over the next decade, at least 7,000 more followed in their wake.

The city of New Orleans quickly set itself apart from other southern cities. In 1727, the city adopted the "Code Noir," a set of rules for the proper treatment of slaves. It made life less oppressive than in other parts of the South, but it was still slavery, and slave auctions continued in the city until the Civil War.

Records show that as early as 1805, Congo Square (now Louis Armstrong Park) was a grassy area on the edge of the swamp and just outside of the French Quarter. It became a place where slaves could congregate and gather for religious rituals and ceremonies. Their African customs were kept alive in this way and many people from various tribal groups discovered a common bond through music and dance. A few years later, the immigration of slaves and former slaves from Haiti served to introduce new tribal customs to the Louisiana slaves.

But not all the Africans living in New Orleans were slaves. There were many free blacks who were either former slaves or free black immigrants from the Caribbean. Between 1840 and 1860, census records show that there were over 7,500 free blacks in the city and the initials F.P.C. (Free Person of Color) came to be used after the name of a person of mixed race who might be mistaken for white. As racist as this was, New Orleans offered free blacks more rights than any other American city, allowing them to own property and to seek justice in the courts.

There was another aspect of free black life in New Orleans that remains one of the most controversial and mysterious customs in the city's history – the Quadroon Balls.

In those days, having any African blood could affect your place in society. Men and women of separate races were prohibited from marriage, but this, of course, did not stop the races from mixing. Shades of skin may have varied, but it had to be kept track of. In other words, the less African American blood you had the better, which may quadroon women (one-quarter African American) the least offensive of the race. But even so, Creole society did not consider them worthy of marriage.

The Quadroon Balls were held at the Salle d'Orleans and during these extravagant events, mixed race daughters were presented by their mothers as potential mistresses to masked white men. The wealthy sons of business and plantation owners sometimes supported quadroon mistresses and families in addition to their "legitimate" white families. Many have assumed these young women to be no better than prostitutes, but this was not the case. The girls were raised to be proper young women and were as well-educated as the times allowed. They were free women and known for their beauty.

After being presented at a ball, the young woman left with a suitable "protector," usually young Creole gentlemen with money, who would then support her in fitting style. The women would own property in a small house in the upper quarter and often these arrangements would last for many years, or perhaps for life. Most of them became renowned for their successful businesses and rooming houses and were usually well-regarded by their neighbors. The upbringing of children from these alliances was prearranged. Most education was taught abroad, usually in France, as there were no schools available for mixed race children in New Orleans at the time.

The Creole called these "left-handed marriages," but they were never technically legal. It was a poorly-kept secret in the city for decades, even though many of the arrangements lasted a lifetime.

The Quadroon Balls lasted until the late 1870s, although since they officially did not exist, little record remains as to what exactly occurred during them. Regardless, they were a principal diversion for white men in those days and many would gather at the Salle d'Orleans to drink, talk, and hopefully make the acquaintance of one of the beautiful young women that he met.

The Quadroon Balls lasted until 1881, when the Salle d'Orleans went up for sale. It was purchased by a man named Thomas Lafon but not for himself. It was a gift for a group of women who had been working diligently nearby for years. They incorporated the ballroom into an orphanage for the convent that had been founded at the site.

And the next chapter in the future hotel's history was written.

In a way, the Sisters of the Holy Family order was created thanks to the notorious Quadroon Balls that were held at the place where they convent would eventually stand. Henriette DeLille was the daughter of a free woman of color and a wealthy Creole man whose relationship had been arranged through one of the balls. Henriette grew up in a world of literature, music, and dancing, raised to someday be escorted by her mother to also become a Quadroon mistress.

But that was not what Henriette wanted from her life. She was drawn to religion. She was raised as a Catholic and had been influenced by Sister Marthe Fontier, who opened New Orleans' first school for girls of color. Rebelling against her mother's wishes, she began working with slaves and the poor of the city, while teaching in the local Catholic school when she was just 14. She became an outspoken opponent of the Quadroon Balls and the "left-handed marriages" they created, believing they represented a violation of the sanctity of Catholic marriage.

By 1836, Henriette had formed a small, unofficial congregation of nuns – seven Creole women who called themselves the Sisters of the Presentation of the Blessed Virgin Mary. That same year, Henriette's mother suffered a nervous breakdown. The court declared her incompetent and all her assets went to Henriette. This allowed her to purchase a small home that became their first convent. In 1842, they became the Sisters of the Holy Family.

Nuns had shaped much of the social landscape of New Orleans. They were not passive, complacent women who stayed in the background of the Church. The Sisters of the Holy Family, like other orders in the city at the time, were outspoken and protested for women's rights and equality. They became the first order of Creole nuns in America and most of them were African American. They gathered to pray each Sunday at the St. Louis Cathedral, after spending each week feeding the poor, teaching neglected children, and instructing the city's people of color.

During the Civil War, the city was captured by the Union and the Sisters of the Holy Family established a hospital for sick and wounded soldiers where a portion of the Bourbon Orleans now stands.

Then, in 1862, Sister Henriette died from tuberculosis, cutting short her life of service and charity. She was buried at St. Louis Cemetery No. 2, but the good works that she began did not end with her death.

In 1881, the Salle D'Orleans was turned into a convent, school, and orphanage. Where once the halls had echoed with music and laughter, for the next 83 years only whispers, the sound of an occasional novena, and the laughter of children would be heard. The nuns felt that the purchase of the building was a fitting one – they had wiped out what Henriette felt was a part of the city's sordid past and replaced it with a place of virtue.

By the 1960s, the convent had outgrown the location in the French Quarter. Pressed by a need for larger facilities for its 1,300 students, they sold the building to a group of investors. One of their first steps was to preserve and restore the Salle d'Orleans. The ballroom had become an integral part of the hotel that replaced the convent that stood at the site. When it opened, the Bourbon Orleans became one of the finest hotels in the French Quarter.

The old walls of the school came down and the ballroom was restored to its former glory. Where there was once a patio for the students, there is now the bleu-green waters of a saltwater pool.

Surrounding the courtyard are 218 guest rooms, some with balconies that overlook Bourbon Street's infamous nightlife.

And contained within those walls are the spirits of children, soldiers, nuns, and guests from the location's history who simply refuse to depart.

Perhaps the most unnerving haunted section of the hotel is the grand ballroom, the former Salle d'Orleans. The ballroom and meeting rooms that surround it boast scores of spirited encounters with the other side. The tales that are told by doormen, bellhops, and staff members make for a chilling laundry list of weird happenings.

During the restoration, John Davis's luxurious gambling room was turned into restrooms. One evening, during a wedding reception, a member of the bridal party went into the men's room and was terrified when a sad-looking man in early nineteenth century clothing appeared from nowhere and walked right through him.

During another wedding, a man in a soldier's uniform was spotted mingling with the guests. Assuming an eccentric reenactor had crashed the festivities, one of the groomsmen walked over to ask him to leave and the man simply vanished.

Staff members report that they have often heard the voices and laughter of children coming from the closed, locked ballroom. Knowing that no one is there, they open the door anyway, only to find the area deserted. Other employees say they have frequently heard footsteps walking and running across the ballroom floor, even when no one is present. Perhaps the sounds of the children from the era of the school are still present in the old building.

The rest of the hotel also has more than its share of ghosts.

The ghost of a young woman reportedly resides in the Gabrielle Room of the hotel. She is often seen gazing down into the pool area. Children are often heard crying in the halls or in unoccupied rooms. Guests frequently complain about the television sets in their room turning on and off or the channel changing on its own. Bathroom sinks and showers mysteriously turn on in the middle of the night. Lights turn on and off, unassisted by living hands. One guest was reportedly awakened by a lady in white who suddenly appeared and sat down on the edge of the bed. When the startled guest sat up, the phantom looked at her, smiled, and then vanished.

One hotel spirit, which seems to favor women, has been nicknamed "Raul." Legend has it that he was killed in a sword fight – likely over a lady – on this site in the distant past. He is frequently seen, appearing next to unsuspecting women with a wide smile on his face. As the lady turns to look at him, his smile turns to laughter – and then he slowly fades away. Staff members say that this ghost's antics unnerve some women, but most find him amusing.

On the top floor of the hotel is a room that staff members have dubbed "the nun's room." It earned its moniker because of the large number of guests who have encountered what seemed to be one of the Sisters of the Holy Family in this dormered room. She is never frightening or threatening in any way. She usually appears in the bedroom mirror and then vanishes. She has also been known to move things around and tap on the walls.

I stayed in this room about 10 years ago and while I never saw the nun, the light in the bathroom had a terrible habit of turning on and off by itself. On one of the nights when I was staying in the room, I woke up in the early morning hours to see that the bathroom light had somehow been switched on. I knew that I hadn't done it when I'd gone to bed. It wasn't some kind of electrical malfunction either. When I got up to turn it off, I saw that the light switch had been manually flipped to the "on" position – by someone with unseen hands.

Guests aren't the only ones who encounter the resident spirits. A staff member who was setting up for a private reception on the sixth floor reported that glasses on a table rearranged themselves while she was working on other things. She believed that the ghosts of children were responsible because she heard the disembodied laughter of a small child just moments before the glasses moved.

A chef that was working alone in the second-floor kitchen one afternoon, getting ready for a special event, accidentally knocked two pans off a preparation table. Irritated at his own clumsiness, the chef cursed loudly. Seconds later, all the lights in the kitchen went out and he was slapped across the face. When the lights mysteriously came back on, he was startled when he saw his face in the mirror and saw the vivid red mark of a hand on his face. Knowing that he had been in the kitchen alone, the frightened man turned in his resignation.

I'm going to blame that one on one of the nuns.

6. THE PFISTER HOTEL
MILWAUKEE, WISCONSIN

Milwaukee got its start back in 1818, when a French-Canadian explorer named Solomon Juneau founded a small village near what is now this Lake Michigan city. Two additional settlements also sprang up nearby in the years that followed, and in 1846, they merged to form Milwaukee, a place that was truly put on the map by German immigrants. There were so many of them that flooded into the area that the city was nicknamed the "German Athens." It was meant to be a place of civility and class, standing out among other nineteenth century towns in the Midwest.

Civility and class were exactly what Guido Pfister and his son, Charles, had in mind when they built their luxurious hotel – a place that became known as the "Grand Hotel of the West." It soon set the standard for what other hotels aspired to be, earning its place in Milwaukee's history.

And in its haunted history, too. The Pfister has become known as one of the most spirited locations in the city, and the stories of ghosts and specters that haunt the building seem to come from a rather surprising source.

Guido Pfister was one of the scores of German immigrants that came to Milwaukee in the mid-1800s. He arrived in the United States in 1845. He was a tanner by trade and first settled in Buffalo, New York, before coming to Wisconsin two years later. He started a tanning and leather store and was immediately successful. It soon became known as one of the largest leather operations in the Midwest.

Guido had other interests beyond leather. He became president of the German Exchange Bank and a trustee of the Northwestern Mutual Life Insurance Company. He was also the director of the Milwaukee and Northern Railroad Company, Northwestern National Insurance Company, and the Milwaukee Merchandise Insurance Company. He dealt with traveling businessmen from all over the country, and he began to believe that the city needed a first-class hotel, a place where people would feel privileged to stay. But he also wanted it to be a grand place that would be affordable to people from all walks of life. He remembered his days as a new arrival to the country and counted his blue-collar workers among his many friends.

Guido's son, Charles, shared his father's vision. He had also done well with his life. He played a prominent role in Milwaukee's financial world and was heir to the tanning business, which he had learned working closely with his father. He became a power broker in the city and state, delving into Republican politics, and he later became the owner and publisher of the *Milwaukee Sentinel* newspaper.

Unfortunately, Guido didn't live to see the grand hotel that he envisioned. He died in 1889, while the building was still in the planning stages. Charles was determined to carry on, though. He hired architects Henry Koch and Hermann Esser to design an eight-story Romanesque Revival hotel on East Wisconsin Avenue, just three blocks from the lake. Guido's original estimates for the cost of the hotel had been

$50,000. Charles ended up authorizing $1.5 million for it -- $42 million today.

Charles insisted that, whenever possible, Milwaukee workers be employed for the project and that Wisconsin materials be used, including the distinct cream-colored bricks of the exterior. The bricks were made from a local yellow clay and so many buildings in Milwaukee used the bricks in their construction that the city earned another nickname – "Cream City."

The Pfister Hotel had its grand opening on May 1, 1893. The interior of the new hotel was as lavish as the exterior of the limestone and brick building was plain. The front doors opened into an enormous, three-story lobby with an Italian-style fresco ceiling. Many of the staircases, decorative pillars, the huge fireplace, and the floors are made from marble. The lobby, hallways, and public areas were filled with dozens of pieces of Victorian artwork from Charles's own collection – more than 80 in all – making it the largest display of original art in any hotel in the country at the time.

When it opened, the Pfister was arguably the most luxurious in America and it was also the most modern. The Pfister was one of the first – perhaps *the* first – hotel to run completely on electricity, using its own generator. It also boasted groundbreaking features like fireproofing and thermostat controls in every guestroom, instantly establishing its reputation for unsurpassed opulence.

In addition to these amenities, the Pfister offered a formal dining room, a gentlemen's lounge with a private bar, and two billiard rooms, one for men and one for women. It quickly became a popular meeting place for the wealthy and elite of the Midwest.

In 1926 – right in the middle of Prohibition, which gives you an idea how much political pull that Charles had – he opened a saloon in the hotel, the English Room.

But he didn't get to enjoy the bar for long. Charles died in 1927, although his legacy continues today. The hotel was his pride and joy, which is likely the reason that he's never left it.

The Pfister Hotel continued its prominence and success after Charles's death. Almost every U.S. president starting with McKinley has either stayed or visited the hotel. It's also played host to performers and celebrities like Sarah Bernhardt, Bob Hope, Elvis Presley, Bruce Springsteen, and many others.

In 1962, Ben Marcus, of the Marcus Corporation, bought the hotel and immediately began restoring it to its original glory. A few years later, he expanded the hotel, adding a new 23-story tower on the north side, raising the guest room count from 200 to 307. The entire structure was renovated again in 1993 and, today, the Pfister remains a historic gem in downtown Milwaukee, offering the kind of hospitality that Guido and Charles Pfister dreamed of in the late nineteenth century. Their vision remains alive and the hotel is truly a place where the past comes to life – perhaps in more ways than one.

The most recognizable ghost of the Pfister Hotel is Charles, who has been seen in many places throughout the original building. And it's no surprise. He loved the place and poured his heart and soul into its creation. It seems almost natural that he would want to remain behind and watch over the hotel, even after death.

He has been frequently seen on the hotel's marble staircase, in the musician's gallery in the ballroom, and even in a storage area on the top floor. A few have spotted him in the elevators and walking his dog, who has also apparently lived on as a resident phantom. He never interferes with guests or staff members. He simply seems to be overseeing operations and making sure that things run smoothly.

Charles may not be the only spirit haunting the hotel. Guests have reported electrical items – televisions, lights, and air conditioners – that turn off and on by their own power. They have complained of hearing noises inside of the walls or banging sounds in their bathrooms. Things move about and disappear with no explanation.

And while they are not the only ones that report strange goings-on at the Pfister, the majority of the spectral complaints seem to come from a certain section of society – professional baseball players. Major League players stay at the Pfister Hotel whenever they are in town to play the Brewers. Many of them have gotten more than they bargained for when spending a night or two at the hotel.

Even the Brewers avoid the place. They've heard so many stories from visiting players that they won't overnight at the Pfister if business requires them to stay downtown. Phil Rosewicz, who was the Brewers Clubhouse manager, often told a story about an out-of-town rookie who stayed at the Pfister. The player woke up in the middle of the night to find that his blinds were up and his window was open. He shut them both and went back to bed, but early the next morning, they were open again. The next night, he slept in the lobby.

When pitcher Dennis Sarfate was called up to the Brewers in 2006, the team put him up at the Pfister. He settled in and then left for the field. "I had put the *Do Not Disturb* sign on the door and when I got back to the room, the TV was on and the pillows were off the bed. And I was like, that's kind of odd, because when I left it wasn't like that." He soon heard about the hotel from other players. "I even asked the people at the front desk, 'Is there a part of this hotel that's haunted?' And they said, 'Well, what wing are you in?' And I told them where I was and they said, 'No, you're fine.'"

I think it's possible that someone may have lied to him about the ghosts.

Michael Young, a former infielder for the Texas Rangers, had a personal experience at the Pfister. "Listen, I'm not someone who spreads ghost stories, so if I'm telling you this, it happened," Young said. "A couple of years ago, I was lying in bed after a night game, and I was out. My room was locked, but I heard these footsteps inside my room, stomping around. I'd heard all these stories about this hotel, so I was wide awake at that point. And then I heard it again, these footsteps on the floor, so I yelled out, 'Hey! Make yourself at home. Hang out, have a seat, but do not wake me up, okay?' After that, I didn't hear a thing for the rest of the night. I just let him know he was welcome, that we could be pals, that he could marinate in there for as long as he needed to, just as long as he didn't wake me up."

Carlos Gomez, who played for the Minnesota Twins, was getting out of the shower in his room at the Pfister and was sure that he heard voices in the other room. He went to investigate but found the place empty. Then, as he was getting dressed, his iPod, which was sitting on a table, lit up and then started to vibrate. Every time Gomez turned it off, it started back up again. Finally, he fled the room – before putting his pants on.

The next time that he returned to the hotel, he made sure that he had a roommate – and brought a Bible with him. "I'm scared to go there," he said. "They should change the hotel. Everybody here doesn't like the hotel. Why they always put us in the same hotel when you can't sleep? Everything's scary. Everything in the hotel, the paintings and pictures, it's a lot of old, crazy stuff. No good, man. No good."

Gomez wasn't the only one who insisted on a roommate. At least two different pairs of teammates who played for the Florida Marlins also insisted on doubling up when they stayed at the Pfister.

Adrian Beltre, a player for the Dodgers, once reported hearing knocking on his door. When he opened it, there was never anyone there. Later, he saw the air conditioner and the television switch on and off by themselves. When he was sleeping, he was awakened by pounding noises from behind his headboard. He was so scared that he took a bat with him to bed for protection. He later said that he only slept for about two hours during his entire three-night stay.

According to teammate Alex Cora, Beltre was so upset that the entire team was affected. "The next year we switched hotels because of him." The Dodgers no longer stay at the Pfister when they're in Milwaukee.

Brendan Ryan, who played shortstop for the St. Louis Cardinals, claimed that his room became inexplicably chilly one night, followed by a glowing light that floated across the room and disappeared.

Stories like these make the rounds between the ball clubs. Before visiting the hotel, relief pitcher Chad Harville said, "Everyone was talking about it. Everybody said, 'Watch out for the ghosts!' You hear the stories before you go." Infielder Joe Randa heard that "other guys were having lights turning off, fire alarms going on, alarm clocks going on and stuff like that." When Adam Eaton was pitching for the Padres, "guys claimed to have their TV turn on." Pitcher Ricky Bottalico was told that "furniture moved around."

But these aren't just ghost stories that are told to scare other team members. Players take the stories of the hotel very seriously.

Felipe Cresto stayed at the Pfister while on a road trip with the Giants in 2000. "I was so tired I left the TV on when I went to sleep, and I left pretty much every light on. Real early in the morning, I heard someone knocking on the door, so I got up. I came out and nobody was there. And I noticed all the lights and the TV were off. And that really freaked me out." Cresto admitted that "a lot of red wine" helped him sleep through his other nights at the hotel. When he returned to Milwaukee later that season, he paid for his own stay at another hotel.

Tim Lincecum, a pitcher for the San Francisco Giants, had his own encounter at the Pfister. "My door was shaking at one point in the night, like someone leaned on it and then leaned on it again. I could hear it. And I could see the door pressing." It was 4:00 a.m. and he didn't know what could be causing this to happen, but he did know one thing: "I'm not answering that door – if it's a ghost or a real person! I'm not answering it!" Instead, he flipped the door latch, hoping that might keep the spirits out in the hallway.

He slept with the lights on for the rest of the night.

Matt Treanor was in town with the Florida Marlins in 2006 and had just dropped by the room of teammate Taylor Tankersley to make plans for dinner. Suddenly, the two heard an odd tapping sound that seemed to be coming from a door to an adjoining room. "After a few seconds, we both acknowledged that we heard it. We opened the door and the tapping stopped. So that was kind of weird." The two looked at the team's rooming list and saw that the adjoining room was unoccupied.

They didn't think anything of it, but as Treanor was returning to his room, they both heard a child scream. "A young kid," Treanor said," maybe seven or eight. And I opened the door and looked down the hallway and there was nobody in the hallway at all. And I was like, 'Did you hear that?' And we both kind of tripped out about that."

The next day, Tankersley told Treanor that after he left the room, the tapping on the door started again. He tried to figure out where it was coming from for at least 15 minutes, but he couldn't find it. But he added that there was a vent on the wall above the television and every time he looked into the vent, hoping to see something in the adjoining room, the sound stopped.

The two ballplayers eventually asked a bellhop what kind of ghost stories the staff heard from guests. "Sometimes you hear children screaming," he told them. "Also, people experience a feeling of cold air rushing across their face while they're lying in bed. And they can't move, they don't know if they're asleep or awake."

Treanor recalled what happened next. "So, Tank and I were talking about this stuff in the clubhouse and, not knowing what we were talking about, our strength coach, Paul Fournier, came in and he's like, 'Man, I had something weird happen to me last night.' We said, 'What happened?' And he said, 'I was in bed. I felt like I was falling asleep. Next thing I know I felt like I couldn't move, and cold air was rushing across my face.' It was word for word what the bellboy was telling us. It sent chills down our spine."

Despite the stories and the room changes and hotel switches, most believe that the ghosts of the Pfister are friendly. A rumor went around for years that one player specifically requested the same room each time he stayed at the hotel because he has an experience each time and enjoys it.

One-time Brewer Ji-Man Choi actually liked staying at the hotel. He spent his first night there when he was in town with the Angels in 2016. Even though he said that his sleep was "not good" because of the restless spirits, he also said that he felt comfortable when ghosts were present.

Even Matt Treanor – who admitted to "chills down the spine" – wasn't really rattled by his experience. "I slept fine," he said. "That was the weird thing about it. It was chilling. And kind of eerie. But it was comforting. I never felt a sense of being scared."

So, who knows? Apparently, something ghostly lurks in the rooms and corridors of the Pfister Hotel, but whether or not it's frightening apparently depends on the feelings of the person who experiences it for himself.

7. THE SEELBACH HOTEL
LOUISVILLE, KENTUCKY

The city of Louisville sits on a line between North and South where the law sometimes becomes a bit of a gray area. Before the Civil War, it was a major hub on the Underground Railroad, offering the last step to freedom for slaves who crossed the Ohio River. During Prohibition, the city sat smack in the middle of where most of the whiskey in the country was distilled. There were strips of riverfront property where lawmen didn't venture, where racetracks, gambling dens, and speakeasies were found. Louisville became famous as the place to find fast horses, beautiful women, and golden, oaky bourbon.

And because all those things are enjoyed more fully in elegant surroundings, the Seelbach Hotel thrived from the time it opened in 1905. The hotel, with its belief that the customer is always right, was as flexible about the law as the city that it was located in. It became a place of history, legend, lore, gangsters, and, of course, ghosts.

There are few hotels with as much history behind it as the Seelbach and even fewer with a resident spirit quite like the "Lady in Blue."

The hotel was the end result of the American dream for immigrant brothers Louis and Otto Seelbach. Their story began in 1869 when the two Bavarian brothers arrived in Louisville to learn the hotel business. By 1903, after years of running restaurants and gentlemen's clubs, the brothers began construction of a new hotel at the corner of Fourth and Walnut Street downtown. In May 1905, the Seelbach celebrated a grand opening, drawing 25,000 visitors to see the place for the very first time.

Designed by W.J. Dodd of Louisville and F.M. Andrews of Dayton, Ohio, the hotel was built in a lavish Beaux-Arts Baroque architectural style, bringing a Paris aesthetic to Louisville. The hotel interiors offered a lobby with combined marbles from Italy, Switzerland, and Vermont, mahogany and bronze details in a classic Renaissance style, and a vaulted dome with 800 panes of glass. Arthur Thomas, the most famous painter of Native American scenes in the world, was commissioned to decorate the lobby with huge mural paintings of pioneer scenes from Kentucky history.

The hotel's reputation for exceptional service, luxury amenities, and perhaps, most important of all, discretion, inspired a multitude of famous and little-known visitors over the years. Some of the more notable names in the registry included Presidents' William Howard Taft, Woodrow Wilson, Franklin Roosevelt, Harry Truman, John F. Kennedy, Lyndon Johnson, Jimmy Carter, and Bill Clinton, along with The Rolling Stones, Whitney Houston, Elvis Presley, Billy Joel, Robin Williams, Russell Crowe, Julia Child, Wolfgang Puck, and many others.

And then there were the "other" guests – the not so savory ones, which we'll take a closer look at soon.

The hotel attracted large numbers of patrons in its first two years, and, luckily, the Seelbach Realty Company—formed in 1902 before the property purchase—had been planning from opening day to expand the hotel. On January 1, 1907, the second phase opened, raising the number of rooms to 500. The lower two floors of the ten-story structure were faced with stone, while the upper floors were brick. Work included enclosing the rooftop garden to allow it to be used as a winter garden.

Louis Seelbach died in 1925, and in 1929 Otto Seelbach retired, and died 4 years later. The Seelbach Hotel Company disbanded with his retirement and the last Seelbach left his management position with the hotel. Subsequent owners remodeled the place, and until 1968 the hotel turned a profit. By July, loss of revenue forced The Seelbach to close it doors, seemingly forever. Through the 1970s, the property was abandoned. Plywood covered the doors and the broken windows and word spread that the once grand hotel was going to be demolished. Public support was stirred by such news and new owners – construction magnate H.G. Whittenberg, Jr. and actor Roger Davis – bought the crumbling hotel and began extensive renovations. They spent more than $28 million and the Seelbach reopened in April 1982. More owners followed, eventually ending up with the Hilton in 1998. Ten years later, another multi-million renovation restored the hotel to its original glory. It has been thriving ever since.

History comes to life at the Seelbach and its not hard to imagine, as your walk through the lobby, or visit the restaurant or bar, what it was like in its early days. Horseman came to Louisville to run their thoroughbred because the Seelbach was – and is – the only place to stay for the Kentucky Derby. Bourbon, cigars, gamblers, debutantes, jockeys, and socialites – the Seelbach has seen it all. People came to the hotel to be seen. Well, some of them did anyway. There were other guests who preferred *not* to be seen. They were some of the most notorious mobsters in American history.

There are many places that make claim to connections with some of the most feared gangsters of the Roaring Twenties, but the Seelbach is one of those spots where every story you hear about mobsters and the hotel is probably true. And there are likely many more stories that have never been told.

During the 1920s, the Seelbach was the city's most glamourous spot for cards and leisure. Situated in the middle of bourbon and whiskey country, it attracted the America's most infamous gangsters and underworld figures, including Charles "Lucky" Luciano, Dutch Schultz, and Al Capone. All of them spoke fondly of their stays at the Seelbach.

The hotel's Oak Room was originally built for billiards, with tables situated between heavily carved square oak columns. The owners, sympathetic to their clientele's desire for liquor and a good time, hid a bar behind an oil painting that was sliced in half so that it could be closed as a quietly as a guest room door. This was Capone's favorite room and it featured a large mirror that he had sent down to Louisville from Chicago, which allowed him to watch his back – and get a peek at the cards held by his opponents across the table. The Oak Room is now a restaurant and guests can eat dinner in the small alcove where Al once played cards.

The speakeasy also had another feature – spring-loaded doors that could be tripped from behind the lobby desk if the police arrived at the hotel unannounced. Card players had time to get their money off the table and pretend they were simply enjoying dinner, or they could hightail it out the secret tunnel that was hidden behind the paneling. This led to other secret passageways – since sealed off – that went under the hotel and out to the street. A secret drinker or card player could make it almost a block from the hotel without being seen.

Louisville police never caught up with Capone, whether he was escaping a card game or from another room he favored: the Rathskeller. Now used for corporate events and parties, the Rathskeller was a big nightclub in the 1920s and 1930s. It was used by the USO during World War I and II, and during Prohibition was – officially – just a dinner club. But, of course, getting a drink at the Seelbach was easy. All you had to do was know someone – or at least know the password to get into the speakeasy.

Al Capone wasn't the only well-known character to frequent the Seelbach in the 1920s. An Army captain that was stationed at nearby Camp Zachary Taylor also gained quite a reputation at the hotel. He was a heavy drinker and was tossed out of the bar on several occasions for causing trouble. As it turns out, the young captain walked into one of the most iconic bars in the Mid-South and walked out with "The Great Gatsby."

F. Scott Fitzgerald discovered what would turn out to be his favorite bar in Kentucky while serving as a young, reluctant soldier at Camp Taylor. Weekend passes allowed him to escape the boring routine of the military base and head into the big city. A college dropout and eager to leave his innocence behind with his bad grades, he put on the tailored uniform that he'd purchased from Brooks Brothers and landed at the Seelbach.

The hotel did its part for the war effort during World War I by turning the Rathskeller into a USO club. Young recruits mingled with the city's society belles in a nightclub that was decorated in Bavarian style with solid wood décor, a copper-topped bar, and a vaulted ceiling covered in hand-tooled leather. It was undoubtedly the fanciest USO in the country. The music was fast, and the drinks were cold. The girls were pretty, and the soldiers were scared. They never knew when they might be shipped out, so every night became their last. Anything might happen at the Seelbach – and a lot of things did.

Fitzgerald, only 21, was already convinced he was a genius, or at least he wanted to be. He expected to die in the war and was already at work on his first novel, which was never published. He went to the Seelbach looking for some worldly wisdom and, of course, for some inspiration.

Legend has it that it was at the Seelbach where Fitzgerald met George Remus, the man who earned the nickname of "King of the Bootleggers." The big man from Chicago, a lawyer who turned his back on the law, took up bootlegging at the start of Prohibition and became fabulously wealthy. Remus managed to find every legal loophole in the Volstead Act, styled himself a pharmacist, bought up pre-Prohibition bonded liquor, dispensed it for medicinal purposes, and then had his henchmen hijack the trucks so that he could sell it at a higher price. Remus made over $40 million in three years.

Remus became known for his lavish parties at the Marble Palace, his Cincinnati mansion. At one party, he presented all his female guests with new cars, and, at another, gave all the male guests a diamond stickpin. Scantily clad aquatic dancers performed in the pool and there were so many flowers delivered for each gala that his order cleaned out entire greenhouses.

If any of this sound familiar, it's because George Remus is said to have been the inspiration for Fitzgerald's most famous character, Jay Gatsby.

And, of course there's more. In the book, Louisville's most fascinating and desirable belle is Daisy Fay. When Gatsby lingers in Europe – or somewhere – after the war, Daisy marries Tom Buchanan. The couple takes an entire floor at the Seelbach Hotel and gets married in the hotel's Grand Ballroom.

But if Gatsby was inspired by Remus, then who was Daisy? Fitzgerald was later transferred from Louisville to Montgomery, Alabama, where he met and wooed the city's most fascinating and desirable belle, Zelda Sayres. Zelda, of course, is every woman Fitzgerald ever wrote, a character no actress has ever captured. None of them have ever quite captured Daisy's mystery, excitement, and glamor. She is always the one who literally got away and the one who is literally too good to be true. The book paints a picture of Fitzgerald's stormy marriage to Zelda, which ended up in alcohol-fueled disaster and Zelda's eventual death by fire in the insane asylum she was living in.

In Fitzgerald's book, Daisy is Zelda transported to Louisville. The backdrop of the Seelbach adds the proper opulence, which the poor soldier transformed in his book into the waterfront mansions filled with the rich and the beautiful. Gatsby, who owns a chain of pharmacies, is George Remus, a bootlegger, gambler, and mystery man. He is rich, which Fitzgerald could have been but never quite was.

It became Fitzgerald's greatest book and might never have been written at all if not for the Seelbach Hotel.

The stories of gangsters and writers, horse racing, and gambling all add to the local color of the Seelbach, but it's the tales of ghosts that give it a special place in the history of the region. There may be a number of hauntings in the buildings. Thanks to past incidents of death and suicide, it's possible that the tales of lights that turn on and off, doors that open and close, and transparent figures who appear in the dead of night can be attributed to the restless souls who checked in and, you know... never checked out.

But there is one ghost who has a special place in the lore of the Seelbach – the "Lady in Blue." She has been seen by staff members and guests alike. She has appeared in corridors, in rooms, and in the lobby. In 1987, a hotel chef was working on Sunday brunch and saw a woman in a blue chiffon dress with dark hair walk into an elevator and disappear. The elevator doors were closed at the time. A few minutes later, a maid saw the same thing.

It's an encounter that has been repeated many times over the years and the story has become so widely known that a myriad of tales have been concocted to explain her presence at the Seelbach. The mainstays are that she was a bride who committed suicide after catching her soon-to-be husband with another woman or that she was waiting for her estranged husband at the Seelbach so they might reconcile, only to find out that he died in a car accident on the way to the hotel. Distraught, she threw herself down the elevator shaft.

But none of that is true. She did fall at least six stories and she did die instantly in the hotel. She was buried in a quiet plot after a nice funeral. She was described as beautiful, sweet, and well-liked by those who knew her.

"The Lady in Blue" was a real person and her name was Patricia Wilson.

On Thursday morning, July 16, 1936, the body of a woman was found on top of an elevator car at the Seelbach Hotel. She was soon identified as Patricia Wilson (born Pearl Mae Elliott), an unemployed divorcee who lived in a boarding house on South First Street. When the cause of her death – was it murder, suicide, or an accident? – could not be determined, several events eventually led to an unresolved police investigation, and Patricia was forgotten until 1987, when the first sighting of the ghost in the blue dress occurred.

An employee of the Seelbach, curious about the flurry of ghost sightings, connected the spirit to Patricia after finding a 1936 newspaper article about her fall down the hotel's elevator shaft. The accompanying photograph showed a beautiful, dark-haired woman with fine features, matching the description of the ghost.

Meanwhile, the sightings of the "Lady in Blue" continued. Stories also claimed that those events were accompanied by chilling cold spots and the lingering scent of a woman's floral perfume. As the stories of the encounters spread, the origins of the specter grew more and more convoluted and dramatic. The true story of the ghost was much less exciting and, if possible, much sadder.

Using city directories, probate court records, circuit clerk records, coroner's inquest records, and newspaper back issues, writer Lisa Pisterman pieced together what she could of Patricia Wilson's life and her death in Louisville.

Patricia was born Pearl Mae Elliott on March 10, 1910. She was one of four children born to Albert and Annie Elliott in Davenport, Oklahoma. Albert passed away when Pearl was just five. Her mother remarried in 1917 to a man named Frank Goff, but then Annie died in 1919. The children were all placed with relatives and foster parents. Pearl with William and Fronia Funnell, who were farmers. Her sister, Ruby, to whom Pearl was especially close went to live with grandparents in Pawnee. The two girls stayed in touch through letters and pictures.

At some point, between 1930 and 1934, Pearl married a man named Charles B. Wilson or perhaps "L.B." Wilson, as he was referred to in newspapers, and they moved to Louisville. She had changed her first name from Pearl to "Patricia." Her husband was a traveling salesman and Patricia, as she was now known, worked as a busgirl at the Blue Boar Restaurant downtown. It wasn't long before the two of them split up, although the exact date remains unclear, as well as what brought them to Louisville in the first place.

Not much is known about Patricia's life after that. When her husband left her, she stayed in Louisville. Perhaps she had always just wanted to get out of Oklahoma and found that new life in the city, away from the farm, suited her. Maybe changing her name from Pearl to Patricia made her feel more sophisticated. We'll never know.

What we do know is that she met with friends at the most glamorous hotel in Louisville on that July day and sipped cocktails. Maybe she hoped that she'd meet a man who would take her away from the low-rent boarding houses and low-paying jobs. We'll never know her dreams, hopes, or fears.

But on July 16, 1936, she met her death at the Seelbach.

At the Jefferson County Coroner's Inquest that followed, a jury listened to the details of the events that occurred on July 16, 1936. According to James Embry, a linen sorter at the Seelbach, he was working on the first floor that morning, dealing with a coating of dust and pieces of plaster that had fallen inside the linen elevator car. This particular car was smaller than an average elevator car and contained a single shelf. Its only purpose was to transport fresh linens upstairs from the laundry. Dirty linens were dropped into a chute down to the laundry room. While trying to find the source of the dust and debris on the floor of the car, James glanced up and saw a woman's glove sticking out from the edge of the car. He pulled on the glove, which then revealed a woman's pocketbook. Baffled, James hurried upstairs to the second floor and opened the elevator door to find the lifeless body of a young woman on top of the car. He called for Dell Burton, a hotel maid, who testified that Patricia was fully dressed in an orchid colored dress and white high heels.

The coroner was called to the scene and Patricia's fatal injuries were detailed as a fractured skull, fractured left leg, and fractures to the right tibia and fibula.

The body was taken to the L.D. Bax Funeral Home, where she was identified by Mary Katherine Berlew, her landlady. She told the police and reporters that Patricia and her husband had moved to Louisville from Oklahoma in 1932. The couple lived on and off at the rooming house that Mrs. Berlew and her husband, Charles, owned. On July 15, she spoke with Patricia as she was leaving the house.

Patricia smiled, waved, and called back to her, "I'll be back later, Ma." When she left, she was carrying her gloves, purse, and hat. Her hat was later found in the hotel bar but where she went during the time when she left the car and her body was found in the elevator shaft the next morning remains a mystery.

Soon after Patricia's death, a Prudential life insurance policy turned up in the amount of $500, with an additional accidental death benefit of $500. Patricia's sister, Ruby Miller, allowed Louisville attorney Edward G. Langan to be appointed executor of the estate. Ruby lived in Cushing, Oklahoma, and was unable to travel to Louisville. Mary Katherine Berlew immediately filed a claim for $350, stating that she had loaned Patricia $100 "for her divorce and a trip to Indianapolis." She added that Patricia had not paid room and board for nearly a year. A friend, Lena Richardson, corroborated Mrs. Berlew's story. After the cost of the funeral and burial – plus the coroner's inquest fees, administrator's fees, and bond and court costs – were paid, Berlew received $280 from her claim against the estate. No grave marker was ever purchased, and Patricia's sister received nothing. Her ex-husband never came forward to claim any of the estate for himself.

However, executor Edward Langan filed a wrongful death suit on behalf of Patricia's estate against the Seelbach on November 9, 1936. In the complaint, he stated that the Seelbach advertised extensively, inviting the public to its bars and restaurants for lunch, dinner, and specialty cocktails. As such, it was not unusual for people who were not registered as guests to be on the premises. He alleged that while patronizing the bar, Patricia may have mistaken the door to the linen elevator for a washroom door. They were simply doors that opened on hinges with glass in the center. They even had a knob on them and looked nothing like standard elevator doors. They were supposed to be locked unless a maid was using them, but, because of the hotel's negligence, were not. He believed that Patricia walked through the door and fell to her death. He sued the hotel for $25,000.

The hotel's attorneys issued a denial of all Langan's allegations and stated that since Patricia was not a registered guest, she was essentially a trespasser, and there was no duty owed to her. Since there were no witnesses to the incident, Langan's suit was based on "surmise, guess-work and theory, and theory based upon theory." Patricia's death was caused by her own negligence, not the hotel's. The lawsuit was subsequently dismissed.

But Langan wasn't giving up. A year later, he and his co-counsel, James Robertson, filed another civil suit on behalf of the estate. This one was for more money and turned the focus to a culprit that was not the Seelbach Hotel. This time, he accused former Brigadier General Henry H. Denhardt of having "assaulted, beat and bruised said Patricia Wilson with force and violence, and malicious acts causing the death of Patricia Wilson and causing her to fall down an elevator shaft in said hotel." He was suing Denhardt for $75,000.

If you're reading this and thinking this came out of left field, you'd be right.

Denhardt was an influential Kentucky politician and retired U.S. Army officer who had served as lieutenant governor from 1923 to 1927. But he was also in the news for having just been charged with the murder of his fiancée, society figure Verna Garr Taylor. The jury had voted 7 to 5 in favor of acquittal in his first trial. He was awaiting his second trial when Langan's lawsuit was filed against him.

There was no real evidence to substantiate the claims of the lawsuit when it was filed. Robertson told reporters that the information that Denhardt was involved in Patricia's death had been given to him by a client. Robertson didn't do anything about it until another client told him the same thing. He didn't believe it at first, but the rumors grew so strong that he felt he could no longer ignore it. He had hoped the filing could be delayed until the matter could be completely investigated, but the statute of limitations was about to run out.

Denhardt scoffed at being served with the suit. On July 28, 1937, he filed a countersuit against Langan and Robertson. In his complaint, Denhardt's attorney alleged that the lawyers had acted improperly in filing the suit. Denhardt said that his enemies were intent on destroying him in all aspects of his life, including "financially, politically and socially." He referred to rumors that had circulated prior to his first murder trial that Denhardt had killed "his former wife, eight other women, and fifteen to twenty men." The rumors, he said, were intended to create public hostility toward him with his second trial approaching. Denhardt was adamant that he had never met

Patricia Wilson and was not at the Seelbach on the day she died. He was suing for damages of $150,000.

He never collected – that sum or any other.

Denhardt was released on bond while awaiting his second trial for the murder of Verna Garr Taylor when he was shot and killed by E.S., Jack, and Roy Carr, Verna's brothers. They killed him on September 20, 1937, the night before the new trial was set to begin.

After Denhardt's death, the case of Patricia Wilson faded into obscurity until she came back to life, so to speak, as the Seelbach Hotel's "Lady in Blue." Whatever brought her to the Seelbach Hotel in the first place, she has apparently never left.

She remains a part of the hotel's history. Since 1905, it has been a place where the weary traveler can lay his head, and where the infamous, the silent, and the mysterious can become a part of the rich fabric that makes this place the most amazing building in Louisville.

8. ST. JAMES HOTEL
CIMARRON, NEW MEXICO

With less than one thousand people as year-round residents, the town of Cimarron is little more than a dot on the map. Its roots date back to the western movement of the pioneers in the early nineteenth century, who crossed lands that once belonged to the Anasazi, Jicarilla Apache, and the Utes.

Everything changed between 1821 and 1880, when the Santa Fe Trail was established as the wagon road for those hoping to make the grueling and dangerous journey from Missouri to New Mexico. This early American highway was also used by traders, soldiers during the Mexican-American War, fortune-seekers looking for gold in California, and later, by stagecoaches. It didn't fall into disuse until the railroad made it obsolete in 1880.

It was because of the Santa Fe Trail that the St. James Hotel exists. It was started in 1872, played host to a bevy of frontier personalities –

from Wyatt Earp to Billy the Kid – and still introduces travelers today to Wild West hospitality. The guest register is never empty, and those who book rooms today come looking for a little taste of history – and for the ghosts.

The town of Cimarron, located along the Santa Fe Trail, dates back to the middle nineteenth century. In 1842, a trapper named Lucien Bonaparte Maxwell fell in love with a local woman named Luz Beaubrien. Her father, Charles, along with Guadalupe Miranda, secretary of the territory's governor, owned the 1.7 million-acre Beaubrien-Miranda Ranch in Northern New Mexico. It had been part of a land grant from the governor. As a wedding present, Charles gave Lucien and Luz 15,000 acres of property, on which, in 1858, Lucien built a two-story mansion in the foothills of the Sangre de Cristo Mountains. It was located in the heart of what is now Cimarron – which was charted four years later and took its name from the Spanish word for "wild" or "unbroken."

Charles Beaubrien died in 1864 and named Lucien Maxwell as his heir. He later bought out all his father-in-law's partners and other family members to eventually own all of the original ranch. He welcomed settlers onto the land and did little or nothing to discourage squatters, even after gold was discovered in nearby Elizabethtown. In 1870, Lucien sold everything – a massive section of land which became known as the Maxwell Land Grant -- except for the house and the surrounding 1,200 acres. He left the area a short time later, moved to Eastern New Mexico, and died in 1875.

Meanwhile, a man named Henri Lambert had arrived in New Mexico. He had come west looking for gold but had an interesting background. He was once the personal chef of President Abraham Lincoln, upon the recommendation of Ulysses S. Grant. He remained in Lincoln's employ until the president was assassinated in 1865 and then came west. He settled in Elizabethtown but, like so many others whose dreams of gold were dashed, he realized there was more money to be made providing services to the other miners. When Lucien Maxwell sold the grant in 1870, the new Land Grant Company men discovered that Lambert, who had a reputation as a French chef, was working in Elizabethtown and enticed him to come to Cimarron. So, Henri moved to Cimarron and opened a saloon and restaurant that drew area miners, as well as travelers, cowboys, and other frontiersmen.

The Lambert Inn opened in 1872 and was an immediate success. It quickly became one of the most notorious bars in the Southwest – and one of the most dangerous. There was little law and order in the region at the time and the saloon earned a reputation as a violent place. Legend has it that 26 men were shot and killed within its adobe walls. The first question usually asked around Cimarron in the morning was: "Who was killed at Lambert's last night?" There are still 22 bullet holes in the ceiling of the saloon, which is now the hotel's dining room. In 1901, when the pressed-tin ceiling was removed during refurbishment, more than 400 bullet holes were found in the beams underneath it. The only reason that people in the overhead rooms weren't killed by stray gunfire was the double layer of wood between the saloon ceiling and the floorboards above.

The saloon became wildly (obviously) popular for locals and travelers on the Santa Fe Trail. Realizing that Cimarron needed a place for travelers to spend the night – whether they'd been on a stagecoach or were a drunk cowboy needing a place to sleep it off – Henri added guest rooms to the structure in 1880. At the time, they were considered deluxe accommodations and even boasted the first running water in a hotel in the Southwest.

Many well-known people stayed at the hotel over the years. Wyatt Earp, his brother, Morgan, and their wives stayed three nights at the hotel on their way to Tombstone. Doc Holliday stayed there and gambled in the saloon. Jesse James stayed there several times, always in Room 14, signing the register with his alias, R.H. Howard. Robert Ford – a member of the James gang before turning against the outlaw and shooting him in the back – also stayed at the Lambert Inn.

One frequent visitor was gunfighter Clay Allison, who liked to dance naked on the bar, which is still in the dining room, after having one drink too many. Allison also liked killing people. According to some accounts, he killed 19 of the 26 people who were shot to death in the saloon.

Willian "Buffalo Bill" Cody, who was a goat ranch manager for Lucien Maxwell for a short time, met Annie Oakley at the hotel and began to plan and rehearse their Wild West Show. When Cody left Cimarron to take his show on the road, he took an entire village of Native Americans from the area with him.

When Henri's son, Fred, was born, Cody nicknamed him "Cyclone Dick" because he was born during a blustery snowstorm, and he was soon asked to be Fred's godfather. When Fred got older, Cody was one of the first to give him instruction in the use of guns. Fred ended up spending most of his life as a lawman – Cimarron sheriff, member of the tribal police, and territorial marshal.

Other notables who visited the hotel included train robber Black Jack Ketchum, lawman Bat Masterson, Billy the Kid, Pat Garrett, artist Frederic Remington, Governor Lew Wallace, author Zane Grey, and General Phillip Sheridan.

The name of the hotel was eventually changed to the St. James, but this came at the end of its original glory days. The Santa Fe Trail died when the railroads came through and by the time the railroad bypassed Cimarron in favor of Santa Fe, gold had been depleted in area mines, and the boom times were over. The population of the town – along with the number of visitors passing through – declined and the elegant St. James fell into disrepair. Henri's sons, Fred and Gene, replaced the roof in 1901 as the hotel struggled on.

In 1913, Henri Lambert died and his wife, Mary, died 13 years later. As the years passed, the old hotel was, at many times, uninhabited and it passed from owner to owner. Finally, in 1985, the St. James Hotel was restored to its former luxury. The new owner laid heavy carpets over the hardwood floors, hung plush velvet drapes and crystal chandeliers, and installed period furnishings.

The hotel has once again become a place that would be immediately recognizable to owners Henri and Mary Lambert and the many guests who walked through its doors during the late 1800s. The St. James Hotel was once again a place they could call home, for a night, a lifetime, or – in some cases – for eternity.

Some of those who once inhabited this place have simply never left.

The St. James Hotel is best-known for two of its resident ghosts – unfriendly spirits who have been known to make the stay of some overnight guests very unpleasant ones – but they don't haunt the old building alone. The owners, staff members, and guests can assure you that the hotel is a very haunted place.

The second floor of the hotel seems to be the most active, with stories of cold spots, lights that turn on and off, doors that open and close, and the sounds of heavy boots tromping up and down the hallways at night, even when the corridor is obviously empty. Many have also reported the smell of cigar smoke wafting through rooms, even though there is no smoking allowed anywhere in the building.

There is also at least one mischievous spirit in the hotel that constantly plays tricks on the staff. On one occasion, the ghost was said to have stuck a knife into the floor between two owners of the hotel. Most often, however, he is blamed for objects that mysteriously disappear, only to be found later in strange locations.

Throughout the building, staff members report that objects fall off walls and shelves and electrical equipment at the front desk often behaves erratically. Some report feeling as though they are being watched and guests' cameras sometimes stop working inside the building, then return to normal when they leave the St. James.

A college student who worked the front desk at the hotel one summer once reported hearing a high-pitched scream come from nowhere in the lobby. He looked up abruptly from his work and was surprised to see that no one else in the room had heard it. There were three guests mingling on the other side of the lobby, but they were complexly unaffected by the bone-chilling sound.

Who are all these spirits? No one knows, but a former manager of the hotel once said in an interview that "you never see them, but you do feel and hear them," although one staff manager did have a face-to-face encounter with what she called a "pleasant-looking cowboy." She was in the dining room and saw the man standing behind her in the mirror behind the bar. When she turned around quickly, he was gone.

One of the sinister specters at the St. James is that of Thomas James Wright, who was killed at the door to Room 18 just after winning the deed to the hotel in a poker game – or so the legend goes. He was shot in the back, stumbled into his room, and slowly bled to death.

This might explain why his spirit is so ill-tempered.

Wright's angry, malevolent ghost continues to haunt the room and he does not like company. Ever since his death, dangerous poltergeist activity has occurred in the room whenever anyone goes inside. A former owner of the hotel stated that she was pushed down while in the room and, on another occasion, saw a ball of orange light that flared in the corner. The room contains only a bed frame without a mattress, coat rack, rocking chair, and a wooden dresser. On top of the dresser is an assortment of items meant to appease the spirit of Thomas Wright – a bottle of whiskey, a hand of cards, a tin of tobacco, and a shot glass. There's also a bad painting of a half-naked woman on the wall. It's said that if anyone goes inside, pouring a shot of whiskey into the glass might protect them from the spirit's wrath – or maybe not.

The staff never enters the room and rarely allows anyone else to go inside it, let alone sleep there. The door is kept locked at all times. There are rumors that say that several mysterious deaths occurred in the room after the hotel was reopened in 1986, but no records exist to substantiate the deaths. There are plenty of stories of "violent hauntings," though, so the hotel owners play it safe by not renting it out.

The other unhappy spirit that resides at the hotel is that of Henri Lambert's wife, Mary. She lingers mainly in Room 17 and it's possible that she is not so much an unpleasant spirit as she is a protective one. She may simply be unhappy with the people who stay in her room, invading the space where she once lived, gave birth to her children, and died in December 1926.

The night for those who stay in this room can often be a sleepless one.

Many guests have complained about the smell in this room – an overpowering floral perfume scent that can be so strong that they are forced to flee the room. When the staff search for a source of the smell, it's gone. It has never been attributed to any kind of cleaner or air freshener. It's simply there one moment and then disappears the next.

Some believe that it's Mary's subtle way of moving people out of her room.

Her other methods are not so subtle. She hates it when guests open the window – even when it is necessary. The original hotel has 13 historic rooms, restored to how they looked in the nineteenth century. There is also an annex that has all the amenities of a modern hotel – but those amenities won't be found in Room 17. There are no telephones, radios, or televisions in the historic section of the building, where Mary's room is found. When guests decide to open the window to let in some nighttime desert air, Mary's spirit will tap loudly on the window until it's closed. There is no mistaking the sound – it's rapping knuckles on glass – and it won't stop until she gets her way.

It's probably just best to give her what she wants.

9. THE HAWTHORNE HOTEL
SALEM, MASSACHUSETTS

The town of Salem, Massachusetts, is not one which initially conjures up the thought of ghosts. It was witches – or at least those accused of being witches – that put Salem on the map, much to the dismay of historians who would rather the city be known for its maritime history instead of for hanging its residents.

But there seems to be little doubt that the hauntings and restless spirits that linger in Salem are because of its violent history and the infamous witch trials of 1692. That history plays a large part in the ghost stories that are told about the Hawthorne Hotel.

The events in Salem began at the home of Reverend Samuel Parris. He had a nine-year-old daughter named Betty, a quiet, nervous child. Also living in his household was an 11-year-old niece, Abigail Williams, who was much bolder and who dominated her cousin. Of the reverend's wife, we know little, except that she was a devout woman who spent most of her time doing charitable work in the village. Parris had lived for a time in Barbados and had brought two black slaves to Salem with him: John Indian, who did outside work, and his wife, Tituba, who cooked and cleaned. The children were mostly cared for by Tituba, who loved them. Often, to entertain the girls, she told stories about her island home, usually involving Voodoo, and showed how to cast harmless spells. The girls were very proud of this secret knowledge and they boasted about it to some of their older friends - Mary Walcott, Elizabeth Booth, and Susanna Sheldon – and later, to several others, including Ann Putnam, the malicious daughter of a neurotic, gossipy mother who was largely responsible for the rumors that soon began to spread.

After an ill-fated "conjuring session" with an egg white and a glass of water, Betty and Abigail – and later, other girls – were allegedly "possessed." They began to suffer from seizures that Reverend Parris claimed went far beyond anything that might have been caused by epilepsy. They were afflicted with memory loss, fits of dizziness, and spells during which they crawled about on all fours and made horrible animal noises. Prayer proved to be of no avail and doctors could find nothing physically wrong with the girls. Accounts stated that the girls screamed as though touched with burning coals whenever sacred words were said over their bodies. Reverend Parris appealed for help and two ministers, Nicholas Noyes and John Hale, hurried to the village.

What was going on? No one knows for sure, but many believe this was a hoax, perpetrated by the girls, while others have suggested that perhaps the girls were poisoned, or accidentally drugged, by something that Tituba had brought with her from Barbados. It's believed that a type of herb that caused hallucinations, used during Voodoo ceremonies, could have been the culprit in the case. Still others support the theory that the girls' hallucinations and bizarre behavior were caused by their having eaten bread made from grain that was contaminated by the ergot fungus. Ergot poisoning – or ergotism -- leads to hallucinations, seizures, vomiting, and prickling sensations under the skin, all of which the girls experienced. Of course, that doesn't explain why only the girls and their friends experienced the strange symptoms, and not the others in their households. More likely, they were simply seized by the same witchcraft hysteria that had been running amuck in New England for the better part of the last seven decades.

But the Puritans of Salem were not seeking a logical explanation. They believed the Devil was at work in their village. They reportedly asked all the girls who their tormentors were but could not get a straight answer from any of them. Mary Walcott's aunt, who suspected Tituba, persuaded the slave to make a "witch cake" from an old country recipe, consisting of rye meal and the urine of the afflicted children. The idea was that if the family dog ate the cake made with the urine of the "possessed" girls, the dog would also behave as if he were bewitched. This meant that the girls were truly under the influence of witchcraft. When Parris learned of this and accused his daughter of being involved with the making of the cake, she went into such terrible hysterics that he feared she would die. Betty and the other girls accused Tituba of witchcraft. Two other women, Sarah Good and Sarah Osbourne, were also charged.

Two magistrates, John Hathorne and Jonathan Corwin, were sent to examine the alleged witches. The prisoners were allowed no defense counsel. It was enough for a witness to declare that he had seen the "shape" of the accused riding through the air on a broomstick for his word to be believed. It didn't matter how much the poor soul on trial protested the testimony.

Tituba, who was considered Parris' property, was savagely beaten by her master as he tried to obtain a confession from her about her evil acts. Eventually, hoping to avoid further punishment, she gave him what he wanted – and confessed to anything that she could think of. Once started, she was nearly impossible to stop. She claimed that a "tall man" had come to her, told her that he was God, and ordered her to serve him for the next six years. He had brought her a book that contained nine names and among them were those of Sarah Good and Sarah Osbourne. She had flown to Sabbaths with the "tall man," accompanied by a hog, two red cats, and the winged head of a cat that belonged to Sarah Osbourne. The "shapes" that belonged to the two witches had tried to force her to harm Betty and Abigail, but she had resisted.

The court readily accepted her testimony. It was evident to them that the slave had been deceived by the Devil and was an innocent victim of the witches. Evidence of this was given as Tituba also became "possessed," rolling her eyes, frothing at the mouth, and screaming that she was being attacked by a demon for having spoken out against the forces of darkness. Her husband also got involved in the ruse and he roared, blasphemed, and threw himself onto the floor of the courtroom, also apparently in agony. The court believed that he, too, was also another victim of the horror that had come to Salem. In truth, it was an effort to save themselves from the same fate that awaited the other accused.

Hysteria gripped the village. A dozen people came forward, including some who may have honestly believed what they were saying, who claimed that they had seen the "shapes" of others sticking pins into dolls and taking a diabolical sacrament of red-colored bread and wine mixed with blood. Rebecca Nurse, a formerly respected old woman, was dragged from her sick bed to be charged as a witch. A farmer named John Proctor had the courage to declare that the girls were liars and that their "possession" was self-induced in order to draw attention to themselves. The result was that he was arrested as a witch and his property was confiscated before he had even been tried.

During each of the trials, the girls were brought into the courtroom. Their behavior had an unsettling effect on the accused. If the prisoner lifted his eyes, the girls all lifted theirs; if he rubbed his face, the girls did the same; if he coughed, the girls all coughed; and so on. If the prisoner denied the charges brought against him, the girls went into a frenzy, howling and throwing themselves on the floor. Still worse, they became the jury and executioner of the accused. One by one, the girls were taken before the prisoner and he or she was forced to take their hands. If the girls continued to rave and thrash about, the accused was innocent, but if they became quiet, it was assumed that he or she had removed the demon that had been sent to torture her, and so was obviously guilty.

The girls had a terrifying effect on not only the trials, but on the people of the village, as well. They were constantly seeing "shapes" all over the place, and so unshakable had the belief in them become that, at the children's direction, the villagers stabbed with swords and pitchforks at the empty air where the "shapes" were supposed to be.

A new governor, Sir William Phips, arrived from England and came to the village with Increase Mather, the father of Cotton Mather and later president of Harvard University. Mather had been prominent in the earlier witch trials in Boston, but Phips was only interested in getting together a military expedition against the French in Canada. After decreeing that all of those who had been accused of witchcraft remain chained in their cells, he left the business of trying them to the courts. A special court was formed with Deputy Governor William Stoughton as president, along with six other judges.

People in Salem who feared being accused began to leave the village. Among them was John Willard, the deputy constable, who had arrested several of the so-called witches. In a sudden fit of disgust, he turned on the girls, accused them of being fakes, and said that they should be hanged for what they had done. The girls retaliated against him by claiming that they had seen his "shape" strangling his own nephew, a young man who had recently died. Willard tried to flee but was captured and chained up in prison, accused of having witched to death several people.

Around this time, the "possessed" girls finally announced the identity of the man who had played the part of the Devil at the local Sabbaths. It was, they declared, Reverend George Burroughs, who had been a minister in Salem a number of years before. Even though they were shocked at the idea that a minister would be involved, the magistrates quickly dispatched officers to the parish where Burroughs now lived. They stormed into his home in the middle of a meal and dragged him back to Salem. To Burroughs' amazement, he was accused of murdering several soldiers who had been killed near his parish while fighting Indians – not physically, of course, but as a sinister "shape," just like the other alleged witches. What possible defense could he offer to prove his innocence?

Rebecca Nurse was brought to trial. Her good reputation served her well – at first. Her numerous friends and family were brave enough to testify on her behalf and she was found to be not guilty of the crimes for which she was accused. Instantly, the courtroom was plunged into chaos. The girls howled, pulled their hair, and rolled around on the floor screaming that the woman was guilty. Unbelievably, she was brought back into court and the jury was ordered to think things over again. This time, they reversed their verdict and she was found guilty. On Tuesday, July 19, she was one of five women hanged as witches in Salem.

The terror continued to spread. Scores of additional people were accused, and the court continued its travesty of justice. Prisoners who confessed could hope for clemency, but those who denied their guilt were condemned. On September 22, eight more were hanged, including a woman named Mary Esty – which led to one of the most bizarre incidents to occur during these hysterical times. According to a servant girl named Mary Herrick, the ghost of Mary Esty appeared to her on the day that she was hanged. She said to her, "I am going upon the ladder to be hanged for a witch, but I am innocent and before a twelve-month be past you shall believe it." Shortly afterwards, Herrick claimed that the ghost told her to denounce the wife of minister John Hale as a witch. Reverend Hale knew the charge to be false, and he suddenly realized how many others of the accused might also be innocent.

This event marked the beginning of the end of the insanity. The governor returned from the Canadian border and was shocked to find that 150 people were chained up in prison, waiting to be put on trial for witchcraft. He decreed that in the future, supernatural evidence would be inadmissible in his courts. This made trying the other defendants impossible. They were found to be not guilty, and the Salem witch hysteria came to an end.

What really happened in that small New England village? Was it fraud, class conflict, village factions fighting against one another, repression, accidental poisoning, actual witchcraft, or merely a product of the hysteria of the times? It's a question with many possible answers. Many can be discarded completely because the evidence is too weak. Several others seem obvious but are not very helpful in getting to the bottom of things. Yes, a few of the "afflicted" may have been acting or lying, even while their fellow accusers were in the grip of a true psychopathology. And yes, Puritan beliefs and practices could be hard on young children. It seems likely, too, that some of the individual suspects did actually attempt the practice of witchcraft, but there is no way to distinguish them from the ones who were falsely accused.

While the list is trimmed down, many possibilities still remain. In the end, there are likely several reasons why things turned out the way they did. Witch-hunts, like most social and historic phenomena, almost always show a pattern of multiple causes – just like in Salem.

One of the main reasons for the panic involved the conflict between the farmers and the merchants in the village, or the old way and new way of doing things. The economy was changing, lifestyles were changing, and the two different parts of society struggled to interact with one another. New arrivals in the community were viewed with suspicion as people began losing touch with the religious strength that once shaped the village. Political issues arose as the royal authority overseas eroded the self-governing traditions that were once part of colonial life. Locals also feared for their property when New England's official charters were revoked between 1684 and 1691, when titles to their lands were put at risk. In 1689, a smallpox epidemic swept through the region. Combine all this with a rising fear of the Indian populace, which was spread through stories of massacres, rumors, and threats, and the result was nothing less than an overwhelming and toxic climate of fear. With all these things affecting the hearts and minds of the people, the New Englanders of the late 1680s and early 1690s must have felt the hand of "Divine Providence" was turning against them.

As the entire region teetered on the edge, these factors converged on the village of Salem. As panic overwhelmed the people, Salem became the center of early America's most far-reaching, deadly, and lastingly famous American witch-hunt.

The Hawthorne Hotel would have several connections to the Salem witch trials. For one, the land on which the hotel is built once belonged to a woman named Bridget Bishop, who was executed during the hysteria. She owned an apple orchard and guests at the hotel have reported smelling apples for many years, even though they're not included on the menu.

Another connection is that of the hotel's name. There were 20 people who were accused of witchcraft who were hanged by the "Witch Hanging Judge," John Hathorne. But the hotel wasn't named for the judge; it's named for one of his descendants, author Nathaniel Hawthorne.

Hawthorne was born in Salem on July 4, 1804. His father died just four years later from yellow fever and he and his mother and two sisters went to live with relatives, the Mannings. At the insistence and with the financial support of an uncle, Nathaniel was sent to Bowdoin College in 1821. Despite his affinity for drinking and gambling, he was able to avoid expulsion and he graduated in 1825. At some point between graduation and 1827, he added the letter "w" to his surname, changing it from "Hathorne" to "Hawthorne." Some speculate that the change was made to distance himself from the "Witch Hanging Judge."

Hawthorne went on to earn his place in the annals of American literature, but the hotel that now bears his name would not be built until many years after his death. His connections to Salem through his life and work made naming the hotel in his honor an easy choice.

The hotel's history began in July 1923, when the people of Salem became interested in a modern hotel that would serve to attract tourists to town. Frank Poor, founder of the local lighting company, helped create the plans for a six-story, 150-room facility, and stock sales raised the money to start the construction. More than 1,000 residents of Salem bought the stock, which meant they owned the hotel until after World War II, when a group of local businessmen acquired controlling interest. The hotel opened for business on July 23, 1925, amidst fanfare. Thousands of people turned up for the parade and flag-raising ceremony.

The hotel was named for Hawthorne, Salem's most famous son, and was located on Washington Square, near three buildings associated with the author – his birthplace on Union Street, the house on Herbert Street where he started writing, and the Mall Street home where he wrote *The Scarlet Letter.*

The chosen ground was already occupied when plans for the hotel were originally drawn up. Since 1766, the site had been used by the Salem Marine Society as a meeting place for sailors. A deal was struck between the society and the hotel promoters that allowed the sailors to meet in a room that was situated at the top of the new hotel. The new headquarters was designed as a replica of the cabin of the *Taria Topan*, one of the sailing ships from Salem's East India trade history. The society is still active today and continues to meet in the room provided to them. This area of the building is not open to the public.

The hotel was constructed in Colonial Revival-style, matching the other buildings and mansions along the square. It has enjoyed great success over the years and has been visited by many celebrities and notable figures, including Presidents Bill Clinton and George H.W. Bush, Colin Powell, newsman Walter Cronkite, film stars Bette Davis, Vanessa Redgrave, Robert De Niro, Jennifer Lawrence, and many others.

In 1970, the cast and crew of the television show *Bewitched* stayed at the Hawthorne and filmed there. The comedy was about Samantha Stephens (Elizabeth Montgomery), who married a mortal, Darrin, played by Dick York. A fire at the soundstage where the show was usually shot created an emergency and the crew needed to find a place to keep filming while the sets were repaired. The writers decided to create a series of shows that were set in Salem. The entire cast and crew moved into the Hawthorne Hotel and while room records don't survive, it is thought that Montgomery and her husband, William Asher, the producer and director of the show, stayed in Room 512. The hotel was featured in some of the episodes and the elevator was used in the episode titled "Samantha's Bad Day in Salem."

Montgomery and Asher loved the hotel. Souvenirs of their stay – pages from the scripts of the Salem episodes and a special menu created by the restaurant for the production – are still on display in the lobby.

Not everyone in town was thrilled with *Bewitched* being in Salem. This was prior to the tourist business that now exists to take advantage of the history of the witch trials. Many at that time felt the trials were a blight on the town and that it should distance itself from any association with witches – real or imagined. They wanted to stress the town's maritime history instead. That didn't work out, though, as any visitor to Salem today will quickly discover. There is also a monument commemorating *Bewitched* -- with a sculpture of Elizabeth Montgomery – at the intersection of Essex and Washington Streets.

The Hawthorne Hotel, like Salem itself, has endured, and in the 1990s, went through a major renovation. Each of the six floors at the hotel now has a theme and the tavern was renamed Parker's -- after Parker Brothers, the toy manufacturer that thrived in Salem and, incidentally, has manufactured the Ouija Board for decades.

With all that history, it's no surprise that the Hawthorne plays host to a ghost or two.

Many of the haunted stories at the Hawthorne seem to surround the captains who were part of the Salem Marine Society prior to their deaths. It's been said that some of these old sailors linger around the society's meeting room. Old charts and maps that are kept under lock and key can sometimes be found moved about after no one among the living has been in the room.

Another sailor-related story surrounds a large nautical ship wheel, which is located inside of Nathaniel's restaurant. Many have claimed that the wheel moves on its own. When physically stopped, it resumes the movements. In an area known as the "Lower Deck," tables and chairs are often found in disarray in the morning. An employee, who was responsible for setting up and arranging the room, performed his duties one night and briefly left the room. Upon his return, he found that all his work had been undone and the room was completely rearranged. This experience frightened him so badly that he requested to be removed from all night shifts after that.

Maritime ghosts aside, the rest of the hotel also seems to have its phantom residents and they seem to be attracted to certain parts of the hotel, or at least certain rooms. The most active spots are Room 325 and Room 612.

In Room 325, a suite, past guests like to turn lights and water faucets off and on. The toilet flushes by itself and the television often switches on in the middle of the night. While lying on the bed, guests have reported experiencing an extreme cold chill. Many have reported feeling as if they have been touched while trying to sleep. Additionally, many have reported hearing a disembodied cry of a child that seems to be searching for its mother.

The elevator made famous by *Bewitched* is said to be haunted by an invisible presence, and the sixth floor of the hotel has cold spots and chandeliers that sway back and forth on their own. One guest and her mother stayed on the sixth floor and witnessed their closet door opening by itself. They also saw a shopping bag on the bed that suddenly crumpled, as though it was squeezed by an invisible hand.

But it's Room 612 where the apparition of a woman has been encountered. She is usually seen outside the door to the room, but many guests have experienced her presence inside, too. They often complain about an uneasy feeling, as if someone was sharing the room with them. Many believe that this woman, seen wearing an old-fashioned dress, may be one of the spirits of those who were hanged as witches in 1692. Some suggest that it might be Bridget Bishop herself, who once owned the land where the hotel now stands. In 1592, she was accused of bewitching five women of the village and was hanged for it.

Perhaps she remains here still, as a spectral way of protesting the injustice that was done to her so many years ago.

10. HOLLYWOOD ROOSEVELT HOTEL
LOS ANGELES, CALIFORNIA

Many of Hollywood's older hotels are much like Hollywood itself. They are aging and slightly faded, still trying to hang onto the shimmer of glamour that they enjoyed in the days gone by. In times past, before you could find hookers on Hollywood Boulevard, the hotels of Hollywood were luxurious pleasure palaces where the stars of the silver screen went to dine, dance, and rendezvous with secret lovers. Like other parts of Hollywood, a few of the hotels have seen face-lifts in recent years, which have stirred up memories and "spirits" of the past. Not all the ghostly stories, and wicked scandals, are products of recent times, however, many of them have been around for years.

I chose to feature the Hollywood Roosevelt in this chapter because it's probably the best known of the local haunts, but there are a few other hotels that still play host to the stars of Hollywood past that are worthy of mention.

Historically speaking, the first hotel in the city was the Hotel Hollywood, which was opened by H.J. Whitley in 1902, before the idea of the area turning into a hotbed for movie stars was ever imagined. It was located on the west side of Highland Avenue and it fronted a dusty, unpaved road that would eventually become Hollywood Boulevard. In less than three years, Whitley was compelled to add an additional wing onto the place, and it continued to expand. It was, after all, the only show in town. Eventually, it covered the entire block and Whitley installed a wide lobby, a chapel, music room, ballroom, and 125 guest rooms.

The Hotel Hollywood soon became the most prestigious lodging house in the region and when the movie colony began to grow, it attracted luminaries like Louis B. Mayer, Irving Thalberg, Jack Warner, Wallace Reid, Gloria Swanson, Greta Garbo, Pola Negri, Rudolph Valentino, and many others. In fact, for many years between 1903 and 1956, when the hotel was razed, it was the social center of Hollywood.

There was a continuous stream of movie stars that arrived at the hotel daily. Many of the great silent movie actors made their homes in the Hollywood Hotel and attended the dances held every Thursday night in the ballroom. It was considered "the" place to be seen. To identify where certain people regularly sat and dined, the hotel had stars with the names of celebrities painted on the ceiling above their tables. Those who didn't live in the hotel lived nearby and the close-knit community made the place their second home.

Soon after the Hotel Hollywood opened, an eccentric millionaire spinster from Iowa, Mira Parker Hershey, who was then staying at a hotel in Los Angeles, rode out to see the new hotel in Hollywood that was being advertised in local newspapers. She became a guest; lured, the legend goes, by the cuisine, particularly the apple pie. She fell in love with the hotel and bought shares, eventually becoming sole owner of the place.

In 1909, Carrie Jacobs Bond wrote her then-famous song, "The End of a Perfect Day" at the Hotel Hollywood, which had inspired the tune. Five years later, opera star Geraldine Farrar was welcomed to Hollywood with the town's first white-tie-and-tails party in the hotel's famous ballroom. The Hearst newspapers' famous gossip columnist

Louella Parsons made the hotel's name synonymous with glamour when she broadcast live over the radio from the lobby during the height of her popularity.

By the 1920s, the hotel was so connected to the film colony's high living that it became a target for the tabloids and scandal rags of the era. The film magazines were correct in assuming that a lot of "hanky-panky" was going on at the hotel and the antics of the stars always made for good gossip. Nevertheless, the Hotel Hollywood attempted to maintain at least a bit of respectability. When John Barrymore climbed into the room of a female companion from the garden, the management ordered cactus to be planted under the windows of all ground floor rooms to dissuade others from trying the same thing. When that proved ineffective, all the ground floor windows were nailed shut.

In 1919, a desk clerk demanded that Valentino produce a marriage license before he could go upstairs with his new wife, Jean Acker, on their wedding night. As it turned out, he needn't have bothered. That night, after he led his bride to her room, Acker slammed the door in Valentino's face, locked it, and wept that she had made a terrible mistake. That was the end of their marriage, although they were not divorced for three years – three years during which Valentino would become one of the most famous screen lovers in history.

Mira Hershey died in 1930. In the early 1940s, developers acquired the historic hotel, planning to tear the place down and redevelop the block. They were only halted because of World War II, having to wait until the release of building materials. By the 1950s, the hotel was run down and faded, only a relic of its former glory. The developers were adamant that renovating and restoring the property was out of the question. Many of the remaining residents of the hotel had been there for years, even decades. Just before the building was torn down, writer Ezra Goodman interviewed many of them. One old woman, who had lived in the hotel for 35 years, was depressed at the idea of leaving a place that she loved so near to the end of her life. "I don't want to go to heaven," she said. "I just want to stay here."

The Hotel Hollywood was finally razed in August 1956, destroying a piece of history from Hollywood's early days. But if the old hotel had ghosts of film stars from days gone by, those stars would be smiling if they learned what replaced their beloved hotel. In 2001, the Hollywood and Highland entertainment complex, which includes the Kodak Theatre, the "official" home of the Academy Awards, opened on the site of the former Hotel Hollywood.

The spirit of Marilyn Monroe haunts the Knickerbocker Hotel. That's probably not the only place, though. Some claim she has been seen standing on the sidewalk outside of the Brentwood home where she died, and others claim that she manifests near her crypt in Pierce Brothers Westwood Village Memorial Park.

Marilyn's association with the Knickerbocker started when she began dating baseball great Joe DiMaggio. She used to enter the hotel through the service entrance to avoid the press and meet up with Joe in the Lido Room, the hotel's nightclub. After the two got married, part of their honeymoon was spent at the Knickerbocker. The nightclub is closed now, but when it was open, women who visited the ladies' room were sometimes surprised to see Marilyn powdering her nose in the mirror.

The Knickerbocker was built in 1925, and throughout the tumultuous decade of the 1920s, it played a key role at the heart of Hollywood. It first opened as a luxury apartment building and became a hotel later in its history. One of the attractions of the place was the Renaissance Revival nightclub (later the Lido Room), which saw more than its share of celebrities. During Prohibition, Los Angeles police often looked the other way and the club became a notorious speakeasy. One frequent guest was Rudolph Valentino, who reportedly loved to dance the tango to the live music performed in the bar.

As time passed, the hotel became home to both scandal and tragedy.

The lobby featured a huge crystal chandelier, which cost over $120,000 in 1925, and it was under this chandelier that epic film director D.W. Griffith died of a stroke in 1948. At the time of his death, Griffith, who was a pioneer in the Hollywood film industry, had been largely forgotten by his peers. He eked out a painful and lonely existence at the Knickerbocker, spending most of his time in the hotel bar, talking to anyone who was willing to listen to him. His dismissal by Hollywood was as great a tragedy as his death, and it would not be until years later that he would be regarded as the genius that he undoubtedly was.

The stories say that author William Faulkner and Meta Carpenter, a script girl from the Fox studios, began their lengthy affair at the Knickerbocker. Elvis Presley often stayed at the Knickerbocker, and in 1956, when he was filming "Love Me Tender," he posed for "Heartbreak Hotel" photos in one of the rooms. Other stars who lived or stayed at the Knickerbocker included rocker Jerry Lee Lewis, Mae West, Lana Turner, Cecil B. DeMille, Frank Sinatra, Laurel and Hardy, and many others.

In 1943, police dragged Frances Farmer, half naked, kicking and screaming from the hotel on assault and DUI charges. At her hearing the next morning, she behaved even more erratically. She claimed the police had violated her civil rights, demanded an attorney, and threw an inkwell at the judge. He immediately sentenced her to 180 days in jail. Frances put up a fight, which led to a policeman being knocked down and another one injured. She managed to get into a telephone booth, where she tried to call her attorney, but was subdued by the police. Thanks to the efforts of her sister-in-law, a deputy sheriff in Los Angeles County, Frances was transferred to the psychiatric ward of Los Angeles General Hospital. She was placed under the care of a psychiatrist who stated that she was suffering from manic-depressive psychosis. She spent most of the rest of her life in and out of mental institutions, enduring insulin treatments, cold water baths, and electroshock therapy.

Character actor William Frawley, who played Fred Mertz on the *I Love Lucy* show, lived at the Knickerbocker for decades. In March 1966, he was walking into the hotel when he dropped dead of a heart attack on the sidewalk outside. His nurse carried him into the lobby and attempted to revive him, but it was too late.

Perhaps the strangest tragedy took place in November 1962 with the suicide of Irene Gibbons, an actress and costume designer at MGM. Gibbons, whose real name was Irene Lentz, started out as an actress under her birth name, appearing in secondary roles in silent films beginning with Keystone Studios in 1921. The director of her first film was F. Richard Jones and the two of them became involved in a relationship that led to a marriage that lasted until his premature death in 1930. Irene decided to leave acting after that and, with skill as a seamstress and a flair for style, she opened a small dress shop. The success of her original designs in her shop eventually led to an offer from the Bullocks Wilshire luxury department store to design for their Ladies Custom Salon, which catered to Hollywood's wealthiest women, including many film stars.

Irene's designs at Bullocks garnered her attention from the film community and she was contracted by independent production companies to design wardrobes for some of their films. Billing herself simply as "Irene," her first screen work appeared in 1933 for the film *Goldie Gets Along*, worn by star Lily Damita. Her big break came when she was hired to create gowns for Ginger Rogers in a 1937 outing with Fred Astaire called *Shall We Dance*. This was followed by more designs for Ginger Rogers, as well as work for Walter Wanger Productions, Hal Roach Studios, and major companies like RKO, Paramount, and Columbia. During the 1930s, Irene worked with most of the major female stars in Hollywood.

Through her work, Irene met and married short story author and screenwriter Eliot Gibbons, the brother of multi-Academy Award winning Cedric Gibbons, head of art direction at MGM Studios. Cedric Gibbons has been generally regarded as the most important and influential production designer in the history of American films and he hired Irene when gown designer Adrian left MGM to join Universal Studios. By 1943, she was a leading costume supervisor at MGM and earned international recognition for her designs. She is best remembered for Lana Turner's avant-garde wardrobe in *The Postman Always Rings Twice* and in 1948, was nominated for an Academy Award for Best Costume Design for *B.F.'s Daughter*.

Despite her success, working under the powerful and arrogant Cedric Gibbons, while being married to his brother, was not easy. In 1950, Irene left MGM to open her own fashion house. She was out of the film industry for nearly 10 years when her friend Doris Day requested her talents for a Universal Studios production, *Midnight*

Lace. Irene earned her second Oscar nomination for her work in this film. The following year, she did another costume design for Doris Day and during 1962, worked on her last production, *A Gathering of Eagles*.

While working with Irene on designs for the 1962 film, Day noticed that her friend seemed upset and nervous. Irene finally confided in her that she was in love with actor Gary Cooper and that he was the only man that she had ever truly loved. Sadly, Cooper had passed away a short time before. Irene seemed unable to get over the loss.

On November 15, Irene took a room at the Knickerbocker Hotel, checking in under an assumed name. She cut her wrists but when this did not prove to be immediately fatal, she jumped to her death from her bathroom window on the 14th floor, landing on the extended roof of the lobby, where she was discovered later that same night (not two days later, as is often reported). She had left caring notes for friends and family, for her ailing husband, and for the hotel residents, apologizing for any inconvenience her death might cause.

By the 1960s, the Lido Room had ceased operations. The nightclub was reopened in 1993 as the All-Star Café and Speakeasy but lost its lease in 2001. During the period when the club was open again, the ghost of Marilyn Monroe was often spotted in the bathroom. Since then, the hotel has been transformed again into the Hollywood Knickerbocker Apartments. With the nightclub out of business and access to the building limited to tenants, there's no way to know if the building's legendary ghosts are still active.

However, there is one link to the supernatural that can never be taken away from the Knickerbocker – the famous Houdini Seances. During his life, the famous magician, Harry Houdini, had been an opponent of the notorious Spiritualist movement but had made a pact with his wife and friends that if contact was possible from the other side, he would attempt it. For 10 years after his death in 1926, his wife, Bess Houdini, continued to hold séances in hopes of communicating with her late husband. Any message had to contain a specific word – *believe* – spelled out in a code that Bess and Harry had used for a mind-reading act they had devised early in their career. No Spiritualist medium was able to break the code so after 10 years, Bess was ready to give up. The last "official" Houdini séance was held on Halloween night of 1936 – on the roof of the Knickerbocker Hotel, a place where Harry and Bess had often stayed while in Hollywood, working on some of Harry's films.

On October 31, a group of friends, fellow magicians, occultists, scientists, and Bess Houdini herself gathered on the roof. Eddy Saint, a former carnival and vaudeville showman and Bess's close friend, had arranged the gathering.

Coverage for the Final Houdini Séance was provided by radio and it was broadcast all over the world. Eddy Saint took charge of the proceedings and started things off with the playing of "Pomp and Circumstance," a tune that had been used by Houdini to start his act in the later years. He noted for radio audiences: "Every facility has been provided tonight that might aid in opening the pathway to the spirit world. Here in the inner circle reposes a "medium's trumpet," a pair of slates with chalk, a writing tablet and pencil, a small bell, and in the center reposes a huge pair of silver handcuffs on a silk cushion."

Saint continued coverage of the event, finally crying out to the late magician: "Houdini! Are you here? Are you here, Houdini? Please manifest yourself in any way possible... We have waited, Houdini, oh so long! Never have you been able to present the evidence you promised. And now, this, the night of nights... the world is listening, Harry... Levitate the table! Move it! Lift the table! Move it or rap it! Spell out a code, Harry... please! Ring a bell! Let its tinkle be heard around the world!"

Saint and the rest of Bess's inner circle attempted to contact the elusive magician for over an hour before finally giving up. Saint finally turned to Bess: "Mrs. Houdini, the zero hour has passed. The 10 years are up. Have you reached a decision?"

The mournful voice of Bess Houdini then echoed through radio receivers around the world. "Yes, Houdini did not come through," she replied. "My last hope is gone. I do not believe that Houdini can come back to me --- or to anyone. The Houdini shrine has burned for 10 years. I now, reverently... turn out the light. It is finished. Good night, Harry!"

The séance came to an end – but with one last surprise.

Almost immediately after Bess spoke her final words, a tremendously violent thunderstorm broke out, drenching the séance participants and terrifying them with the horrific lightning and thunder. They would later learn that this mysterious storm did not occur anywhere else in Hollywood --- only above the Knickerbocker Hotel! Some speculated that perhaps Houdini did come through after all, as the flamboyant performer just might have made his presence known by the spectacular effects of the thunderstorm.

The Oban Hotel – now known as the Hotel Hollywood, an homage to the city's first hotel – was built in 1922. However, the small, three-story peaked structure didn't have its grand opening until five years later. It stands on Yucca Street, one block from Hollywood Boulevard and around the corner from the Knickerbocker.

For many years, aspiring actors stayed at the Oban as they struggled their way to the top. Among the many guests were James Dean, Clark Gable, Fred MacMurray, Glenn Miller, Paul Newman, Orson Welles, and many others. The rooms were simple – a bed, desk and chair, lamp, dresser, ceiling fan, and a private bath with a toilet, sink, and shower. It wasn't much but it was a luxury for those just starting out.

Of course, times have changed, and the hotel was completely remodeled in 2002. It has all the amenities guests could possibly want now – along with at least two ghosts.

One of the lingering presences in the hotel is that of Hollywood hopeful Charles Love, a failed actor who eventually settled for a prop manager's job and as a double for silent film comedian Harry Langdon. On February 15, 1933, after a fight at the studio, followed by a drinking binge, Charles returned to his cramped hotel room, wrote a farewell note to Langdon, and then shot himself in the head, instantly ending his life. He was dead but, of course, didn't leave the hotel. Rather than stay behind in the room where he lived and died, his spirit has become trapped in the hotel's basement, on the stairs leading down to it, and on the landing at the top of the steps. He is usually encountered as an intense cold spot and an incredibly foul, pungent stench but his apparition is sometimes spotted, as well.

Charles doesn't haunt the building alone. There is also an unidentified woman – believed to be a former guest – who wanders the hallway on the second floor. She has been seen by scores of guests over the years, who often mistake her for another customer. When she turns and walks into a room through the door, however, they realize that they have just seen a ghost.

The most famous haunted hotel in Hollywood is, without a doubt, the Hollywood Roosevelt. Today, the hotel has been refurbished and remodeled to capture the spirit of its early days, but the new furnishings and decor don't stop the stories of the old spirits from being told.

The Hollywood Roosevelt opened in 1927 and was, from the beginning, designed to serve the new movie industry as a luxury hotel. The most famous movie stars of the day, Douglas Fairbanks and Mary Pickford, helped bring the hotel to life and the grand opening hosted the biggest celebrities of the day like Gloria Swanson, Greta Garbo, Will Rogers, and Clara Bow, among others. The hotel remained popular for many years and then in 1984, underwent a restoration. Since that time, the ghosts, they say, have been putting in frequent appearances.

The first strange event to be reported occurred in December 1985, about two weeks before the grand re-opening. Alan Russell, personal assistant to the general manager, was in the Blossom Room, where the first Academy Awards banquet was held in 1929. He was sweeping the floor when he noticed an extremely cold spot in one part of the room. He and the other employees who were present were perplexed to find there were no drafts or air conditioners to explain away the chill. Psychics who have investigated the hotel believe there is a man in black clothing who haunts this room, although who he may be, no one knows.

On that same day, another employee named Suzanne Leonard was dusting a mirror in the manager's office. She looked into the glass and saw the reflection of a blond woman. She turned quickly around but there was no one behind her, although the reflection remained for some time before fading away. It turned out that the mirror once hung in Suite 1200 of the hotel – the suite frequented by Marilyn Monroe.

Suzanne was the first person to spot Marilyn's image in the mirror but would not be the last. Soon, others were spotting her, too. The mirror was eventually moved to the lobby, near the valet stand and then near the gift shop, and the sightings continued.

But Marilyn did not confine herself to the mirror. She has since been seen all over the hotel. She has been spotted in Suite 1200, as well as Room 229, another of her favorite spots. Some claim to have seen her in Cabana 246 and around the deck chairs in the pool area, where she did modeling shoots.

But Marilyn is not the only spirit wandering the hotel, or the only celebrity ghost. As guests began to arrive at the refurbished hotel, the staff was told of other encounters. They frequently heard complaints about loud talking in nearby rooms and of voices in hallways -- rooms and corridors that would prove to be empty. Phones were lifted from receivers in empty suites and lights were turned on in empty, locked rooms. A maid was inexplicably pushed into a supply closet. A typewriter began typing in the middle of the night in an empty, locked office. A man in a white suit (who was seen by three different people on two different days) walked through a door and vanished. Extra bedspreads that were hung on a rod in the basement began moving on their own and a little girl was seen playing in the lobby and she vanished before the eyes of a startled staff member.

And there was more. Some employees also reported strange shadows on the ninth floor, prompting many of them to refuse to work on that level. Strange things were especially connected to Room 928. There, housekeepers reported cold spots that brushed by them and others felt a strong presence watching them or walking beside them. One night in 1992, a female guest reported that a man's hand patted her on the shoulder while she was reading. She turned, thinking that it was her husband, only to find him sound asleep.

Room 928 has been most prominently connected with actor Montgomery Clift, who lived in the room for three months in 1952 while filming *From Here to Eternity*. Clift was said to restlessly pace his room and the corridor outside, rehearsing his lines and practicing the bugle. Some say that he still does.

On screen, Montgomery Clift exuded an aura of vulnerable masculinity that appealed to both men and women alike; however, his real life was filled with insecurities that were often too much for him to bear. His gradual deterioration was once described as "the slowest suicide in show business."

Clift was born in Omaha, Nebraska, in 1920. He grew up the privileged son of a Wall Street stockbroker and traveled all over the world with his family and private tutors. When Wall Street crashed in 1929, the Clifts changed their lifestyle and moved to a small home in Sarasota, Florida. There, Clift would try acting for the first time at the age of 13. He joined a local youth theatrical group and his mother, realizing his natural talents, pushed him toward an acting career. After the family moved to Massachusetts, Clift was able to audition for a part on Broadway. He won the role and his new career was started at the age of 17.

Over the next three years, Clift played a number of leading roles on Broadway, while members of the film industry tried to lure him to Hollywood. He rejected every offer until he finally was able to get the studios to agree to hire him on his terms. United Artists cast him alongside John Wayne and Walter Brennan in what became one of the most famous westerns of all time, *Red River.*

After that, Clift began to work in other roles and became friends with actress Elizabeth Taylor, who he appeared with in *A Place in the Sun*. He would later appear with Taylor in two other films, *Raintree County* and *Suddenly Last Summer.* He accepted both roles without even looking at a script. He just wanted to act with Taylor. After a two-year hiatus following *A Place in the Sun*, Clift returned to the movie screen with *From Here to Eternity*, with Burt Lancaster and Frank Sinatra. The film would be nominated for eight Academy Awards and Clift would be nominated for Best Actor. After that, he starred in the Alfred Hitchcock film, *I Confess*, and in *Indiscretion of an American Housewife*. He would not be seen on the stage or screen again for more than three years.

About this time, Clift's personal life began to be plagued by his own inner demons. Despite his talents, he was utterly insecure. His mother controlled his life until he was in his 20s and he constantly tried to hide the fact that he was a homosexual, which was a "career-killer" in the Hollywood of the 1950s. His emotional difficulties were enhanced by his rise to stardom and he became an alcoholic and habitual drug user. Soon, the booze and pills began to interfere with his work and during the making of *From Here to Eternity*, the cast and crew began commenting about his drunken behavior on the set.

One night in May 1957, Clift attended a dinner party at the home of Elizabeth Taylor during the shooting of *Raintree County*. As he was driving home, he veered off the road and his car collided with a telephone pole. Taylor arrived at the crash scene and discovered that Clift was having trouble breathing. She forced her hand down his throat and pulled out two of his broken teeth, which were blocking his airway. The accident left Clift with a broken jaw and nose, a crushed sinus cavity, two missing teeth, and severe facial lacerations that required plastic surgery. Somehow, he recovered and returned home from the hospital after just eight weeks. He was able to complete filming on *Raintree County*.

Clift had other problems apart from his self-destructive personality. He suffered from various illnesses including colitis and a thyroid condition, the symptoms of which were almost indistinguishable from the effects of alcohol and drugs. When Clift co-starred in *The Misfits* – both Clark Gable and Marilyn Monroe's final movie – Marilyn said of Clift, "He's the only person I know who is in worse shape than I am."

In 1962, Clift was hired for the title role in John Huston's *Freud* and Universal sued him because he was incapable of remembering his lines. Studios were now in the habit of insuring their productions and Clift's shaky track record made him a liability. He didn't act for three years after that, until Elizabeth Taylor got him a part in the 1967 production, *Reflections in a Golden Eye*. Clift was also offered a part in *The Defector*, which he felt was an inferior film, but he was so desperate to prove that he was worthy of *Reflections in a Golden Eye* that he signed on. He did all his own stunts in *The Defector*, just to show the studio that he was able to work.

On Friday night, July 22, 1966, Clift went to sleep and never woke up again. When a friend entered his bedroom and found Clift naked except for his glasses, he planned to cover him up and leave him alone. He was used to Clift's drunken stupors, but this time was different. Clift did not seem drunk, but dead. Unable to find a pulse, he called a doctor, who pronounced that Clift had died in his sleep. Although many assumed that he succumbed to alcohol or a drug overdose, Clift actually died from a heart attack.

All of Clift's friends from his long career on stage and screen had encountered him once or twice before his inevitable demise and each had a heart-breaking story to tell about the once-intelligent and gifted actor who was destroyed by drink, drugs, and poor health. Clift's life was ruined, but his film work remains the product of one of the greatest actors of all time.

That's how he is remembered today – along with being one of the continued guests at the Hollywood Roosevelt Hotel.

11. THE SKIRVIN HOTEL
OKLAHOMA CITY, OKLAHOMA

Built in 1910, the Skirvin Hotel has long been one of the great landmarks of Oklahoma City. The majestic building at One Park Avenue was constructed by an Oklahoma oilman who was determined to make it one of the finest hotels in the Southwest.

Some say it may also be one of the most haunted.

William Balser "Bill" Skirvin moved his family to Oklahoma in 1906. He had already made money in Texas, but when the government opened up the Indian Territory in the early 1900s, he participated in the land runs that would eventually lead to his tremendous wealth in oil and property. In 1910, he decided to build a hotel on one of his properties in Oklahoma City after an investor from New York City offered to buy the lot in order to build the "biggest hotel" in the state. Oklahoma City had only one luxury hotel at the time, and Skirvin thought it was an excellent investment.

He approached Solomon A. Layton, a famous area architect who had designed the Oklahoma State Capitol building, and plans were finalized for a 6-story, U-shaped hotel. But in late 1910, just as construction of the fifth story neared completion, Layton convinced Skirvin that the city's growth justified 10 stories rather than six. With money to burn, Skirvin agreed to the plan.

On September 26, 1911, Skirvin opened the newly completed luxury hotel to the public. The lobby was decorated in English Gothic, and the wings of the hotel contained a drugstore, retail shops, and a cafe. The hotel had 225 rooms and suites, each with a private bath, telephone, hardwood furniture, and velvet carpet. It was one of the first buildings in Oklahoma City to have "iced air," as well as running ice water in each room. The ballroom, which could seat 500, boasted imported Austrian chandeliers that cost more than $10,000 each.

The hotel became the center of Oklahoma City society and attracted celebrities, businessmen, and politicians from across the state. Skirvin began to expand the hotel, slowly at first, building a new 12-story wing and then eventually raising all wings to 14-stories by 1930. This increased room total to 525 and added a roof garden and cabaret club as well as doubled the lobby size.

As much of the country was hit with a depression, the oil boom in Oklahoma City kept the Skirvin Hotel going strong, and despite failed extension attempts and family problems, William Skirvin operated the hotel until his death in 1944.

During its heyday, Skirvin's daughter, Pearl Mesta, brought the hotel a national reputation. She was a well-photographed Washington, D.C. socialite and U.S. Ambassador to Luxembourg. She was known for her extravagant parties and connections to celebrities and politicians. She even had a Broadway musical written about her that starred Ethel Merman.

After Skirvin's death, his children inherited the property but decided to sell it to Dan W. James in 1945. He immediately began modernizing the hotel, adding numerous amenities such as room service, a beauty shop, a barber shop, a swimming pool, and a house physician. The Skirvin only grew in prominence as it hosted Presidents Harry Truman and Dwight D. Eisenhower. But by 1959, suburban sprawl was severely hurting downtown Oklahoma City, and James sold the Skirvin hotel to Chicago investors in 1963. It was then sold again in 1968 to H.T. Griffin.

Griffin spent millions remodeling the Skirvin Hotel, but business continued to suffer. Griffin filed for bankruptcy in 1971. After changing hands a few times, the hotel underwent more renovation in the 1970s, then again in the early 1980s, but by then, it was too late to save it. The once grand hotel closed in 1988.

It sat empty for the next nearly 20 years, with sealed off doors and boards over the windows. It slowly decayed, with the only occupants being security guards who had been hired to keep away trespassers and vandals.

Finally, in 2002, the city of Oklahoma City acquired the property and put together a financing package to "renovate, restore, and reopen" the Skirvin Hotel. In February 2007, the place came back to life as a Hilton property and remains a jewel of downtown Oklahoma City today.

A jewel that is tarnished only by rumor and ghost stories, of course.

The hauntings at the hotel – as well as its somewhat tarnished history – can all be traced back to Bill Skirvin and his reputation as a womanizer with a history of gambling and carousing. During Prohibition, Skirvin had a speakeasy at the hotel for many of his fellow oilmen and well-heeled friends. There were also stories of a gambling den and a brothel on the hotel's 10th floor.

It was in the 1920s that Skirvin allegedly began an affair with one of the hotel's maids, a beautiful young woman named Effie. Unfortunately for both of them, the maid became pregnant. Afraid that the scandalous affair would ruin him, Skirvin supposedly kept the maid locked in a private room on the top floor of the hotel. She was not allowed to have contact with anyone except for Skirvin and a doctor that he trusted. She remained there until she gave birth to the child, but even after that, Skirvin would not allow her to leave.

The legend claims that the maid became so depressed by the isolation that she lost her sanity. Out of her mind, she took her child in her arms and flung herself out the window to the street below.

Or so the story goes.

Over the years, strange incidents have occurred at the Skirvin, which are believed to be connected to the luckless maid and her child. Guests claim to have seen a maid's cart moving down the hallways on its own. Others have complained about being unable to get a good night's sleep because of the incessant crying of a baby. When the security staff investigates, they never find the weeping child. There are also reports of a ghostly woman walking around on the hotel's top floor.

And things get even weirder than that. Men who have stayed alone at the hotel claim they have heard a disembodied female voice who propositions them. Others say they have seen the misty form of a naked woman joining them in the shower. One man even claimed that he was sexually molested by a female ghost during his stay.

It's said that this rowdy spirit is none other than the ghost of Skirvin's mistress, Effie, unable to leave the hotel where she died. But is it really? And was there really an Effie who took her own life by throwing herself out of a hotel window?

There has never been any historical documentation about a woman fitting Effie's circumstances who committed suicide at the hotel. Years of newspaper articles and obituaries have failed to substantiate the legend, but witness statements tell a different story. They have seen the woman and have heard the crying child – could this be Effie and her baby, or another specter entirely?

Who knows? Despite her tragic story, Effie is considered a playful prankster these days, knocking on doors, opening drawers and causing commotion in the halls. Oh, and one other thing – causing mayhem and panic among the NBA players who come to Oklahoma City to play the hometown, the Thunder.

Effie has sort of become a mascot for the Thunder, haunting the team's opponents who stay at the Skirvin Hotel when they come to town. Large men who are unafraid of attacking the lane, diving headfirst into the seats, or shooting pressure-packed shots shudder at the mere mention of Effie. More importantly for the home team, they lie awake on the night before the game, their much-needed rest undone by a restless spirit.

For more nearly a decade, Effie has wreaked havoc for visiting teams. The Knicks blamed creaks and groans for a sleepless night before a loss. A Bulls player could not explain why his bathroom door slammed shut on its own. A player for the Phoenix Suns woke up to find his bathtub mysterious filled with water.

"Everyone in the league knows about her," said Caron Butler, an NBA veteran who stayed at the Skirvin many times before joining the Thunder.

The story began to spread among NBA players back in January 2010, when some of the Knicks said that a loss in Oklahoma City could be blamed, in part, on a wakeful night at the Skirvin. "The place is haunted," Jared Jeffries told reporters. "It's scary."

His teammate Eddie Curry admitted that he only slept two hours one night. He was the only player assigned to the supposedly spirit-infested 10th floor, and he spent most of his time in Nate Robinson's room, afraid to be alone. "I definitely believe there are ghosts in that hotel," Curry said later.

A few weeks later, Chicago's Taj Gibson said that the bathroom door in his room had slammed shut in the middle of the night for no reason. His teammate Derrick Rose was among the Bulls who heard strange sounds in the night and became a believer. "It was scary last night," he said the next day – after a loss to the Thunder.

That spring, basketball commentator Craig Sager did a report about the hauntings and his own experiences there. Bill Simmons of ESPN wrote about a chilling night at the Skirvin, when he was startled awake by the sound of a baby crying in his room.

In 2012, Jordan Hamilton of the Denver Nuggets confessed, "This hotel creeps me out every time we come here." In 2013, Wesley Johnson of the Phoenix Suns said he awoke to find his bathroom door closed and his tub inexplicably filled with water.

What does the management of the Skirvin have to say about all the ghost stories being shared by NBA players? Nothing. They don't talk about ghosts and desk clerks have been told to dismiss the rumors.

Employees do know about the legends and while, officially, they're supposed to laugh off the tales as nothing but a story, off-the-record, some will admit to their own strange encounters. One banquet worker said she sometimes heard a crying baby, mostly in the basement or on the 10th and 14th floors. It is not scary, she said, because it is something she only hears, not sees.

The first stories about Effie didn't appear until the middle 1990s, when the hotel was closed, and its future was in doubt. The accounts appeared in a few books and articles and mostly rattled around on the internet until the Knicks brought them back to life in 2010. After that, similar stories began to spread across the NBA.

The place may be spooking basketball players, but it remains as popular as ever with the public. Visiting today, you'll usually find that the place is sold out. Each night, the two-story lobby, with its dark-wood columns and rich tones, is filled with sounds of conversation and melodies from the piano bar. The Skirvin's restored elegance makes it easy to imagine an era when the guests included oilmen, actors, and presidents.

And what about Effie? Is she real, or merely imagination? If you ask any NBA player who has spent a night without sleep at the Skirvin, he'll assure you that she is real. But is she really the ghost of a maid who died here years ago, or is she the ghost of someone else, forced to spend eternity at the hotel?

No one can say for sure, but whoever this ghost might be, she doesn't seem to be in any hurry to check out of the Skirvin Hotel.

12. REVERE HOTEL BOSTON COMMON

BOSTON, MASSACHUSETTS

This isn't a place where you'd expect to find ghosts.

Unlike so many other hotels that have appeared in these pages already, this is not an old hotel, steeped in history. Until just a few years ago, this was a Radisson property and looked like just about any other hotel you'd find in a city or at an exit from the expressway. It was renovated and reopened as a unique, boutique-type hotel near the Boston Common in 2012 – but that hasn't stopped all the strange stories.

It's the people, you see. It's the tired, confused, disheveled people who appear from nowhere, stumbling through the lobby or down a hallway. Many of them smell like smoke. They were often seen at the Radisson and now they appear at the Revere, blackened by soot from a fire that doesn't exist.

Well, it doesn't exist anymore. But it did. In fact, it was one of the most devastating fires in American history and it happened right where the Revere now stands.

It's as if these scorched figures refuse to let that long-ago fire be forgotten.

In the 1930s and 1940s, it was *the* place to be in Boston. The Cocoanut Grove was the city's most elegant nightclub and everyone wanted to be seen dancing, drinking, and listening to music there. Named after the famed Cocoanut Grove nightclub in Los Angeles's Ambassador Hotel, it started out as a restaurant and semi-speakeasy. Musician Mickey Alpert convinced California mobster Jack Berman – then hiding out in Boston – to put up the financing for the club. Mickey found a vacant building near the Boston Common and used the cash to open a fine eatery with top-notch entertainment. On advice from his attorney brother, George, Mickey refused to serve alcohol in the club. But he had no problem with guests bringing their own. The place opened in October 1927 and flourished for the first few years providing a safe place to eat, dance, and drink during Prohibition.

But the Great Depression hit the club hard. Business nosedived and the partners could no longer afford to book new acts. Desperate for cash, they sold the club to Charles Solomon in 1930 for just $10,000.

Solomon was a Russian-born Jewish gangster who had risen through the ranks of New England organized crime to become one of the most powerful crime bosses in the city. He ran most of Boston's illegal gambling, prostitution, and narcotics operations and, most importantly, controlled almost all the bootlegging in the region. He bought the Cocoanut Grove for his own personal amusement but turned it into a lucrative speakeasy where the liquor was always flowing. He hired popular performers to entertain the crowds that packed the place, like Rudy Vallee, Guy Lombardo, Jimmy Durante, and Sophie Tucker. Despite the crowds and the booze, the soaring entertainment budget caused the club to operate at a loss. Solomon didn't care, though. He used the club to hobnob with celebrities, politicians, and the Boston elite.

But his time at the Cocoanut Grove didn't last long. In 1933, he was gunned down in the bathroom at Boston's Cotton Club. His business was divided up by rival gangsters, but his estate was handled by his attorney, Barney Welansky.

Welansky had worked for Solomon for years but kept himself well-insulated from the dead man's mob dealings, only handling his legitimate business. A private meeting with a probate judge and some cash under the table led to Welansky becoming the new owner of the Cocoanut Grove.

By then, Prohibition had been repealed and he turned the former speakeasy into Boston's most important and stylish nightclub. He made many changes to the operation, too, reducing the cost of the entertainment by hiring musicians and establishing a house band that was led by none other than Mickey Alpert, the Cocoanut Grove's original creator and owner. Angelo Lippi had worked as maître d' at the Grove since it had opened and agreed to continue to work for Barney. He managed the floor employees and kept the customers happy and eager to return.

The floor space of the Cocoanut Grove was enlarged several times as adjacent buildings were acquired and added to the Grove. Barney bought three more buildings and brought in famous nightclub designer Reuben Bodenhorn to renovate the new spaces. His ultimate vision for the interior of the club was a theme reflecting the tropical settings of Casablanca, as well as elements of Tahitian jungles and Arabian Nights. The walls were lined with imitation leather and the ceilings were draped with thousands of yards of satin. Six pillars, three on each side of the dance floor, were designed to look like palm trees, with large paper palm fronds extending far out over the floor in a circular pattern. An elevated area called "the terrace" was inside the main dining room just off the foyer. Wrought iron railings had been installed along the edges of the terrace which created a feeling of separation and maintained prime views of the floorshow for VIP customers. He also added a bar – since there hadn't been one during Prohibition – that was covered with red leatherette and commanded an excellent view of the floorshow.

Barney then decided to add a new bar, away from the floor show, in what used to be the storage room in the basement. It was meant to be dark and private, with only a piano on a revolving floor for entertainment. It became immediately successful, so Barney decided it needed an upgrade. He brought in Reuben Bodenhorn again to design a look for the space. The designer wisely decided to embrace the dark, windowless space and created a dim, intimate lounge with an exotic feel. There was one soft light in the center of the room, aimed at the floor and neon lined the underside of the bar. The only other illumination was from tiny lights that twinkled out from the fronds of the imitation palm trees in the corners. He hid the concrete walls with flimsy paneling and covered the ceiling by draping nearly 2,000-square-feet of dark blue satin over wooden slats along the low ceiling. This was meant to give the customers a feeling of sitting beneath a star-filled night sky. He placed zebra print settees along the outer walls of the lounge along with several tables and chairs.

In 1942, Barney bought another building and added the New Broadway Lounge onto what was now an entertainment complex. As with his two previous renovations, he didn't bother to apply for a building permit. He did submit plans to the city, however, which called for an emergency exit to be built that could accommodate the New Broadway Lounge patrons. However, as the renovations progressed, Barney decided to keep the door locked and to have a coat check room built across the exit, thus blocking the door and concealing it from sight. Since the new lounge was connected to the main dining room through a narrow corridor next to the stage, the liquor license board required a fire door to be installed. Barney didn't bother with that either, but he got a license because his brother was on the board.

The club grew larger and as it did, it became a confusing maze of coat check rooms, dressing rooms, restrooms, service rooms, kitchens and store rooms connected to each other and to the three large public rooms by winding and twisting corridors, and to the basement Melody Lounge by a single narrow stairway. Barney didn't pay much attention to Boston's building or fire codes because he didn't have to – his best friends and customers were the politicians and commissioners who ran the city.

By the time of the fire, the Cocoanut Grove was made up of six interconnected buildings, nearly tripling its original size. There were three large public rooms with three bars, a dining room, a dance floor, and a stage for the band. During fair weather, the roof above the dance floor could be electrically rolled back, revealing the night sky and allowing patrons to dance under the stars.

Saturday nights were always packed at the Cocoanut Grove and November 28, 1942, was no exception. Even though the legal occupancy of the building was 460 people, extra tables and chairs had been added to allow over 1,000 people to enjoy a night out at the Grove. Among the patrons was Buck Jones, the famed cowboy celebrity, star of more than 200 movies. In town promoting war bonds on a war bond tour, he was having dinner with a group of fellow promoters. As a VIP, he was seated with his party on the terrace.

The nightclub was packed but two key people were conspicuously absent. Club owner Barney Welansky had been admitted to the Mass General Hospital 12 days earlier after suffering a heart attack, leaving his brother Jimmy in charge. Also missing was the Grove's long-time maître d' Angelo Lippi, who was home suffering from arthritis.

Customers drifted back and forth between the dining room, the dance floor, the restrooms, and the basement's Melody Lounge, which filled up with about 400 people. In one corner of the lounge, a sailor and his date were enjoying the privacy created by the dim lighting in the room. To make things a little darker, the sailor reached up and unscrewed the tiny light in the palm tree over their heads. Head bartender John Bradley looked over and noticed that the corner was now pitch dark. Annoyed, but too busy with his customers to deal with it, he sent Stanley Tomaszewski, a 16-year-old bar boy, to get the light back on right away. Stanley walked over to the corner and politely explained that it was dangerous having the light out and he had to turn it back on. Unfortunately, the bulb had fallen completely out, and it was far too dark for Stanley to see the socket inside the tree. Striking a match, he found the socket and got the bulb back on. He blew out the match, dropped it to the floor and stepped on it to make sure it was out.

As Stanley returned to work, he heard someone shout that there was a fire in the top of the palm tree. John Bradley ran from behind the bar and he and Stanley pulled and batted at the tree attempting to put the fire out. Other employees ran to help by throwing pitchers of water on the tree. It might have been comical if not for what happened next. Just as the burning fronds were pulled down, Bradley looked up to see the stain fabric on the ceiling above the tree start to burn. A wave of flame erupted from the corner, engulfing the fabric on the ceiling, and spreading across the room toward the open staircase. The ceiling had been turned into a sheet of blue and orange flame, dripping fire onto the patrons below.

Almost immediately, the crowd panicked as hair and clothing began to burn. The crowd moved toward the only exit they knew - the narrow staircase, where the fire was also spreading. It swept up the stairs, burning away at the fabric on the ceiling. The staircase quickly jammed with the 400 panicked people trying to escape the basement.

The way to safety wasn't easy. The frightened patrons had to make their way up a narrow flight of 15 steps, past the locked emergency exit at the top, then around a U-turn to the right and down a 10-foot hallway, then another right turn around an office and coat check room for 28-feet, then another right turn and 12 more feet across the foyer to the revolving door opening onto Piedmont Street.

This had to be done with a fire raging over their heads and thick black smoke filling the air around them.

And it got worse. Barney Welansky had ordered all the service and emergency exits, to which the public had access, be locked while the club was open. This was intended to keep patrons from sneaking out without paying their check.

Many terrified, confused people never made it out of the Melody Lounge. They were overcome by the thick choking smoke or by the tremendous heat from the fire. They weren't aware that there was an exit door in the back of the lounge, as it was disguised with the same paneling used on the walls. It would have taken them down a hallway, up three steps and to an outside exit. Not a single person found this door.

When Melody Lounge customers finally stumbled to the main entrance off the Piedmont Street foyer, only the first few were able to make their way through the revolving door before it was completely clogged by the crush of people behind them. They were unaware that there was a conventional exit door right next to the revolving door. Welansky had installed a coat check room in front of it, with a large wooden coat rack blocking the door from sight. Even if they had seen it, it probably wouldn't have helped them to escape – the door opened inward, not out. It would have been forced shut by the crush of the crowd.

The fire had started in the fake palm tree in the lounge at 10:15 p.m. At that exact same time, the fire department was responding to an alarm for a car fire just three blocks from the Cocoanut Grove. It only took a few minutes to put out that small fire, and a firefighter noticed what he thought was smoke coming from the area of the Grove. As the firefighters headed toward the club to investigate, people started running toward them to report the fire. When they arrived, they found heavy black smoke pouring out of the building and patrons and employees scrambling out into the street. The battalion chief on site ordered a third alarm to be issued, skipping the second alarm as he realized the scale of the disaster.

While the fire department was assembling on the outside, the fire continued to rage inside the club. When the blaze reached the main floor, several hundred unsuspecting revelers were just beyond the foyer, not knowing that many of them would be dead within minutes, and the rest would be frantically searching for any way out of the blaze. Just as the fire entered the main public room, the lights went out, plunging everyone into total darkness. A cry of terror went up in the room when they saw the flickering of the approaching flames.

The fire roared into the main public room, where the dining area, dance floor, bandstand, and bar were located. The fire was still feeding off the fabric on the ceilings and now devoured the wall coverings, too. With the flames came extreme heat that seared flesh. The thick, acrid smoke made it impossible to breathe. The flames moved through the room so rapidly that many were overcome with heat or smoke before they even had a chance to leave their chairs. In the aftermath, bodies were found burned beyond recognition, while others were found next to tables without any signs of external injury.

Movie star Buck Jones was one such victim. He was trapped on the terrace as the fire advanced across the room. He was overcome by the heat and smoke and fell to the floor beneath his table. Firefighters found him there, barely alive. He was taken to the hospital but died a short time later.

No one knew where the emergency doors were located. They only knew the doors by which they had entered the club – the revolving door in the main foyer on Piedmont Street and the exit leading from the New Broadway Lounge opening onto Broadway Street. This exit entailed a single, inward swinging door that led into a small vestibule then double doors opening onto the street. Most of the patrons had entered the club through the Piedmont entrance with only a single revolving door. These two exits were nearly a full city block apart. All but 20 of the club's employees survived the fire, largely because they knew where the hidden exits were, and which windows would open. Some of the patrons were able to follow employees to safety. The rest were on their own.

As the foyer at the Piedmont Street entrance continued to fill with people, bodies began to pile up against the revolving door. Eventually, the door mechanism gave way and the door collapsed outward onto the sidewalk. However, as it did, a wall of fire followed the crowd through the opening, seeking the fresh air outside, and scorched most everyone who was in or around the doorway.

A set of emergency doors was located along the Shawmut Street wall behind the terrace. These double doors were hidden behind wooden-slatted venetian doors and were blocked off with tables that were added to accommodate the large crowd. Even so, several people were able to find the doors. Each door was only 20-inches wide and the door on the right was bolted near the top of the frame. At first, no one could find the bolt in the dark but then it was released, and they rushed forward, knocking people down in their panic. Many of those who made it outside reached back and forcibly pulled others through the narrow doors, then shoved them aside on the sidewalk, injured, but alive.

One group of people descended a service stairway to the kitchen. They searched for an exit in the dark and found a small window above the counter that had been boarded up. Knocking the boards away, they found a pipe blocked most of the opening. They struggled through and into a blind alley behind an apartment building. Margaret Foley, sitting in her living room, was unaware of what was going on only a few feet from her home when a woman burst through her back door, ran through her apartment, and out the front door. Stunned, Margaret watched as others followed. She later estimated that at least 50 people escaped the fire through her home.

Two more exits were located on the main floor but proved to be useless. One was a service door located to the left of the stage platform. It also opened inward and it was locked. The other door was in the New Broadway Lounge, locked and well hidden behind a coat check room.

The nearly 250 customers enjoying themselves in the New Broadway Lounge remained blissfully unaware of the horror that was taking place on the other side of the adjoining wall for several minutes. Meanwhile, the fire in the dining room was getting hotter. When it reached the velour-lined passageway into the Broadway Lounge, extreme heat built up a massive amount of pressure which blasted the flames and hot gasses down the short passage and into the lounge. Even without all the flammable decorations that were in the rest of the club, the hallway acted like a blowtorch, obliterating everything – and everyone – in the lounge. There were 25 bodies found, burned to blackened cinders, found where they fell. Dozens of bodies were piled against the only unlocked exit in the room.

Next to the Broadway Street entrance, two large windows had been replaced by glass block. One man was able to break a small hole through the glass block and attempted to crawl out but became stuck. Firefighters found the man reaching through the hole but could not pull him through. They doused him with water but in the end, they had to watch helplessly as he burned to death.

A long wall on the Piedmont Street side of the building contained four large plate glass windows. These windows, if broken out, would have provided an excellent escape route for those trapped in the dining room area. Unfortunately, they had been covered with wood panels and no one knew they were there. It was later suggested that if the windows had not been covered, hundreds might have been saved.

Firefighters needed to get hoses into the building quickly to save anyone trapped by the fire. Early on, wherever they tried to break through, they were driven back by the extreme heat and thick black smoke. When they were finally able to enter, they went through the area where the revolving door had collapsed. They had to climb over a six-foot-high stack of bodies to get to the dining room area. By the time they were able to enter the foyer, the fire had nearly burned itself out.

The fire was out in less than a half hour. Clearing the entrances, rescuers pulled body after body from the stack that blocked the doorway, lining them up on the sidewalk. Police Officer Elmer Brooks later remembered rescuers lifting bodies and having arms and legs come off in their hands.

Clearing the entrance was a harrowing job but nothing prepared the firefighters for the gruesome task that awaited them. As they worked their way through the building, they found bodies everywhere. Some were piled up against locked doors, while others were by themselves. Some were horribly burned, while others were unmarked by flames. Some were found where they were sitting when the fire started while others were found in the far reaches of the club. Firefighter Winn Robbins saw a woman, propped up in one of the Grove's phone booths, dead but still holding the telephone receiver in her hand.

Firefighters, police officers, and volunteers began removing the bodies, piling them on the sidewalks. Some of the victims were still alive but there wasn't time to separate the living from the dead and so those not badly charred were all loaded into ambulances and trucks and taken to area hospitals. Medical professionals triaged the victims as they arrived, sorting out the dead and determining the level of medical care required by the living.

Everyone who died at the Cocoanut Grove, died as a result of the fire, but there were several causes of death. The most straightforward were those who were physically burned. Others died from smoke inhalation or carbon monoxide poisoning, and still others died from internal burns - burned lungs and nasal passages from breathing the fiery air. Several bodies showed signs of being crushed on the floor or against doors because so many people were pressing against them. Even more disturbing was the number of people who had fallen and were simply trampled to death by the stampeding crowd.

As first responders went about their work inside with a kind of stunned calmness, the scene outside the club was becoming more chaotic. The temperature was falling and the water from the hoses was making everything icy. Family members, friends, and bystanders pushed toward the building, forcing officials to form a human chain to stop people from entering the club to search for loved ones or to satisfy morbid curiosities. Unfortunately, some of the bodies piled on the sidewalk suffered the further indignity of being stripped of their money and jewelry as they lay dead or dying by ghouls in the crowds.

In the hours that followed, hundreds of victims were taken to hospitals. Hundreds were dead when they arrived or died soon after. Some were sent directly to temporary morgues but were found to be alive and transferred to hospitals. A few of those eventually made it home.

In the days that followed, the newspapers were filled with stories of those who lived and who died. The fire had involved 187 firefighters, 26 engine companies, 5 ladder trucks, 3 rescue companies, and countless volunteers. The property loss was in the hundreds of thousands of dollars.

The cost in human suffering was immeasurable.

Hearings began within days of the fire. More than 100 witnesses gave testimony, including several public officials and over 90 survivors. The results of the inquest revealed that Barney Welansky manipulated local politicians to his advantage and cut corners, putting his customers at risk, to save a buck or make a buck. At the same time, politicians and public officials were ducking blame and trying to make the fire someone else's responsibility. A Suffolk County grand jury eventually handed down 10 indictments, ranging from neglect of duty to manslaughter. Barney and Jimmy Welansky received the harshest charges. Several public officials were also indicted, along with interior designer Rueben Bodenhorn.

The only person exonerated in the entire mess – and, in fact, was commended for his actions – was Stanley Tomaszewski, the young man who tried to put the fire out in the first place. Even so, he received scores of death threats and had to be placed in protective custody for an extended time. He escaped the fire without injury but was scarred from it anyway. For decades, he had been threatened, harassed, and awakened by late-night telephone calls. Shortly before his death in 1994, he said he had suffered enough and wished to finally be left alone.

In the end, only Barney Welansky was found guilty at trial. He was convicted of 19 counts of manslaughter and sentenced to 15 years in prison. Nearly three years into his sentence, he was diagnosed with lung cancer. Governor Tobin, mayor of Boston at the time of the fire, quietly pardoned Welansky. When he walked out of prison, Barney was a sick, bitter man, who told reporters that he wished that he had been at the fire and died with everyone else. Nine weeks later, he was dead.

The burned-out shell of the infamous Cocoanut Grove nightclub was finally demolished in September of 1945.

Years ago, the streets that used to surround the Cocoanut Grove were reconfigured to allow for the construction of the Boston Radisson Hotel and Theater Complex – now the Revere Hotel. The original site of the nightclub has been swallowed by the much larger hotel and its parking lot. The only physical reminder of what happened that night in 1942 is a small bronze plaque that was embedded in the sidewalk next to the parking lot in 1993. You have to look for it, but it's there.

Even though the physical reminders of the Cocoanut Grove are gone, there are other reminders that still linger. So many lives were snuffed out that night, before they could know what was happening, leaving their remains in chairs where they had been sitting or lying on the floor nearby. It is believed by many that these unfortunate victims are still wandering the site, trying to find their way to safety, or maybe to a friend or loved one.

A few blocks away from the site of fire is Jacques Cabaret. On that night, some of the victims were taken directly to hospitals while others were taken to a temporary morgue or to one of the designated mortuaries in the city. Many who were believed to be still alive and taken to hospitals were already dead, and conversely, some of those taken to the morgue or mortuaries were still alive. A film distribution garage located near the Cocoanut Grove was set up as a temporary morgue on the night of the fire. The bodies were laid out side by side in rows on the tile floor to await identification and transportation.

That garage is now the Jacques Cabaret.

Not everyone at the club is willing to discuss the ghostly happenings there, but one former bartender said that "spooky stuff happened there all the time." The most significant experience he had while working at the bar happened late one night when he was cleaning up after closing. He had left the bar area for a moment and when he returned, he saw bodies lying in long rows all across the floor. He turned to switch on the overhead lights and when he turned back, everything had returned to normal.

During the time when the hotel located on the site of the Cocoanut Grove was still the Radisson, a large number of employees admitted that they had witnessed strange appearances throughout the hotel. Disheveled and confused men or women, seeming to appear out of nowhere, wandered past them and disappeared just as mysteriously as they had appeared. They also spoke of experiences in the hotel bar and in the kitchen, where they saw bright flashes and heard odd noises and loud popping sounds that had no discernible cause.

And the eerie events continue today. Current employees at the Revere have revealed that fire victims are still making their presence known. On occasion, the quiet, shadowy form of a man can be seen passing a doorway or walking down an empty hall. When approached by employees, he fades away to nothing. Apparitions – like those reported previously wearing dirty, soot-stained clothing – are often encountered by staff members and guests alike.

Other ominous events have also been reported, like unexplained flooding in different areas of the hotel and a water faucet in a restroom on the second floor that repeatedly turns itself on, even when no one is in the room. Some staff members have described hearing their name called while working at the hotel at night, especially when no one else is there.

This is a relatively new hotel with a terrible history. It's not the history of this lovely hotel but of the place where it now stands. The horror of 1942 still lingers at this site. Perhaps one day, this is a haunting that will fade away, but the event that took place will never truly be forgotten.

13. THE BULLOCK HOTEL
DEADWOOD, SOUTH DAKOTA

In the early days of Deadwood, in the Dakota Territory, the town was sometimes referred to as the "wildest gold town in the West." It was a place where murder was sometimes a daily occurrence and where many men had their lives cut short in the streets, saloons, and brothels of the violent settlement. Thanks to the blood that was shed here in days gone by, Deadwood today is known as a very haunted place.

The first modern hotel in Deadwood was opened in 1896 by a businessman and sheriff who would eventually achieve legendary status. He died in 1910, but no one is ever very surprised when they hear the rumor that he's never left his grand hotel.

The town of Deadwood, the seat of Lawrence County, in the Black Hills of western South Dakota was incorporated in 1876. The city was named for the dead trees that were found in the narrow canyon (Deadwood Gulch) and homes and building were constructed along its rugged and steep sides.

Deadwood came into existence thanks to the Black Hills gold rush of 1874. At the time, the Black Hills belonged to Native American nations and prospecting in the mountains was forbidden. Thanks to secret incursions by soldiers and gold hunters, though, it was discovered that the Black Hills were rich with gold. Soon, packs of men were squatting illegally in the region and had to be removed by the authorities. The military quickly realized they were unable to keep the prospectors out, so the government embarked on another round of treaties with the Indians. They tried to postpone the settlement of the area, but the onslaught of gold hunters made it impossible. Eventually, the land was simply seized, and the Indians were moved out.

The prospectors flooded the area and settlement came to Deadwood Gulch. Tents and shacks began to sprout up in the area and were quickly serviced by saloons, suppliers, opportunists, and prostitutes. In early 1876, freight hauler Charlie Utter led a wagon train into Deadwood containing what were deemed to be needed commodities for the new camp -- including gamblers and a fresh batch of prostitutes -- and made a small fortune.

Demand for women was very high and prostitution proved to be one of the most profitable businesses in town. Madam Dora DuFran eventually became the richest brothel owner in Deadwood, followed closely by Mollie Johnson. The first grand saloon, with gambling, liquor, and prostitutes, was the Bella Union, which was operated by businessman Tom Miller.

Miller's rival was Al Swearingen, who owned the Gem Variety Theater. He also controlled the opium trade in town. Swearingen used his reputation for brutality and his uncanny instinct for forging political alliances to survive as one of Deadwood's leading citizens for more than two decades. Swearingen arrived in Deadwood with his wife, Nettie, in the summer of 1876. Nettie later divorced him on the grounds of spousal abuse and Swearingen married two more times. They also ended badly.

Swearingen represented the second wave of Deadwood residents – those who came not to prospect but to earn their money from the pockets of those who toiled in the gold fields. His Gem Variety Theater saloon, which offered alcohol, stage shows, prize fights, and, of course, prostitutes, was just the place for those men to spend their money.

When the saloon burned to the ground in September 1879, Swearingen rebuilt it larger and more opulent than before. His talent for political affairs, along with payoffs, kept Swearingen shielded from attempts to clean up Deadwood until the Gem burned down again in 1899. After that, he left town and never returned. What became of Swearingen over the course of the next five years is unknown, but according to newspaper accounts, he was found dead in the middle of a suburban Denver street in late 1904. His death was caused by a massive head wound but who killed him, and why, will never be known.

As the economy of Deadwood changed from gold rush to steady mining, much of the rough and rowdy character of the town began to vanish. In September 1879, a devastating fire swept through the town, destroying more than 300 buildings. Many of the residents moved on to other places, but the more settled locals decided to stay and rebuild. Soon, Deadwood was back on the map, attracting railroads and new residents.

The town would always be known for the notoriety that it attained for murder and for attracting notables like Buffalo Bill Cody, Calamity Jane, and others. But there are two men connected to Deadwood whose names have become permanently attached to the town. These men are James "Wild Bill" Hickok and Seth Bullock, and while both may have passed on many years ago their spirits still remain here in Deadwood.

James Butler Hickok was born in what is now Troy Grove, Illinois, and was raised with a taste for danger, having been exposed to it throughout his life. His father, William Alonzo Hickok, was an ardent abolitionist and allowed his farm to be used as a station on the Underground Railroad. As a boy, Hickok often helped lead slaves to safety.

In 1855, he moved west to Kansas with his brother. At the time, the territory was being torn apart by disputes over slavery. Hickok joined up with an anti-slavery militia group and eventually became marshal of a small town called Monticello.

There was little to do as a lawman, aside from locking up the occasional drunk, so he kept busy by homesteading and then took a job as a stage driver on the Santa Fe Trail. He moved freight in Kansas and Nebraska, where he befriended a hunter and cavalry scout named William Cody, who went on to be known as "Buffalo Bill." During the Civil War, he was a scout for the Union army and served as a sharpshooter, where he earned the nickname of "Wild Bill."

After the war was over, Hickok settled in Springfield, Missouri, and during his time there, he made history by gunning down a rival during the first recorded showdown in the West. After that, he ran unsuccessfully for election as a lawman and then returning to scouting and hauling freight.

In 1869, he became sheriff of Hays City, Kansas. Hays City was a wild town in those days, serving as a freight and cattle center, and it attracted some of the most bloodthirsty gunmen in the region. Hickok killed at least two men – both ruled as justifiable homicides – but left town in 1870 after being forced to gun down two drunken soldiers from nearby Fort Hays. General Phillip Sheridan, commander at the fort, was furious and ordered Hickok arrested. Hickok had already left town.

He ended up in Abilene, Kansas, following the card games and the rich pockets of the inebriated cowboys who ended up in town after months on the trail. Hickok found easy pickings for his card-playing skills. Abilene was one of the roughest towns in the west at the time, so it's no surprise that Mayor Joseph McCoy tapped Hickok to serve as the town's sheriff. He was appointed with a salary of $150 a month, which supplemented his poker games. His first act as sheriff was to ban firearms within the city limits. Of course, that didn't always work out well.

On October 5, 1871, a dangerous gunman and gambler named Phil Coe led about 50 cowhands into Abilene, where they proceeded to start drinking and generally raising hell. Hickok warned Coe and the others to behave themselves, but at about 9:00 p.m., a shot was fired outside the Alamo Saloon and Hickok went to investigate. When he arrived, he saw a dozen of the cowboys, including Coe, with guns in their hands. Coe admitted that he had fired the shot after a stray dog had nipped at his ankle. Hickok drew his guns, ordering Coe to give up his pistols. Coe drew his own guns and immediately fired twice at Hickok. Both bullets cut through Hickok's coat. Hickok only fired one time, but his bullet plowed into Coe's groin. He was carried away and died in agony three days later.

In the confusion, Hickok's friend Mike Williams rushed to help. Hickok saw only a flash of movement and thought that he was being ambushed by one of the other cowhands. He spun and fired and shot Williams dead by mistake. Hickok paid for his friend's funeral and plunged into a dark depression. He was said to have never fired another shot at any man.

By 1872, Hickok was both famous and broke. Books and stories had been written about him and were widely read across the country. But being the subject of tall tales didn't pay the bills. Hickok decided to try and cash in on his image and he launched a theater production in Niagara Falls, New York, called "The Daring Buffalo Chase of the Plains." It had a number of western characters, Indians, and even real buffalo, but no audience. The show soon closed, and Hickok sold six of the buffalo to pay train fare home for the Native Americans, who retired from show business.

The following year, Hickok joined up with Buffalo Bill Cody for a stage show called "Scouts of the Prairie." This endeavor proved to be much more successful and Hickok stayed with the production for seven months. Although steadily working, Hickok took to drinking, depressed at the idea of having to "play act" to earn a living, he soon left the show.

Although no one knew it, Hickok's drinking wasn't just because of depression – he was losing his vision to glaucoma. He drifted across the West, playing poker, and winning enough money to stay just ahead of the game. In 1874, he was in Cheyenne, Wyoming, when he ran into an old flame named Agnes Lake. The two of them were married on March 5, 1876, but after a short honeymoon in Cincinnati, they parted ways. Hickok was off to hunt gold in the Dakota Territory and in April 1876, rode into Deadwood.

Legend had it that Hickok had a premonition of death as soon as he arrived at the rough and tumble mining camp. He reportedly said to Charlie Utter, whose wagon train he arrived with, "Those fellows over across the creek have laid it out to kill me. And they're going to do it or they ain't. Anyway, I don't stir out of here unless I'm carried out."

Hickok had several friends with him in Deadwood, including Charlie and the famed military scout, Martha Jane Cannary, who was best known as "Calamity Jane." Jane had been born in Missouri but spent her formative years in Wyoming, raising her younger siblings after the death of their mother. She received little or no formal education but was literate and taught her siblings to read. In 1870, Jane signed on as a scout and adopted the uniform of a soldier. In 1875, Jane's detachment was ordered to the Big Horn River, under General Crook. Carrying important dispatches, she swam across the Platte River and traveled 90 miles to deliver them, even though she was exhausted, soaked, and cold. Not surprisingly, she became very ill afterward and spent weeks recuperating at Fort Laramie, Wyoming. In July 1876, she joined up with Charlie Utter's wagon train, heading to Deadwood. It was here that she first met Wild Bill Hickok and they became close friends.

Hickok had earned himself many enemies over the years, working as a lawman, but none of them hated him as much as a small, cross-eyed man named Jack McCall. On August 1, McCall lost $110, his entire savings, to Hickok in a card game. Even though Hickok loaned the man enough money to have breakfast, McCall swore revenge.

On the afternoon of August 2, Hickok walked into the No. 10 Saloon and found a game in progress between Carl Mann, the owner of the establishment, Charles Rich, and an ex-riverboat captain named William R. Massie. They invited Hickok to sit in and Bill said he would if Rich would switch him seats. Bill was always uneasy when he was unable to get a chair that faced the door. Rich made a joke about it and rather than pursue the issue, Hickok sheepishly took a chair with his back to the door.

By late afternoon, Hickok was losing badly to Massie. Still, he held a promising hand: two black aces, two black eights and a jack of diamonds. Just a little after 4:00 p.m. Jack McCall entered the saloon and ordered a drink at the bar. He slowly walked up behind Hickok, pulled out an old six-gun and aimed it at Hickok's back. He shouted, "Damn you, take that!" McCall then jerked the trigger.

The bullet slammed into the back of Bill's skull, exited just under his right cheekbone and struck Captain Massie's forearm, just above his left wrist. (Massie never had this slug removed and carried it with him until his death in 1910. It is now buried in Bellefontaine Cemetery in St. Louis) Hickok died without knowing what had happened to him. He fell forward onto the table and his cards, known today as the "Dead Man's Hand," slipped out of his fingers and fell to the floor.

McCall ran out the rear door of the saloon and cries of anger and dismay followed him into the alley. Hickok's friends found McCall hiding in a butcher shop less than a half-hour later. A trial was organized by the following morning, only to adjourn in the afternoon for Hickok's funeral. When the hearing went back into session, McCall claimed that Hickok had killed his brother in Hays City in 1869 but could offer no proof of this. Regardless, a jury found him not guilty, much to the dismay of basically everyone in the courtroom.

McCall remained in Deadwood a free man, but he became nervous thanks to threats from Hickok's friends and angry local residents. The prosecutor in the case, an attorney named May, claimed that the jury had been paid off in the trial and he harassed and followed McCall everywhere. He would not rest, he vowed, until justice had been done.

May tracked McCall to Laramie and had him arrested. He had found a loophole in the law that said that since Deadwood wasn't supposed to exist because of the Indian treaties, no court decision made there was actually legal. A new trial was held in Yankton, Dakota Territory, and on January 3, 1877, McCall was sentenced to death. He went to the gallows on March 1 – justice delayed but eventually carried out.

Hickok was buried in Deadwood's Mount Moriah Cemetery, but the local legends say that he does not rest there. Many believe that because he died unaware of what was about to happen to him, his confused and angry spirit still walks in Deadwood.

It has even been suggested that Hickok knew that he might die soon and that if possible, he planned to return to this world. A short time before that fateful day in the No.10 Saloon, Hickok posted a letter to his wife, Agnes. In it he wrote, "Agnes Darling, if such should be we never meet again, while firing my last shot, I will gently breathe the name of my wife--- Agnes---and with wishes even for my enemies I will make the plunge and try to swim to the other shore."

Whether he planned to stay behind or not, some say that he remained in Deadwood. A shadowy figure is sometimes still seen at the old No. 10 Saloon, a landmark in town. Others claim to have glimpsed a figure in the doorway of the building, looking out and perhaps still looking for the man who shot him in the back after all these years.

Just down the street from the No. 10 Saloon is the sturdy-looking Bullock Hotel. Named for its original owner, this grandly restored establishment has played host to several generations of visitors and, it's widely believed, remains home to the spirit of Seth Bullock himself.

I've stayed at the Bullock Hotel and had my own experiences there. If it's not haunted by Seth, it's haunted by someone – and they have no interest in leaving.

Seth Bullock was born in Canada, just across the river from Detroit, in 1847. His mother was Scottish, and his father was a retired British officer named George Bullock. As a young man, Seth became tired of his father's military discipline and ran away several times, including once to Montana, where he lived with an older sister and her husband. By 1867, he was living in the territory full-time. He became involved in business and local politics, worked as an auctioneer, a commission merchant, and chief engineer of the Helena Fire Department. After an unsuccessful run for the territorial legislature at age 20, he was elected as a Republican member of the territorial senate of Montana. During the 1871 and 1872 sessions, he introduced a bill that would later result in Yellowstone being named a National Park.

In 1871, he also met the man who would be his long-time partner and friend for life, Sol Star. Sol was born in Bavaria to Jewish parents and when he was 10 years old, his family came to America and settled in Ohio. When he grew older, he moved to Helena, Montana, where he served as territorial auditor and as a personal secretary to the governor. After meeting Seth, the two of them partnered in a hardware business.

In 1873, Bullock first pinned on a badge when he was elected sheriff of Lewis and Clark County in the Montana Territory. Most of the wild days of the Montana gold rushes were over by that time, which made things a little easier for the 26-year-old lawman. It was during this time that one of Bullock's legends was born. He was tasked with overseeing the first legal hanging in Montana and, supposedly, a mob tried to take the doomed criminal from him. He held them off with a gun and proceeded to hang the man single-handedly. Bullock himself told this story himself in his later years but it probably isn't true. Newspapers from the time say the execution went off without a hitch, as did another hanging Bullock supervised. However, killing those men didn't sit well with Seth and he didn't run for re-election.

He also had other plans. Bullock and Star were heading east to Deadwood to make their fortunes – not in the gold fields, but by supplying the miners. By this time, Seth had married his childhood sweetheart, Martha Eccles, and had a daughter. He sent them to Michigan to live with his parents until he could get settled in the new town.

They set out for Deadwood in the summer of 1876. It was a dangerous journey. Native Americans wiped out George Custer's troops while they were on the road and there was a very real threat of further attacks. It took weeks to reach their destination, but they arrived on August 3 – the day after Jack McCall had murdered Wild Bill Hickok. The town was still in an uproar when they rode into Deadwood.

The settlement that Bullock and Star found was a wretched place. Streets were muddy and nearly impassable, even at the best of times. There were plenty of saloons, lots of drunks, lots of violence, and no law enforcement or even a jail. The place reeked of rotting animal carcasses, open sewage, and just about any other smell imaginable.

But almost immediately upon arriving, the two men built their hardware supply company, which would outfit the miners and settlers who were flocking to the region. The new store included a fireproof, brick storage area in the back, which would be used for other purposes in the future.

Even as new arrivals, they made an impression. Eleven days after getting to town, Bullock was appointed to the Board of Health and Street Commission, which basically ran the town. And because Seth had been a lawman in Montana, he became the county sheriff on August 21 without a vote being cast. He'd been in Deadwood just two and a half weeks.

By September, Deadwood residents had set up a government, although it wasn't officially recognized by U.S. officials, since the town was still on Indian land. Sol was elected to the city council. Bullock didn't run for anything. Instead, he went east to retrieve his family and new stock for the hardware store. He was gone for five months. Some Deadwood residents started to doubt his commitment to the town, but Bullock was unfazed by this.

By the time he returned, the U.S government had removed the land from the Indian treaty and Territorial Governor John Pennington began appointing various county officials, a move that upset those who'd wanted elections. Pennington and Bullock were friends, which cemented his official appointment as sheriff of Lawrence County, which included Deadwood.

The Star and Bullock Hardware store doubled as the sheriff's office. The fireproof storage facility in back became the jail. Bullock had every intention of keeping the peace in town, but it was a challenge. The population of Deadwood had doubled in the first year and so did the number of murders. Bullock made numerous arrests, but he did so fairly. He rarely took drunk and disorderly offenders into custody. He usually just sent them home to sleep it off.

Unfortunately, not all his acts as sheriff were heroic. On March 25, 1877, a band of outlaws held up the Deadwood stage a few miles outside of town. In the process, driver Johnny Slaughter was killed. One of the owners of the stage line asked Bullock to lead a posse in pursuit of the robbers. He spent months tracking them but had no luck. The gang went on to rob other stages and a train six months later. One of the outlaws was Sam Bass, who went on to greater infamy in Texas in 1878.

Then, later that same year, Bullock was called on to end a labor strike. Miners had put aside their picks and shovels and camped in one of the local mines, hoping to force the owners to pay them back wages. Bullock tried several approaches to get them out. Finally, he put burning sulfur into the mine and the choking strikers left. Mine owners were grateful but working men in town, who identified with the miners, were angry with Bullock, which was a factor in his losing a bid for re-election in November.

He lost the sheriff's job, but he'd already been appointed as a U.S. deputy marshal two months earlier. He kept that position for the next decade.

He also turned his attentions more toward his business interests in town. Over the next 30 years, he would be a merchant, bank president, town promoter, forest supervisor, and also got involved in ranching, raising horses, mining, and real estate. He became a captain for the Black Hills Rough Riders during the Spanish-American War in Cuba. He is credited for introducing the first alfalfa crop into South Dakota, and as a conservationist, he secured a federal fish hatchery for the Black Hills at Spearfish. In addition, he and Sol Star founded the town of Belle Fourche, which became the seat of Butte County and one of the largest livestock shipping points in America. He enjoyed great success in many of his ventures, and a fair number of failures. He was always an idea man, looking for the next project that might bring in money, and earned great respect from people all over the region.

During these years, a friendship developed between Bullock and Theodore Roosevelt. The two of them had met years before on the trail near Roosevelt's ranch. At that time, Roosevelt was a deputy sheriff in Medora County in the Dakota Territory and had just apprehended Redhead Finnegan, a horse thief. Later, as vice-president under McKinley, he appointed Bullock the first forest supervisor of the Black

Hills Reserve. In 1905, Bullock and 75 cowboys rode their horses in Roosevelt's inaugural parade.

The two remained good friends until Roosevelt's death in January 1919. Saddened, Bullock established a memorial to his friend. A tower was constructed of Black Hills stone and was erected on Sheep Mountain, which was later named for Roosevelt. The memorial was dedicated on July 4, 1919, and two months later, Seth Bullock himself died from cancer at the age of 70.

The former lawman was laid to rest in Deadwood, but the stories say that Seth Bullock still watched over the former frontier town, lingering at the hotel that he built there in 1896.

Seth Bullock had not planned to go into the hotel business. The site that would someday be his hotel was the originally the location of the Bullock and Star Hardware store, which sometimes doubled as the town jail. In 1879, the first of the great fires swept through Deadwood, destroying stores, businesses, and homes. The hardware store was damaged, but the fire didn't put them out of business. They rebuilt, adding a brick warehouse in back, replacing the storage area where prisoners were sometimes locked up.

The business continued to thrive until 1894, when another fire destroyed the store, leaving the warehouse intact. Rather than rebuild, the partners decided to build a hotel on the site instead. Constructed from sandstone in an Italianate-style, it was the first modern hotel in Deadwood. When the doors opened in April 1896, the Bullock Hotel offered a 100-seat restaurant that served lobster and game birds, a Turkish Bath, a luxurious lobby that was decked out with red velvet carpets, brass fixtures, a grand piano, and a library that could be used by guests. The 63 rooms upstairs offered comfortable brass beds, a bathroom on each floor, central heat, and hot and cold water. A few years later, an adjoining building was purchased and turned into the Gentleman's Bar. There was no question that, outside of San Francisco, it was the finest establishment in the West.

The partners sold the business in 1904 and it continued into the new century under a series of owners, becoming more timeworn as the years passed. In the 1990s, though, new owners completely refurbished it to its former glory and, of course, added all the modern amenities that travelers could want. It's this mix of old and new that has allowed the Bullock Hotel to endure the test of time as a fine western hotel – and a haunted one.

For years, staff members and guests have encountered the ghostly figure of a tall man with a thick mustache in the corridors, rooms, and public spaces of the hotel, but strangely, one person who told of Bullock still haunting his former hotel had never been to South Dakota at all.

In 1990, a psychic from England named Sandy Bullock claimed to receive messages from someone with the same surname as his own. The spirit said that his name was "Seth Bullock" and that he had once lived in Deadwood. The medium was puzzled. He had never heard of such a place, or person, so he went to the library looking for information. Unable to find much, he wrote letters to the Deadwood Sheriff's office and to the local chamber of commerce and told them of his eerie messages. He received no reply and simply assumed that they had dismissed his correspondence as the work of a lunatic.

Finally, in March 1991, he sent a letter to the owner of the Bullock Hotel, Mary Schmit. He assured her that he had a good reputation in England as a psychic and that before receiving the messages, he had no knowledge of Deadwood or of Seth Bullock. And he certainly had no awareness of his ghost.

According to the medium, the old lawman was concerned that Deadwood was turning into another Las Vegas (limited stakes gambling was legalized in the city in 1989, just before the spirit messages were first received). He also said that Seth believed Deadwood was heading towards a major crime problem and he urged the local sheriff to get more help, as he would need it in 1993.

The medium added: "He has been back in spirit to Deadwood many times. There's one person in particular that he's given the frights to, but the bangings going on now means he can't haunt the same place, but he will be back, and they'll know it's Old Seth."

Mary Schmit was startled by the letter. The reference to "bangings going on" made sense to her as the hotel was undergoing major restoration at the time. She was also intrigued by the mention of

"Old Seth." That was the nickname she and her Aunt Jerri had privately given the former sheriff. During the remodeling, when they were the only occupants of the hotel, the two women had often heard someone calling their names. Jerri often laughed and said that it was "Old Seth up to his tricks again."

Mary Schmit later said that her sister, Susan, had fallen victim to Old Seth's pranks. She was in the building alone on one occasion when she was spooked by the sound of pots and pans banging together in the kitchen. She was so scared that she locked herself in the vault, fearing that intruders had broken in. It later turned out, though, she was in the hotel alone. Was it Susan that Seth Bullock had "given the fights to?"

As word of Sandy Bullock's spirit communications spread, hotel employees began to come forward with their own strange experiences in the place. Two men claimed to see a lanky figure in western clothing one night. Others had heard footsteps or had heard their name being called when no one else was around. One night, the construction manager on the restoration project, Terry Kranz, came to take photographs of the hotel. He moved lights from room to room, leaving doors open as he went down the hallway. On three different occasions, he opened doors and then walked down the corridor to get his equipment. All three times, the doors banged shut behind him, one by one. There were no windows open, no wind blowing, and no one else in the hotel. Kranz left without taking the rest of the photos.

In 1991, a writer for *Deadwood* magazine, Reba Webb, interviewed Sandy Bullock about the mysterious messages from Seth Bullock. She decided to see if he could answer something about which he had no knowledge. She asked him questions during a telephone interview, "Who was a well-known person who was a close friend of Seth Bullock, and how is Bullock's grave positioned in regard to that friendship?"

The psychic passed the question on to Seth before replying, "Trees block the view from his old bones, but they cannot block the friendship, as Teddy and he still meet." He then asked her if the reply made any sense to her.

Amazingly, it did. Before Bullock had died, he had chosen a burial plot high above Mount Moriah Cemetery. It was a site that offered an unobstructed view of the memorial to the president on Roosevelt Mountain. In the years since Bullock's passing, ponderosa pines had grown up around the cemetery and now blocked the view of the memorial.

Mary Schmit's brother, John, visited the psychic in England and one of the things he asked him was whether there was something that could be done for Seth. Schmit later said that the medium went into a deep trance, looked at the floor, and then spoke in a low voice, "There's no gate on my grave." The words from Sandy Bullock's mouth, although John Schmit always maintained that the words had come from Seth himself.

Back home, John asked his sister if she had ever visited Bullock's grave site. She described it to him, "It's high on a hill above the other graves and it faces Roosevelt Mountain. There's a bench there and a fence around it."

He asked her, "Anything else?"

She replied, "Yes, there's no gate on his grave."

Mary Schmit has always maintained that there was no way that the medium could have known such a thing, unless he had heard it from Seth Bullock himself.

Seth Bullock's spirit may have become particularly active during and soon after the restoration of the hotel, but he is still restless today. Perhaps his lifetime of hard work, new enterprises, and drive for success have kept him from resting in peace. Or perhaps he's simply watching over the town that he loved and the hotel that became a symbol of the friendship between himself and Sol Star.

Whatever the answer, he's still here. He has been seen and heard often, and he is an unmistakable figure when described by visitors who know nothing of his role in the history of Deadwood and the Bullock Hotel.

A former hotel manager named Ken Geinger told a story about a little boy who went downstairs one night looking for his father, who was gambling in the casino. Later, the boy told his father that when he went back upstairs, he became lost and a tall man with a mustache helped him to find his room. The next day, the boy pointed out a portrait of Seth Bullock in the hotel lobby as the man who helped him get safely back to bed.

I last visited Deadwood in 2016 and stayed at the Bullock Hotel for a weekend. My partner, Lisa, was along on the trip, as well as her daughter, Lux, who was not quite three-years-old at the time. We had a suite on the second floor with separate sleeping areas so that Lux could have a portable crib set up for her. We spent a lot of hours in the car getting to South Dakota and after stops at the Corn Palace in Mitchell, the Badlands, Wall Drug, and Mount Rushmore, that little girl slept very well during the night at the Bullock Hotel.

Unfortunately, I couldn't say the same.

Don't misunderstand, it's a great hotel. It's very comfortable, historic, and a wonderful place to stay. In all my years of travel, I can honestly say that some of the nicest people that I've met on the road work at the hotel. The entire staff was great but the folks at the front desk made us feel very welcome and went out of their way to make sure we had everything we needed.

But, as anyone knows who travels with a small child, it's hard to rest easy in a hotel. You never know when they might wake up and you're always conscious of them disturbing other guests. I don't know about Lisa, but when Lux was sleeping, I wasn't – not very well anyway.

And that's probably the reason why I heard the sounds.

By 2:00 a.m. on the second night, the hotel was pretty quiet, or at least the second floor was, which is why someone walking up and down the hallway outside of the room became increasingly annoying. It sounded like a man wearing heavy boots, tromping back and forth. I would hear them up close to the door and then the sounds faded as he walked down the corridor in the opposite direction. A short time later, he'd be back, passing the door again.

This went on for at least 20 minutes. I couldn't imagine what this person could be doing. Drunk? Nervous? Worried about money he'd lost in one of the town's casinos? No idea, but it was keeping me awake.

Finally, I got out of bed and went to the door. I was irritated but promised myself that I'd be calm. Whoever it was, I'd ask them to quit walking around and suggest (nicely) that they go back to their room. When I heard the footsteps approaching again, I unlocked the door and opened it, ready to confront them.

You've probably guessed already – the hallway was empty. And silent. The footsteps had stopped. I looked up and down the corridor, even walked around a corner to see if there was anyone in another hall. There wasn't. I was alone – well, with someone that I couldn't see. Whoever it was, they didn't walk anymore that night. We checked out the next day and headed back to Illinois.

Was it Seth Bullock, walking the halls and making sure things were orderly in his hotel? I don't know, but I know that I'd like to think that it was.

14. THE HOTEL CHELSEA
(MANHATTAN) NEW YORK, NEW YORK

At the start of this chapter, I'm going to tell you that the Hotel Chelsea is unlike any other place that you'll find in this book. Built between 1883 and 1885, it has become known primarily for three things – its famous residents, the number of deaths that have occurred inside its walls, and its ghosts.

The 12-story, red-brick building was one of Manhattan's first private apartment cooperatives and actors, film directors, and musicians have all called it home. Mark Twain lived here and so did Alan Ginsberg. Madonna lived at the Chelsea in the early 1980s and Leonard Cohen and Janis Joplin had an affair there. Some of the survivors of the *Titanic* disaster stayed there. Dylan Thomas drank himself to death at the Chelsea and author Charles R. Jackson committed suicide in his room.

And there's been worse – much worse.

Is it any wonder that the Chelsea has become famous for its ghosts?

The roots of the legendary hotel date back to the middle eighteenth century, when New York was still confined to the southern tip of Manhattan. In 1750, Captain Thomas Clark and his family settled along the Hudson River, about two and a half miles north of the city. His homestead, which he named Chelsea, was located near what is now Twenty-Third Street, between Ninth and Tenth Avenues.

The city slowly grew. Meanwhile, the Clarks' daughter, Charity, married Benjamin Moore, an Episcopal bishop. Their son, Clement, became famous for a poem that he wrote called "A Visit from St. Nicholas." Clement took advantage of the increasing demand for real estate and by 1850, had subdivided and sold off the Clarks' property to form the district that is known as Chelsea today.

In 1884, the Hotel Chelsea opened on West Twenty-Third Street, between Seventh and Eighth Avenues, in the busy theater district. It was one of the first co-op apartment buildings in New York, designed for long-term residents, although rooms were also available for short-term lease. At the time it was built, the twelve-story building was the tallest in Manhattan, and it remained so until 1902.

The hotel was designed by Philip Hubert in a style that has been described variously as Queen Anne Revival and Victorian Gothic. Among its distinctive features are the flower-ornamented iron balconies on its façade and its grand staircase, which extends upward 12 floors. Hallways on the guest floors were tiled in marble. No two apartments were alike; some were particularly spacious, with up to seven bedrooms. All had tall doors and windows and ceilings that were 10- or 12-feet high. The walls were thick, designed so that sound didn't carry between them, a design that would appeal to scores of musicians in the building's future.

While initially successful, a few years of economic stress, the suspicion of New York's middle class about apartment living, the opening of Upper Manhattan and the plentiful supply of houses there, and the relocation of the city's theater district all combined to bankrupt the Chelsea. The company went under in 1903, and the building was put up for sale. Two years later, it reopened as a hotel, although long-term residents were still welcome.

Soon, there was an ever-changing whirlwind of famous and not-so-famous guests passing through its doors. The hotel's reputation as a haven for artists of every kind started almost immediately. Early visitors included actresses Lily Langtry and Sarah Bernhardt, who traveled with and slept in her own coffin instead of a hotel bed.

The parade of performers and artists who called the Chelsea home cemented its reputation as a sanctuary – and even as an asylum – for creative souls. Visual masters who lived and worked here included Willem de Koonig, Jasper Johns, Robert Mapplethorpe, Diego Rivera, Bernard Childs, Yves Klein (who wrote his *Manifeste de l'hôtel Chelsea* there in April 1961), Robert Crumb, Ellen Cantor, Jasper Johns, Tom Wesselmann, Moses Soyer (who died there in 1974), and many others. Experimental filmmaker and ethnomusicologist Harry Everett Smith lived and died in Room 328 and painter, Alphaeus Philemon Cole, lived here for 35 years until his death in 1988, at age 112, at which point he was the oldest verified man alive. Charles James, credited with being the first American fashion designer to create clothing tailored to individual client's needs in the 1940s and 1950s, moved into the Chelsea in 1964. He died here of pneumonia in 1978. When Billy Reid started his brand in 1998, it was a one-man operation and while he lived elsewhere, he used a room at the Chelsea as his office, studio, and showroom.

The Hotel Chelsea is often associated with Andy Warhol. In 1966, he and Paul Morrisey directed *Chelsea Girls*, a film about his Factory regulars and their lives at the hotel. This made Edie Sedgewick, Viva, and her daughter, Gaby Hoffman, regulars at the swinging hotel.

Stage and film personalities who passed through the Chelsea include Jane Fonda, Milos Forman, Elliott Gould, Ethan Hawke, Uma Thurman, Dennis Hopper, Eddie Izzard, Russell Brand, Michael Imperioli, and others. Author Arthur C. Clarke was living at the Chelsea when he met with Stanley Kubrick to collaborate on the screenplay for *2001: A Space Odyssey*.

But the hotel's musical history has probably colored the Chelsea more than anything else. Bob Dylan wrote "Sad-Eyed Lady of the Lowlands" while living here. A stay prompted Joni Mitchell to write "Chelsea Morning." Dee Dee Ramone wrote songs here, taking advantage of his soundproof room. He also wrote a novel – *Chelsea Horror Hotel.* Leonard Cohen wrote two songs – "Chelsea Hotel" and "Chelsea Hotel No. 2" -- here and while he never mentions the name of the woman with whom he had a tryst, it almost certainly referred to Janis Joplin, who lived down the hall in Room 411. Madonna lived here in the early 1980s and then returned in 1992 to shoot photographs for her book, *Sex,* in Room 822. Bruce Wayne Campbell, known by his stage name Jobriath, spent his last years in a pyramid-shaped apartment on the Chelsea's roof, where he died of complications due to AIDS in August 1983. The Kills wrote much of their album "No Wow" at the Chelsea between the years 2003 to 2005.

And there were many others who stayed at the Chelsea, like The Grateful Dead, Tom Waits, Patti Smith, Jim Morrison, Iggy Pop, Chick Corea, Jeff Beck, Marianne Faithfull, Cher, Robbie Robertson, Alice Cooper, Pink Floyd, Jimi Hendrix, Canned Heat, Frank Zappa, and the list goes on.

But the most notorious music couple to darken the door of the Chelsea was undoubtedly Sid Vicious, bass player for the Sex Pistols, and his girlfriend, Nancy Spungen. Their relationship was the very definition of a codependent, destructive one, and it ended, eventually, in both of their deaths.

And a haunting at the Hotel Chelsea.

The punk rocker at the center of the blood-soaked incident was born Simon John Ritchie in 1957. His friend, John Lydon, gave him the stage name of Sid Vicious partly as a joke when Lydon's pet hamster, named Sid, "viciously" bit his musician pal. After working with two other bands, Sid was hired to replace Glen Matlock in The Sex Pistols in 1977. He first performed with them in April of that year.

In November 1977, Nancy Spungen ended up in his orbit. Nancy already had a reputation as a groupie with an abrasive attitude and a nasty drug habit. She had been a pretty 17-year-old from Philadelphia before moving to New York, where she became a hardcore partier in the punk scene. She was constantly in trouble as a child. She was expelled from school after school for talking back to teachers and school officials. Eventually, she graduated from boarding school at just 16. She briefly attended college in Colorado but decided schooling wasn't for her and went back east to get involved in the New York music scene.

Nancy was always honest about what she did – she bought drugs for the bands. She wasn't like the usual groupies. She wasn't tall and skinny in fashionable clothes. She didn't try to be cute or charming. She didn't claim to be a model or a dancer. She traded drugs for sex with famous musicians – and that was it.

Most of her fellow groupies were turned off by her crass exterior, but Nancy didn't care. She followed Johnny Thunders and Jerry Nolan of the Heartbreakers around New York and eventually to London. There, she began following a newer band, The Sex Pistols, taking a special interest in their bassist, Sid Vicious.

Unlike the rest of the band, who disliked her so much that they banned her from their tour, Sid found Nancy's abrasive personality captivating. When the two met, he took an instant shine to her and, despite her reputation as a junkie and troublemaker, the two of them became inseparable.

Sex Pistols manager Malcom McLaren later said, "Nancy taught Sid all about sex and drugs and the lifestyle of a New York rocker." Though, really, Sid didn't need much of an education.

Sid was a mess even before he met Nancy. The band wasn't shy about making it known that his addiction created problems for the group and interrupted several of their shows. His relationship with Nancy just made things worse. Eventually, in January 1978, The Sex Pistols broke up, citing Sid's addiction and his relationship with Nancy as the reasons. Sid tried to continue with a solo career, but by then, he was falling apart.

In August, Sid and Nancy moved into the Hotel Chelsea and for the next two months, it was the couple's hideaway. They got high and escaped from the world for days and sometimes weeks at a time.

Friends were worried, fearing their addictions would get the best of them.

In the early morning hours of October 12, they finally did.

During the previous evening, several friends were in the couple's hotel room and they watched Sid take copious amounts of drugs, including as many as 30 tables of Tuinal, a barbiturate. It was a larger dose than most people could survive. He didn't die ,but it put him into a deep state of unconsciousness for hours, leaving him almost comatose until the early morning hours.

Around 2:30 a.m., Nancy awoke and asked Rockets Redglare, Sid's bodyguard/drug dealer, for Dilaudid, an opioid painkiller that can cause respiratory distress and death when taken in high doses or when combined with other substances, especially alcohol.

Five hours later, a number of the hotel's residents heard sounds coming from Sid and Nancy's room. Of course, it wasn't unusual to hear screams, moans, and cries in the hotel in those days, but these cries were different – something they realized when they saw the body bag being carried out of the building a little while later.

At 10:00 a.m., Sid woke in Room 100 and called down to the front desk to ask for help. Hotel staff arrived to find Nancy, half-naked on the bathroom floor. She had been stabbed in the stomach with Sid's knife and had bled to death. When the police arrived, they found Sid wandering the halls, out of his mind, and they arrested him for Nancy's murder.

At first, several sources reported that he confessed to the crime, which is why the police hadn't suspected anyone else. However, after his arrest, Sid recanted, stating that he had been asleep when the murder occurred. The public – along with his friends and family – believed him. "She was the first and only love of his life," Malcolm McLaren said. "I am positive about Sid's innocence."

Sid was released on bail, but 10 days later, he attempted suicide. In December, he was sent to Riker's Island for 50 days for assaulting Patti Smith's brother, Todd. By the time he got out on February 1, 1979, he had gotten clean but wouldn't stay that way for long. The next morning, he was found dead from a heroin overdose. He had spent the night partying in a Greenwich Village apartment and his body was discovered by his mother and his new girlfriend.

With Sid dead, the police dropped Nancy's case. The prime suspect was gone, and it was decided that it was pointless to pursue it further. Despite the fact that his time with Nancy was marked by bouts of terrible violence, Sid denied to the end that he had killed her. He swore that he had no memory of that night because of the number of drugs he had taken. He said that maybe Nancy had fallen on the knife during an argument or that someone else had come into the apartment and killed her – he claimed he just didn't know.

Other theories were suggested, including that Nancy's death had been a botched double suicide or that the bodyguard/drug dealer was involved. Neither theory was investigated and to this day, Nancy's murder remains unsolved.

It doesn't seem to be her ghost who lingers at the Chelsea, looking for justice, though. It is Sid who has been seen in and standing near the elevator. He doesn't engage with anyone, however, so we'll never know the reason why he refuses to leave the hotel. Perhaps he is trying to find the real killer or, more likely, perhaps he has chosen to stay behind in hopes that Nancy's spirit will return, too. This was the only place during their short, volatile relationship that they ever had any peace, even if it was a peace that was created by heroin and narcotics.

And Sid Vicious does not walk the corridors of the Chelsea alone.

During its heyday, the hotel also hosted some of America's most famous writers, in addition to Mark Twain and Alan Ginsberg. They included William Sydney Porter (better known as O. Henry), Sam Shepard, Arthur Miller, Tennessee Williams, Jack Kerouac, William S. Burroughs, and many others, like Joseph O'Neill, who moved there with his wife in 1998 and raised three sons. The Chelsea plays a large role in his novel *Netherland*.

Charles R. Jackson was another literary resident of the Chelsea. In his early days, he worked as a freelance writer and wrote radio scripts. In the 1940s, he wrote a trio of novels, starting with *The Lost*

Weekend in 1944. A year later, Paramount Pictures adapted it to film starring Ray Milland. The book chronicled a struggling writer's five-day drinking binge – a subject that Jackson knew a lot about. He struggled with his own addiction to alcohol and pills.

He published two more books in the 1940s – *The Fall of Valor* and *The Outer Edges* – but neither was as successful as his first. They were both certainly dark, though. The first dealt with a professor's obsession with a handsome, young Marine and the second was about the gruesome rape and murder of two young girls. He later also published two collections of short stories.

Jackson tried repeatedly to kick his addictions. Throughout the writing of *The Lost Weekend*, he drank heavily and took pills. He later told his wife that unless he was taking the sedative Seconal, he suffered from writer's block and became depressed.

In September 1952, he attempted suicide and was committed to Bellevue. He was back four months later after suffering a nervous breakdown. After his release, he went on a drinking and drugs bender that resulted in a book of short stories.

By the mid-1950's, he was sober but was unable to write. As a result, he struggled financially. He sold his New Hampshire home and moved to Connecticut. His wife found a job while Jackson moved to New York, where he rented an apartment at The Dakota. He stayed sober but still struggled to write. He managed a few short stories and eventually got a job teaching writing at Rutgers University.

Soon after, he moved into the Hotel Chelsea and managed to get an advance from MacMillan to finish his book, *A Second-Hand Life*, which he had started years before. When it was released, it received poor reviews but sold well.

But Jackson was unable to stay sober. He began drinking again while working on a sequel to *The Lost Weekend.* On September 21, 1968, he died of barbiturate poisoning in his room at the Chelsea. His death was ruled a suicide.

Jackson may not haunt the Chelsea, but at least two of his fellow writers have been encountered there. One of them is Thomas Wolfe, who was born in North Carolina in 1900. He is best remembered today for the autobiographical novel *Look Homeward, Angel*, which coined the phrase, "You can't go home again."

Wolfe first visited New York in 1923, when he made his first attempt to have his plays produced on Broadway. The following year, he accepted a brief position teaching English at New York University, and remained in Manhattan for the rest of his life. While there, he lived at the Hotel Chelsea.

Wolfe developed pneumonia while visiting his brother in Seattle in July 1938, and that September, he was admitted to Johns Hopkins in Baltimore for tuberculosis of the brain. He died there on September 15, just a few weeks before his 38th birthday.

While the author only lived at the Chelsea for a few years, he obviously developed some kind of deep connection to it that drew him back to the place after death. He has been reported walking the eighth-floor hallway, outside of the apartment where he lived, many times over the years.

The other author who chose to remain at the Chelsea spent even less time in the hotel than Wolfe. He was the Welsh poet Dylan Thomas, who first came to the Chelsea in 1953 while touring the United States and performing poetry readings. His most notorious visit occurred on November 3. After returning from a reading at the White Horse Tavern, he famously told a desk clerk, "I've had 18 straight whiskies. I think that is a record."

Perhaps it should be noted that Thomas was already a well-known alcoholic by this time of his career.

Thomas had already toured in America earlier that year. Then, he returned to England for four months before his return to Manhattan and the Chelsea. When he returned in October 1953, he was already suffering from respiratory problems. He managed to get through a series of personal appearances, including his whiskey-fueled one at the White Horse Tavern. By midnight on November 5, he was unable to breathe. He was rushed from the Chelsea to St. Vincent's Hospital, where doctors discovered that he had acute bronchitis and pneumonia. He died there on November 9, 1953. Though it's widely assumed that his drinking killed him – it was a contributing factor – he actually died from swelling of the brain due to a lack of oxygen from the pneumonia.

Thomas's body was sent home to be buried in Wales, but his spirit has remained at the Chelsea. Guests have often come face-to-face with the poet as he stumbles along through the hotel corridors. He seems to still be drunk, even in death. Some have also blamed his ghost for beer and cocktail glasses that mysteriously empty and for objects that move around on their own.

Or could some of those events be blamed on other resident spirits? There are plenty of other eerie happenings that occur at the Hotel Chelsea. People encounter unexplained cold spots or feel sudden chilly breezes that come from nowhere. Lights and televisions turn on and off by themselves and bathroom taps have been known to spurt water when there is no one nearby to turn them on. Residents have also reported hearing voices and footsteps echoing in rooms and hallways when no one living is present. A few have even claimed to feel the touch of an unseen hand while they are alone in the hotel.

Based on the amount of passion, drama, and tragedy that has occurred at the Chelsea, it's no surprise that unearthly events take place. As mentioned, the hotel is not only famous for the number of deaths that have occurred within its walls, it's famous for its spectral occupants, too.

Want to spend a possibly sleepless night there? Well, that may be a problem.

Throughout the crazy years of writers and musicians, the hotel remained under the auspices of the same management team. After it went bankrupt in the 1930s, it was purchased by Joseph Gross, Julius Krauss, and David Bard in 1939. They managed the hotel together until the early 1970s. With the passing of Joseph Gross and Julius Krauss, management was taken over by Stanley Bard, David's son. In June 2007, though, the hotel's board of directors ousted Bard and the hotel's manager. He was replaced by Dr. Marlene Krauss, daughter of Julius Krauss, and David Elder, grandson of Joseph Gross. A few years later, they were gone, too. The hotel was sold in May 2011 to a real estate developer.

In August, the hotel stopped taking reservations in order to begin renovations, although long-time residents were allowed to remain. Most of them were protected by the state's rent regulations and couldn't be forced out. It wasn't long before complaints were filed by the tenants about health hazards caused by the construction. The complaints were investigated but no major violations were found. This became part of an ongoing battle between the tenants and owners that lasted for the next two years. In 2013, the building was purchased again, and the renovations continued. As of 2019, though, it still has not reopened, despite the promise of a 2018 opening date.

It's unknown when the hotel will finally reopen for business, but when it does, you might want to add it to your list of places to stay when you're looking for ghosts.

You have a very good chance of finding them here.

15. MONTE VISTA HOTEL
FLAGSTAFF, ARIZONA

There is no greater highway in American history than Route 66 – the legendary "Mother Road" – which began in downtown Chicago and stretched all the way to the Pacific Ocean. Officially, it no longer exists today. Its demise began in the 1960s and was finally put out of business for good by the interstates in 1984.

But we've never forgotten the road because so much of it still exists, in real life and in our imaginations. For millions of us, Route 66 represents a treasure trove of memories and a link to the days of two-lane highways, family vacations, lunches at roadside tables, and greasy-spoon diners that ceased to exist decades ago. For many, it conjures up images of souvenir shops, tourist traps, and cheesy roadside attractions that have since crumbled into dust.

One of the biggest attractions for travelers during the heyday of Route 66 were the hotels, motels, and cozy motor courts that dotted the landscape along the road. A few of them were already there when Route 66 began but as the years passed, more and more of them popped up – and many of them became haunted. There were, it seems, many roadside hotels and motels along the Mother Road where travelers came face-to-face with unexpected fellow guests.

The Monte Vista Hotel in Flagstaff was just such a place. It has a rich history that included stays by famous guests like Bing Crosby, Gary Cooper, and John Wayne. In fact, the Duke was the first person to suspect that the Monte Vista had a bit of a ghost problem because he saw one!

Today, the Monte Vista is considered to be the most haunted hotel along all of Route 66. Getting "your kicks" at this place just might include a few ghosts.

As America entered the modern times of the 1920s, the citizens of Flagstaff became eager to start improving the amenities for visitors that came to town. At the time, overnight accommodations were pretty sparse, and the city had little to offer travelers in the way of comforts. Community leaders decided the best way to attract more visitors was to build a comfortable, upscale hotel.

In 1924, local businessman V.M Slipher helped kick off a fundraiser to gather the money needed for the hotel. His efforts led to a city-voted ordinance that established a municipal bond to build the hotel. Donations also flooded in. One of the most prominent of the donors was Zane Grey, the prolific author of western novels and whose books were turned into more than 100 motion pictures. In just a few months, they had raised more than $20,000, far more than was needed to get the project off the ground. It would become one of the very few American hotels to ever be built using public funds and community donations.

On New Year's Day, 1927 -- one year after Route 66 got its start – the 73-room Community Hotel opened its doors. The structure also housed the local post office and the offices of the *Coconino Sun* newspaper. Locals and visitors alike were impressed by the luxurious accommodations, but they didn't much care for the name. A contest was held to come up with a new one. A 12-year-old submitted the winner – "Monte Vista," which in Spanish means "mountain view."

The hotel quickly became a popular spot with vacationers on Route 66 and with the locals, who coined the phrase, "Meet me at the Monte V." During its first year in operation, Mary Costigan – the second woman in the world to obtain a radio broadcast license, call letters KFXY – began hosting her three-hour daily radio show from Room 105 of the hotel.

Even though it had opened during Prohibition, this didn't stop the hotel's lounge, the Cocktail Bar, from keeping local whistles wet. Eventually, a profitable bootlegging operation began operating from the network of secret tunnels that run beneath downtown Flagstaff's streets. They had easy access to the Monte Vista and years later, evidence of a moonshine still, an opium den, and a gambling parlor would be found in the tunnels. As for the Cocktail Bar, it was raided by Prohibition officials in 1931 and closed. It resumed business two years later, when Prohibition finally came to an end. Between 1935 and 1940, the lounge also offered slot machines for the guests, the only ones ever in Flagstaff.

The lounge was also the site of a death in 1970 – which might explain another resident phantom. The date of this story is a little vague (some say 1970, others say in the 1970s) but it involved a bank robbery that occurred in downtown Flagstaff. One of the robbers was shot during their escape and they ended up at the hotel. Lying low and celebrating their success, they decided to have a drink in the lounge. While lifting a glass, it was discovered that the wounded man's gunshot injury was more serious than they thought. Before he could finish his first drink, he fell to the floor and died in the lounge.

Staff members and hotel guests began to believe that the dead bandit stayed behind in the lounge as a ghost. One manager reported that he often heard an eerie voice that said "Hello" or "Good Morning" to him when he opened the bar for the day. Others have told stories of feeling a presence near them while enjoying a drink or of seeing barstools spin around, glasses move up and down the bar, and bottles mysteriously drained of their alcohol. The ghost of the unlucky gunman seems to be making the best of being eternally attached to the place where he died.

And he may not be here alone. On several occasions, lounge staff and patrons have witnessed a spectral couple on the dance floor. They are reported in formal clothes, laughing and smiling as they make a circuit across the floor and vanish. Who this couple might be remains unknown.

In the 1940s and 1950s, during the height of popularity for western films, more than 100 movies were filmed in nearby Sedona and Oak Creek Canyon. During the shoots, the Monte Vista hosted famous guests like John Wayne, Gary Cooper, Jane Russell, Spencer Tracy, and Bing Crosby. There were many other films made in the area, too. Even a scene from *Casablanca* was filmed in one of the rooms of the hotel.

It was while John Wayne was at the Monte Vista in the 1940s that he had several encounters with one of the resident ghosts – the "phantom bellboy." He wasn't the first person to encounter the spirit, nor the last. Guests have reported a knock at their door and a muffled voice that announces, "room service." When they open the door, no one is there. Others have seen the figure standing outside of Room 210, which is the Zane Grey Room. He is always described as a young man in a red coat with brass buttons. When John Wayne was at the hotel, he experienced this ghost several times, inside of his room and outside of it. He did not feel threatened by its presence and, in fact, said that he "seemed nice." The apparition is frequently spotted by the housekeeping staff, even today.

The hallway outside of Room 201 is also believed to be haunted by the ghost of a woman who paces back and forth. Supposedly, the hotel staff avoids putting guests with pets in this room because, in the past, dogs have become crazed with fear in the room and have damaged it.

The second floor of the Monte Vista seems to be a hub for ghostly activity. Just down the hall in Room 220, an assortment of strange activity is reported. In the early 1980s, this room was rented to a long-term – and very eccentric—resident who had a strange habit of hanging raw meat from the overhead light fixture. He died in the room, but his body was not discovered for three days. Not long after, a maintenance man was working in the room on some repairs. When he needed a part, he left the room, turned off the lights, and locked the door. He returned only a few minutes later and found the television turned up to full volume and the linens pulled off the bed and scattered around the room. No one could have entered during his absence.

Today, guests in this room often complain of hearing a man coughing, along with other noises, in the room. The television set turns on and off by itself and guests complain of being touched with cold, unseen hands in the night.

Perhaps the only truly ominous haunting in the hotel occurs in Room 306. In the early twentieth century, Flagstaff's Red Light District could be found south of the railroad tracks downtown, just two blocks from the Monte Vista. In the early 1940s, two prostitutes were allegedly killed in Room 306 and their bodies were dumped in the street below. Apparently, though, the dead women don't rest in peace.

Since that time, the two women have been reportedly sighted in the pool hall and the lounge but spend most of their ethereal time in the room where they were murdered. Guests frequently report the feeling of being watched in Room 306 and hearing what sounds like two women whispering. Some report waking up to a menacing feeling in the night, which causes them to be unable to go back to sleep.

But its male guests who have the most frightening experiences in this room. There have been many who have reported being awakened by a hand being pressed over their mouth and nose, making it impossible to breathe. They struggle but the hand often remains in place until its almost too late, then suddenly, it's gone.

There is, of course, no living attacker in the room.

All types of other strange phenomena are reported in the hotel. Noises are heard, furniture moves around, apparitions are seen, the lobby telephone rings with no one on the other end of the line, objects vanish, doors slam, and both employees and guests have heard band music coming from the second-floor lobby, when there is no band at the hotel. The staff has become accustomed to it, even if many of the incidents still leave them unnerved and with the hair standing up on the back of their neck.

Some guests have seen a ghostly little boy wandering the halls of the hotel, and a few claim that they have felt him touch their hand. His voice is often heard directly behind those who encounter him, as if he was following them. A few staff members who have seen this spirit say that he sometimes appears to be speaking to someone, perhaps an adult, because he is looking upward. His lips move, but no sound emerges from them. A number of children have also reported seeing the little boy and he always approaches them in a friendly manner, leading some to believe that he's simply looking for a friend to play with.

Monte Vista staff members have heard the disturbing cry of an infant in the basement. This is reported primarily by the maintenance and laundry staff, who will talk about how frightening it is. Many confess that they have actually run upstairs to escape from the cries.

One helpful phantom staff member – perhaps less annoying than the bellboy – is the elevator attendant who seems to be forever at his post. Many people, particularly housekeeping and desk clerks, have reported this polite man in the elevator, which has been self-service for many decades. He seems to be a remnant from the early days of the hotel. Sometimes when people step into the elevator, they'll hear the voice of a man who asks, "Which floor may I take you to?" They have also seen a phantom hand closing the elevator's gate.

The most active room in the hotel – or at least the most famous one since it was featured years ago on the television show *Unsolved Mysteries* – is Room 305, which is better known as "the room with the rocking chair."

The legend of this room states that it was once rented to an elderly woman on a long-term basis. She sat in the rocking chair for hours at a time, day after day, looking out the window. One day, a member of the housekeeping staff found that she had passed away, still sitting in the chair, her glazed-over eyes still staring out the window. Since then, many guests have reported being startled when they enter their locked room and find an old lady sitting in the chair, slowly rocking back and forth. If they speak to her, or approach her, she disappears.

Some guests have reported being awakened in the middle of the night by a creaking sound and then look over to see the chair rocking by itself. Staff members report that a few of them have abandoned the room in the early morning hours and demand a different place to spend the night.

The hotel's housekeeping staff say that if they move the chair to another part of the room, they will later return and find it sitting in front of the window again. While cleaning the room, many have also reported seeing the chair rocking back and forth, even though they have not been anywhere near it.

Whoever the old lady had been waiting for, watching out the window, remains a mystery but she is apparently still waiting for them, even after death.

If you're hoping to encounter a ghost while traveling along old Route 66, then I'd suggest a night at the Monte Vista Hotel. It's often been said that "seeing is believing" and there is a very good chance that this place will make a believer out of you.

16. BILTMORE HOTEL
CORAL GABLES, FLORIDA

The luxurious Miami Biltmore Hotel made its debut in 1926 – the era of F. Scott Fitzgerald lifestyles, when Packards and Pierce Arrow motorcars lined the hotel's drives while uniformed chauffeurs cooled off in the shade of palm trees. Limousines delivered statesmen, financiers, captains of industry, wealthy gadflies, and gangsters to the hotel's front door, where bellmen stood at attention, ready to serve.

Inside, the strains of music could be heard drifting in from the afternoon dance on the garden patio. The lobby, with its arches and columns, was brilliant and striking and the drapes and furnishings alone cost more than $1 million. The Biltmore offered nothing but the best.

The vast kitchens were manned by gourmet chefs from all over the world. They were men who had pleased the palates of kings and queens, geniuses of business, and patrons and practitioners of the arts.

A tower of penthouses – the Giralda Tower – reached up beyond the Spanish-tiled roof that topped the first 10 floors. The tower was filled with suites that had played host to some of the most famous and infamous people in the country from President Coolidge, Eddie Rickenbacker, Cornelius Vanderbilt, Jr. to Jesse Lasky, Adolph Zukor, the Duke and Duchess of Windsor, Douglas Fairbanks, and Al Capone.

The Biltmore's elevator – unlike most hotels of the era – indicated that the tower had a thirteenth floor. It was there where the Royal Penthouse Suite was located and it also included the fourteenth floor, as well. These were two floors of luxury that outshined even the elegant lobby. It was this suite that the rich and famous often called their temporary home. It was lodging for America's elite for decades.

But it also served as home to some of the hotel's more sinister guests and, more than once, it became the setting for terror and death – leaving behind a haunting that would grow and infest the entire hotel.

The story of the Biltmore Hotel in Miami – when it was built, Coral Gables was still part of the larger city – began in the early 1900s, when Florida was experiencing a rapid land boom. George E. Merrick, a speculator and developer, was one of the men at the heart of the action. Besides founding the University of Miami, he was also responsible for the creation of many of the city's surrounding neighborhoods, including Coral Gables.

The upscale community, which was nicknamed the "City Beautiful," was planned as a haven for the wealthy. Huge mansions appeared along the wide, palm-lined boulevards. Merrick realized that a luxury hotel was necessary to cater to the needs of affluent visitors to Coral Gables and he convinced John McEntee Bowman, head of the Biltmore hotel chain, to join him in building one in 1924. The announcement was made at a gala dinner and the proposed hotel would be amazing, even by Biltmore standards.

The plans called for a $10 million, 400-room hotel on 150 acres that would also offer tennis courts, a polo field, an 18-hole golf course, and the largest hotel swimming pool in the country.

Bowman entrusted the job to architects Leonard Schultze and S. Fullerton Weaver, designers of New York's Grand Central Station and Biltmore hotels in Atlanta and Los Angeles. The new structure would be Mediterranean Revival – and mixture of Spanish and Italian influences – and would feature a signature tower. Each of the suites located there would be accessible by a private elevator and would take up an entire floor and have several bedrooms and bathrooms.

The hotel had its grand opening on January 15, 1926. For the event, railcars dubbed "Miami Biltmore Specials" transported the wealthy from New York and Boston to Miami. More than 1,500 guests arrived to be stunned by the breathtaking lobby. There was a high vaulted ceiling covered with frescoes, tall marble columns, travertine and terrazzo floors, mahogany railings, leaded glass chandeliers, and a lush courtyard and center fountain. Three orchestras were engaged for the festivities.

The hotel was an immediate success and from the Roaring Twenties through the years of World War II, it was one of the most fashionable destinations in America. In additions to presidents and royalty, the hotel attracted Hollywood stars like Bing Crosby, Judy Garland, and Ginger Rogers, and the aforementioned Al Capone, the mob boss who had a mansion on nearby Palm Island. He liked to entertain at the Biltmore, often renting out the Thirteenth floor of the tower.

The Great Depression of the 1930s had some effect on the Biltmore, but it remained open. It largely remained afloat thanks to his famed swimming pool. Sunday afternoons were set aside for aquatic shows that drew crowds as large as 3,000. The programs featured little Jackie Ott, who dove into the pool from an 85-foot platform, and synchronized swimmers, including one named Esther Williams, who later found fame in Hollywood. Interestingly, another person who later made a big splash in the movies was a swimming instructor at the Biltmore at the time – Johnny Weissmuller, who went on to become the screen's most famous *Tarzan.*

The hotel also sponsored gold tournaments, beauty pageants, fashion shows, and even alligator wrestling. They did anything to keep the doors open and the lights on. Even the wealthy had to watch the way they spent their money during the Depression.

Eventually, though, the Biltmore's initial glory days came to an end. During World War II, the War Department took over the hotel and converted it into the Army Air Forces Regional Hospital. Most of the windows were covered with concrete for their protection and the marble floors were covered with linoleum. When the war ended in 1945, the Veteran's Administration took the building over as a hospital for men returning sick or wounded from overseas. The bottom floor of the building was turned into a morgue, which would lead to an accidentally shocking discovery a few years later.

In the 1950s, a fire swept through a section of the hospital's ground floor. When firefighters broke into the gutted section, they were greeted by a grisly scene – a room filled with bodies that were charred beyond recognition. They didn't learn until later that what seemed to be "fire victims" were actually part of the hospital's cadaver collection. There were several large tanks of formaldehyde that had been designed to hold as many as 100 bodies at a time. They were stored at the hospital for medical students from the University of Miami.

In 1968, a new Veteran's Administration hospital was completed at a modern complex in Miami and the old Coral Gables structure was abandoned. The city took possession of the former Biltmore Hotel in 1973, but it remained unoccupied for the next decade, slowly being allowed to crumble into disrepair.

A decision was finally made in the 1980s to restore the hotel and more than $55 million was spent on a complete renovation. The hotel's grand opening took place on New Year's Eve, 1987. Five years later, the Seaway Hotel Corporation was granted a contract to manage the facilities. As part of their commitment, they spent another $40 million on a complete refurbishment. A spa and fitness center were added, and the legendary pool was updated with a stunning waterfall. The city also spent $3 million upgrading the golf course.

The Biltmore has been restored to its original glory, with all modern amenities. It boasts 275 guestrooms, 130 of which are suites. Visitors still come from all over the world to stay here and the spend the night where the rich and famous have also laid their heads.

And some of them get a little more than they bargained for.

It was during the 1970s, when the hotel was vacant, that it achieved its ghostly reputation. In those days, the majestic lobby was forlorn and empty. The main desk, where so many movie stars, politicians, and businessmen had once signed the registration book, was covered with dust and debris. Hand-carved mahogany panels were hidden under layers of gray government paint.

And yet, as abandoned as the hotel seemed to be, it wasn't empty. Stories circulated of weird, unexplainable lights in the building and of voices and macabre laughter that could be heard coming from inside.

The old hotel was haunted, those who experienced it insisted, and many knew the source of the haunting – it was a murder that had occurred there during the first years of operation.

It was a murder that left a troubling haunting behind.

The story didn't start in Florida – it started in New York, with a man named Arnold Rothstein. He would never become the well-known underworld name. He was no Al Capone, no Meyer Lansky, or Lucky Luciano. He was the man that made them. The millionaire gambler could fix things behind the scenes. He fixed court cases, gambler's bets, a night in bed with a Broadway actress, a murder that needed to happen, and even a sporting event, like the 1919 World Series, in which players for the Chicago White Sox threw the game in exchange for bribes. He was the king of the underworld at the time, although few people knew it. His ideas would outlive him. It was Arnold Rothstein who envisioned a national crime syndicate. He saw that the vast profits being made from bootlegging would forever change the relationship between the underworld and the average citizen. In the 1920s, he saw how the underworld controlled enough money to be able to buy protection directly from politicians and he saw how it became almost like a legitimate lobbying group, but one more powerful than most legitimate concerns. Rothstein himself had political connections in New York that were so good that he could get almost any court case dismissed. In fact, until 1928, when he was killed over a gambling debt, almost every bootlegging case that came before the New York courts -- almost 6,000 of them -- was thrown out through his intervention.

Rothstein financed Meyer Lansky's first enterprise, a trucking rental firm on the Lower East Side of New York. The trucks were in great demand during Prohibition and Lansky was joined by Charles "Lucky" Luciano in a number of bootlegging operations. After Prohibition came to an end, a national Syndicate was created by Luciano and Lansky used many of Rothstein's ideas, which included clearly defined territories and a board of directors.

But it was one of Rothstein's closest comrades who would eventually have a direct influence on the Biltmore Hotel.

Almost every night, Rothstein had his chauffeur-driven Packard parked at the curb at 49th and Broadway in New York. He'd then get out and walk the seven blocks to Times Square and back, stopping along the way to bet with the many sharpies who courted his trade. It was not unusual for him to carry more than $200,000 in his pocket, placing his bets with crisp, new $1,000 bills. In those days, Times Square and the adjacent blocks were the theater district – the place where anybody who was anybody in show business was headed. It was filled with tourists, would-be actors, and everyone who wanted to see the bright white lights of the city.

Even so, Rothstein was always flanked by his bodyguards. These were dangerous men and every one of them was rough, tough, and well-armed. They were highly paid, dressed in the finest suits, and ready to kill if needed. Rothstein's number-one bodyguard was Thomas Walsh, a man that everyone knew by his nickname, "Fatty." He was big, balding, and had been in the rackets since he was a teenager. Wherever Rothstein went, Walsh went, too.

In October 1928, Walsh decided to go out on his own. Rothstein set him up with some of his own operations and he left Rothstein's direct employ on good terms. They remained friends and a month later, on November 4, when Rothstein was mortally wounded at the Park Central Hotel after a disagreement about a bet, it was Walsh who was at his hospital bedside when he died. He was questioned by the police about who might have killed his friend and former employer, but Walsh said nothing.

Several weeks later, the NYPD was looking for Walsh again, although this time it was about his knowledge of a jewel heist. Thinking that Florida's sunshine might offer a healthier climate, Walsh headed to Miami before the police could track him down. He was accompanied by a close friend and fellow mobster, Arthur Clark. In appearance the two men presented a stark contract. Walsh was six-feet-tall and heavy, while Clark was a head shorter, skinny, dark, and weasel-faced.

When the two men arrived in Miami, they rented an apartment on Ferdinand Street in Coral Gables. The only issues they had with the law were about noise complaints from their loud parties. At one party, Walsh connected with an old friend, Edward Wilson, a wealthy gambler with places in New York and Chicago.

Wilson had leased the Royal Penthouse Suite on the thirteenth and fourteenth floors of the Biltmore's tower. With the knowledge of the hotel's owners – and probably local law enforcement – he'd turned the place into a speakeasy and casino. It had become quite a draw for underworld figures and the well-to-do in Miami. Wilson knew about Walsh's many underworld connections and offered to cut him in the operation. One of his best connections was the Federal Liquor Company in Havana, Cuba, which was a major supplier to south Florida. Soon, Wilson had even more liquor flowing at his hotel operation.

But things didn't go well at the Biltmore. The relationship between the two men turned ugly. Wilson thought he'd given "Fatty" Walsh too much of the partnership, and Walsh didn't think he'd gotten enough. One night, the tension between the two men boiled over.

Shortly after midnight on Thursday, March 7, 1929, there were over 100 people at the bar and gaming tables in the penthouse at the top of the Biltmore tower. Black ties, tuxedos, flowing gowns, and mink stoles were everywhere. One the finest liquor from Cuba was being served. A trio of musicians on the balcony were competing with the sounds of dice, roulette wheels, and laughter as they played "Alexander's Ragtime Band."

Fatty Walsh and Ed Wilson were in the card room off the main casino hall. Their voices were raised but no one could hear what they were saying over the noise of the room, but it was obvious from their flushed faces and flashing eyes that they were arguing about something. It likely had something to do with money. The two men swore at each other and then Wilson walked away and sat down to watch several men at the blackjack table. Fatty was pacing back and forth on the other side of the room and then he walked over and sat down in a chair next to the card table with his back to Wilson.

Just as the band hit the last notes of the song, Wilson jumped up from his seat and pulled a .38-caliber revolver from his jacket. As he backed toward the door that opened to the main room, silence fell over the small group in the card room.

As Walsh started to turn around in his seat, Wilson shot him. A bullet passed through his right side and ricocheted off the table behind him. Fatty started to pitch forward out of his chair and Walsh shot him again before he hit the floor. He landed hard, face down under the gaming table, and the chair that he'd been sitting in toppled across his legs. His friend, Art Clark, rushed across the room and knelt at his side. Wilson fired again, this time hitting Clark. The bullet stitched through his left arm and struck a rib, deflecting it out of his chest.

Still gripping the gun, Wilson fled from the room, bumping into a group that was standing next to a roulette table. Women screamed and men yelled, but no one made an effort to stop him. Wilson charged into the entry hall and ran upstairs. The crowd panicked. No one wanted to get involved in a police investigation. As they rushed from the penthouse, one woman – the wife of a New York City subway official – was thrown against the sharp edge of a table and ended up with lacerations to her face and right arm.

Wilson himself was last seen running across the downstairs lobby and sprinting across the parking lot.

A rookie police officer had just reported for duty when his sergeant, a veteran named Brasher, told him to get the car ready – there had been a shooting at the Biltmore. The two officers sped to the hotel, entered the lobby, and went straight to the elevators. Both cars were on upper floors. They were forced to wait and watch as the elevators only moved a floor or two at a time, never getting closer to the lobby than the fourth floor. After a few minutes, Brasher realized that someone was stalling the elevators to keep the police away. They headed for the stairs – only to find the door to the stairwell locked. Brasher went to the front desk and demanded to know what was going on. He threated to call the fire department and have them break down the door. It turned out there was no need. His rookie partner called over to let him know that both elevators had come down.

When the two policemen entered the Royal Penthouse Suite, they found large, open, vacant rooms. All the furniture was gone. Even the rugs had been removed. There were certainly no gambling tables and the well-stocked bar was empty. In a smaller room off to the side, there was a dead body lying on the floor. It was covered with a white linen sheet. Standing next to the corpse was a man with his arm and chest patched up with bloodstained bandages.

The sergeant pulled back the sheet from the dead man's face. It was Thomas "Fatty" Walsh. As Art Clark was taken away to an ambulance, he sobbed, "He was shot down like a dog. He never had a chance."

Obviously, the elevators had been intentionally delayed so that the liquor could be removed from the bar and the gambling equipment could be hauled away from the crime scene. Six people were held and questioned as material witnesses to the murder. One was a man named M.D. Simpson. Another was Demaris Dove, an 18-year-old nightclub hostess who had seen Wilson shoot Fatty and was nearby when the big man died. After the shooting, she had fled screaming upstairs to a room on the fourteenth floor. She was questioned for 10 hours before she was finally released.

For several weeks, Wilson was sought by various law enforcement agencies, but he was nowhere to be found. Almost a month later, rumors spread that on the night of the murder, Wilson had been seen at the Miami airport being placed aboard a Ford Tri-Motor airplane by Dade County District Attorney's office agents, bound for Havana. The rumors went on to suggest that certain local law enforcement officials had been receiving a percentage of the profits from Wilson's casino, which explained how it so easily operated at the Biltmore.

No one knows what happened to Clark after he left the hospital, but Wilson remained out of sight until many years later. In 1946, the Coral Gables police chief received a called from the FBI office in Los Angeles. They were checking on a man named Wilson. He was apparently connected in some way to Paramount Pictures. He had confessed to the FBI that he was the same Wilson connected to the murder of Fatty Walsh. The FBI asked for a report on the incident, but the chief told him there was no report. He was only a detective at the time and his bosses refused to let a report of the murder be filed.

By the 1970s, when the Biltmore was abandoned and reportedly haunted, Thomas "Fatty" Walsh had been dead for nearly 50 years. But many believed his spirit still roamed the vacant hospital that was once the finest hotel in Miami.

And there were some who were determined to prove it.

In May 1978, authors Richard Winer and Nancy Osborn took five psychics – Patricia Hayes, Jan Clema, Ann Phillips, Jean Barr, and J.R. Worden – to the Biltmore. They were all members of either the Arthur Ford Academy or the Spiritual Frontiers Society and each had earned an impressive reputation for being able to communicate with the spirit world. None of the five were informed ahead of time about where they were being taken.

After entering the building, all of them sensed something in the lobby, near the elevators. Something had happened that involved the elevators, they said, and felt they should go upstairs. One floor up, in the main lobby, the psychics again picked up strange vibes near the elevator. "Something happened in this building," Worden said, "and the elevators were somehow involved."

"There was a lot of commotion here," Phillips agreed.

Barr touched the elevator button. "Whatever they were excited about didn't happen here. It took place upstairs."

They decided to work their way up, floor by floor, to see what they picked up. They climbed the stairs, which were littered with debris. Between the time when the hospital moved out and the city of Coral Gables took over the building, it had attracted squatters and homeless people.

Between the ninth and tenth floors, the group came to a stop. Hayes looked around before speaking. "We're being followed. We're not alone. There are others on these stairs." Of course, there was no one around – she believed they were being followed by spirits.

Worden agreed. "There are four men following us. They've been with us since we left the lobby.

When they reached the thirteenth floor, some unseen energy was felt by the entire group. There was no signal or communication between them. They simply all reacted at the same time. "There's something on this floor," Worden said.

The group silently left the stairwell and entered the open suite. It was a huge room, surrounded by a balcony and mezzanine that made up the fourteenth floor. All the psychics agreed that there was something in the room – an entity that wanted to talk with them. When asked, they said that it was not the four spirits that had followed them up the stairs. They had left when the group entered the suite because they didn't like it.

Nancy Osborn unfolded a blanket that she was carrying, and they spread it out on the floor. The group sat down in a circle and joined hands for a séance. Almost immediately, they spoke of being able to feel a strong energy. Moments later, for no apparent reason, a set of venetian blinds on one window crashed to the floor. Osborn and Winer both jumped but the others were so deep in thought that they were oblivious to the falling blinds.

Once the séance began, the psychics began to communicate with the spirits that were present. Winer recorded the event. They knew there had been a lot of drinking and partying in the room, even though none of them knew the history of the hotel, or what the suite had been famous for in the 1920s. They soon made contact with a young woman, around 30, who was looking for a child – a little boy who had seen her die. The woman had not died in the room but somewhere nearby. She had been murdered and was looking for her child, they said. She was trapped there because of unfinished business. Apparently, the true story of her death had never been reported.

But the woman wasn't alone. There were other spirits in the room, including an older man with a cane who they said walked around them but would not participate in the séance. The tapping of the old man's cane was bothering the psychics.

They also sensed some sort of traumatic event that had occurred that cause people to run screaming from the room, including a young woman who hid upstairs and later committed suicide, although not in the hotel. They sensed that there had been a lot of gambling in the suite. They received images of violence and of two men who were having a serious argument. They came up with a name that was something like "Fats." One of the men was killed, which caused a serious commotion in the room. They believed the murder was caused by a handgun. Two shots were fired. Patricia Hayes blurted out, "The killer wanted to make sure Fats was dead!" There was a lot of blood and after that, the killer fled. The police were involved, but there were problems with them getting to the scene. They described people who were present that night, including a "weasel-faced man" who had something to do with stolen jewelry and a witness named "Simpson."

They had, with no prior knowledge, described what happened on the night that Edward Wilson had murdered Thomas "Fatty" Walsh in that very room.

After the séance was over, the group gathered around the suite's fireplace. Jan Clema walked over to one of the windows that faced south and put both hands on the glass. "Someone jumped from this window," she said. She added that it had happened in the late 1930s.

The psychics all agreed that there were many spirits haunting the building, from many different time periods in its history. "From all the force and activity going on in here, there are probably hundreds of them," Patricia Hayes said. She told Winer that she couldn't be sure of the number, though. "Some come and go. They don't necessarily hang around a place just because they died there. More often they'll haunt a locale where something significant happened to them while they were alive. But that's not to say that they don't ever return to their place of death. Who can say for sure how many are here. We are dealing with a different concept of time and space. Our reality contains one dimension, but it's a multi-dimensional universe."

Later that evening, Winer received a telephone call from Osborn, who was transcribing the tape from the séance. There was a problem with it – a terrible ticking noise that occurred during a large portion of the session. They listened to it several times but couldn't figure out what it was – and then suddenly they knew. The tapping started about the same time that one of the psychics mentioned the arrival of the old man with the cane.

It was the sound of the cane tapping on the marble floor as he walked around and around the circle of psychics.

In the days that followed the séance, Winer and Osborn did more research into the history of the hotel, digging through newspapers, archives, and microfilms. They also did several interviews with people about the history of the Biltmore and the veteran's hospital. One of the interviews was with William Kimbrough, who had retired from the Coral Gables Police Department after 50 years of service on December 31, 1977. He had been the Chief of Police for many years and had received numerous awards and citations during his time with the department. He had joined the force in 1928 as a replacement for an officer who had been killed in the line of duty.

Kimbrough had been the rookie called to the Biltmore Hotel with Sergeant Floyd Brasher on the night of Thomas Walsh's murder.

Kimbrough was skeptical when they first began to describe the séance but as he looked over the transcript his skepticism turned to surprise. He was especially astonished at the section about the elevators and their connection to the shooting. He told them, "It was something no one, not even the newspapers, knew about." He also confirmed the witness named M.D. Simpson who had been questioned by the police and the identity of Arthur Clark, the jewel thief who looked like a "weasel."

The newspaper archives helped with other parts of the story revealed by the séance. Clema said that she sensed that someone had jumped from a window on the thirteenth floor, but Winer could find no record of a suicide in the 1930s. He did, however, discover that, in 1938, a window washer's safety belt had broken, and he had fallen to his death from the thirteenth floor.

The psychics also mentioned a woman running upstairs in a panic immediately after the shooting – just as Demaris Dove had done. But did she later commit suicide, as described in the séance? If she did, they found no record of it.

And what about the spirit of the woman who first appeared to them at the start of the séance, looking for her child? She didn't seem to be connected to any of the events in the hotel but, oddly, Winer may have discovered who she was. In late 1925, a few weeks before the hotel opened, a young woman was found murdered on a rock ledge that overlooked the hotel's golf course. She left a small child behind. Could she have been the spirit trying to communicate with her little boy after all these years? Possibly, but we'll likely never know.

The hotel was, of course, rescued from its abandonment and restored. The lights are on now, the lobby is once again magnificent, and the place draws people from all over the world. It's a much different place than it was in the 1970s, but some things have stayed the same – it's still very haunted.

Reports of ghostly activity began again in earnest as soon as the updated and revived hotel opened its doors again. A phantom couple is often seen in the ballroom, dancing to music that no one else can hear. In the clubhouse building, a phantom in a top hat and tails has been seen playing the piano. A woman in a white dress has been seen in various rooms throughout the hotel.

Doors open and shut by themselves, often wreaking havoc on servers who are going back and forth from the kitchen with heavy trays in their arms. Lights operate on their own. Lampshades, telephones, ice buckets, and more disappear and then show up again in unusual spots. Many guests have reported the appearance of mysterious, usually illegible messages in the condensation on steamy bathroom mirrors.

And, not surprisingly, the story of Fatty Walsh lives on. He is blamed for all the strange occurrences that take place on the thirteenth floor. Although he lived and died by violence, he was a likable man in life and his ghost continues to be. Although his ghostly pranks might be annoying, they are never mean or destructive.

Occasionally, guests will catch an unexplainable whiff of his cigar smoke and the penthouse is prone to cold spots. Items left on tables sometimes fall on the floor, or shift positions without being touched. They sometimes vanish and turn up in a nonsensical place like in the bathroom or in the refrigerator. Guests have also heard muffled laughter that comes from nowhere and have caught glimpses of a shadowy figure looking out the window at night. When a light is turned on, he vanishes.

The most famous person to encounter Fatty was President Bill Clinton. He was trying to watch a football game on the television while staying in the suite, but the set refused to work correctly. It started changing channels and then switching on and off by itself. It had worked perfectly the day before and it was fine the following day. There was no reason for it to malfunction – unless it was Fatty Walsh. President Clinton chose to go somewhere else to watch the game.

Fatty also likes to play tricks on those who use the private elevator to the tower. Guests have said that the lift will frequently bypass other floors and go straight up to the thirteenth floor, even though a special key is required to go beyond the eleventh level. On one occasion, the doors stayed open on the thirteenth floor for so long that the couple in the runaway car decided to investigate. As soon as the woman stepped out of the car, the doors slammed shut behind her, and the elevator immediately started back down to the lobby with her husband inside. She was rescued but not until after several nervous minutes alone in the hotel's most haunted spot.

Who lingers at the Biltmore Hotel?
Or perhaps we should ask -- how many spirits remain here?
Psychic Patricia Hayes suggested that there might be hundreds of spirits who checked in here and never checked out, and since she was right about so many other things from the hotel's turbulent history, maybe she was right about that, too.

17. THE COPPER QUEEN HOTEL
BISBEE, ARIZONA

Bisbee, Arizona, is one of my favorite places in the country. Located about as far south in Arizona as you can go and not cross the Mexican border, it's a weird, eclectic little town that's been revitalized in recent years by hippies, artists, and the kind of folks that you find in towns like Key West and Provincetown, Massachusetts -- towns that are literally the last stop on the line from the ordinary. The people are a part of what makes Bisbee so great and the history is probably what makes it so haunted.

The Copper Queen Hotel is an integral part of the town's history and it offers a look back in time to when Bisbee was one of the most profitable places in the West. It was built to offer the management of the booming copper mine a place to stay that was elevated above the living conditions of the men who did the real work in the rough mining community. The days of taking wealth from the rocks below the town are long gone now but the Cooper Queen remains.

And so do the spirits of those who once walked its halls.

Mining had been a part of the development of the Arizona Territory since the 1860s. However, things had moved slowly for a variety of reasons, not the least of which was the hostile terrain, weather, and the Apache tribes that had called the area home for centuries. It wasn't until the 1870s that miners, usually working in conjunction with military troops, began to make great discoveries.

In 1877, members of an Army search party from Fort Bowie staked the first claim in what would later be the site of the great copper camp in Bisbee. Or, well, that is sort of what happened – there also turned out to be double-crossing, gambling, and alcohol in the story.

The cavalry patrol from Fort Bowie was in the area tracking Apache and camped at what today is Iron Springs. The men didn't like the quality of water so that sent a scout named Jack Dunn to look for better water. During his search, he found a spring along a large cliff of limestone, as well as an outcrop of rock in Tombstone Canyon containing lead carbonate, which was known to carry silver. Dunn told his commanding officer, Lieutenant John Rucker, and a packer named Ted Byrne of his discovery. They planned to file a claim on it but were delayed when their patrol was ordered to resume pursuit of the band of Apache. Before leaving the fort for the second time, they met with a man named George Warren and persuaded him to file the claim on their behalf, with the agreement that Warren would name Dunn in all notices of locations for the claims. They provided him with money, provisions, and a map to the mining claim site.

Warren immediately decided to cheat them, but he didn't even do that right. On his way to the claims office, he stopped in a saloon, got drunk, and gambled away the money that Dunn and the others had given him. On September 27, 1877 – 56 days after Dunn had located the site – Warren filed his own mining claim. But don't worry, he got what was coming to him. While drinking with an acquaintance a short time later, he made a drunken bet that he could outrun a man on a horse. He couldn't. The bet cost him his interest in the mine claim, which went on to be worth millions.

At that time, though, miners who flocked to the area were focusing on gold and silver. The area was too remote to develop and transport copper ore, and national demand for copper was not yet strong enough to warrant the large investment it would take to haul it out of the middle of the desert.

In the late 1870s, the area around the mines was known as Mule Gulch Camp, a settlement of no more than a few hundred people. It was eclipsed by its neighbor to the north, Tombstone, which had grown into a boomtown of thousands of residents. Tombstone's silver mines initially allowed for more rapid growth, but all that changed when the electrification began sweeping the nation in the early 1880s. Arizona mine owners needed to be able to meet the demand and in August 1880, the new Copper Queen Mine was launched.

Mule Gulch Camp was renamed Bisbee after DeWitt Bisbee, a San Francisco attorney and one of the investors in the Copper Queen Mine. Ironically, Mr. Bisbee never set foot in the town named in his honor, even after it became one of the greatest mining towns in the West.

The Phelps Dodge Company entered the Bisbee mining scene in 1881 and four years later, bought out the Copper Queen and created the second largest producer of copper in the nation during the last two decades of the nineteenth century.

Phelps Dodge had been founded in 1834 as an import-export firm by Anson Greene Phelps and his two sons-in-law, William Earle Dodge and Daniel James. They began by exporting cotton from the South to England and importing various metals to the United States that were needed for industrialization. With the expansion of the western frontier, they turned their attentions to acquiring mines and mining companies, including the Copper Queen.

This was not what most miners would consider a great company to work for. The work was extremely dangerous, and the company routinely demanded unpaid work, subjected miners to intrusive physical strip searches, and followed dangerous practices, like blasting while men were in the mine and not permitting safety operators on drills and elevators. Things only got worse as demand for copper continued to increase across the country.

But as the demand for copper increased, more people came to town. Bisbee experienced even more growth after the railroad arrived in 1889. From 1899 to 1918, the town's population grew from 4,000 to over 25,000.

This didn't mean that it was always a wonderful place to live, though. Smelting had started in Bisbee in the 1880s. The hills around the town were once covered in trees, but the thousands of cords of wood needed by the smelters each year quickly stripped the hills of trees and the smelter fumes killed off much of the remaining vegetation. Bisbee was described as a "dirty, smoke-filled camp." It was a boomtown with no regulations or public services, jammed into the canyons of the Mule Mountains.

Drunkenness and violence were common. Before 1900, Bisbee had 50 saloons, along with gambling halls and brothels. Trash was thrown into the streets and open sewage pits added to the stench that was already lingering in the noxious air. To make matters worse, since the trees had all been stripped from the hillsides, there was nothing to stop the water that poured down the mountains during the summer rainy season. Disastrous floods also became common.

After the turn of the century, as demand for copper continued to rise, Bisbee continued to grow. By 1905, two more copper companies were operating in town and turned copper into big business. The frontier camp transitioned into an industrial city and conditions in town started to improve as upgrades were made to accommodate the new influx of miners and their families.

Flood control measures were implemented that helped with the flooding and Phelps Dodge moved their smelter out of town, drastically improving the air quality. A sewer system was built in 1908, eliminating the problem of the open waste pits. A pipeline was built to bring fresh water from springs six miles away, replacing the need to haul water to town by burro. Many of the hastily built – and now ramshackle -- buildings from the 1880s and 1890s were replaced by substantial buildings built of brick and stone. Electrical and telephone services were expanded to most parts of town. In 1908, a streetcar line was built between Bisbee and the adjacent town of Warren.

With all the families now in town, other changes were made, too. The first ordinance passed after the city was incorporated in 1902 was to ban women from saloons. By 1910, gambling and prostitution had been outlawed.

In 1908, Bisbee experienced a devastating setback after a horrific fire left hundreds of people homeless and burned half of the commercial district. However, with the mines still employing thousands of men, the destroyed sections of the city were quickly rebuilt.

With the goal of processing lower grade ore profitably, Phelps Dodge began open-pit mining. Sacramento Hill, an iconic landmark at Bisbee, was first blasted in 1917 and would become the Sacramento Pit, one of the first open-pit mines in the United States. It would be excavated until 1929 but a second pit – Lavender Pit – was opened in 1950 and remained in operation until 1974.

But trouble was coming to Bisbee and it's likely no surprise that it started at the Phelps Dodge Mine.

The start of World War I caused a dramatic rise in the price of copper. While increased commodity prices were generally seen as a positive thing in western mining towns, the reality for the miners was that they were now expected to work harder and longer for the same amount of pay. The influx of new miners into Bisbee had driven up the cost of living, which made things even tougher for the thousands of miners working in town.

In May 1917, the miners' unions, one of which was affiliated with the radical Industrial Workers of the World (IWW), presented a list of demands to the Phelps Dodge Company. They were immediately rejected by the company and a strike became inevitable.

Around 3,000 miners went on strike on June 27. The strike was peaceable, but rumors quickly spread that IWW members were going to start trouble. While the IWW had been responsible for violence and sabotage in other towns, only a small percentage of the miners in Bisbee were members of the IWW. Even so, any IWW members at all allowed Phelps Dodge to use the union as an excuse for drastic action.

The company tested the waters in Jerome, Arizona, by rounding up 67 members of the IWW and deporting them by train to Needles, California.

They got away with it, so on July 12, 1917, 2,200 armed men, led by the local sheriff, went out onto the streets of Bisbee during the early morning hours. They had a list of strikers and residents who were members of, or sympathetic with, the IWW. At least 2,000 men were arrested, some of them local business owners. They were marched two miles to the ballpark in Warren, escorted by the armed men and a car that had been outfitted with a belt-fed machine gun. Once at the ballpark, they were offered the chance to denounce the IWW, end the strike, and return to work. About 700 men accepted the offer.

The remaining men were forced, at gunpoint, onto 23 railroad cattle cars. The train carrying the strikers traveled east to Columbus, New Mexico, where the men were unloaded. Public officials in Columbus protested and the train turned around and traveled back to Hermanas, New Mexico. The men were dumped there at 3:00 a.m. They had spent 12 hours on the train, traveling in 90-degree heat with little water and no food. With almost 1,300 men with no money or belongings stranded in the desert, New Mexico had to deal with the crisis.

New Mexico Governor Washington Ellsworth Lindsey contacted President Wilson and asked for assistance, but no one had any idea what he was talking about. Phelps Dodge, in collusion with Cochise County Sheriff Harry C. Wheeler, had closed all access to outside communications from Bisbee, so the story of the deportation had not been reported. Eventually, federal troops were sent to escort the miners to Columbus, where they were housed in tents for the next two months, unable to return home. By now, Phelps Dodge was claiming that their actions had been taken as a way to reduce threats to the United States during World War I.

The government would not agree. In October 1917, President Wilson appointed a commission to investigate the dispute. The commission concluded "The deportation was wholly illegal and without authority in law, either State or Federal." In May 1918, 21 executives of the Phelps Dodge company were arrested for their role in the deportation, but none of them were convicted.

And none of the deported men were allowed to return to their homes or jobs.

But mining continued in Bisbee for many years. In time, the Copper Queen closed down, and when the mining at the Lavender Pit stopped in late 1974, it was the first time in nearly a century that no mining was taking place in Bisbee. Unlike the other great copper towns of the West, Bisbee had been spared complete destruction because of open-pit mining. Even so, the open pit didn't employ nearly as many people as the underground mines and thousands of jobs vanished over the years. When the pit closed, Bisbee lost its only industry.

The resulting loss of population in the area was a mixed blessing. Real estate became very inexpensive, and with the attractive climate and beautiful scenery, Bisbee began to attract preservation-minded people who bought the historic homes and buildings, like actor John Wayne, a frequent visitor who partnered in several real estate ventures during the transition from a mining economy. The cheap property prices and remote location also appealed to the artist crowd and the eccentrics, who were looking for a place where they could escape from everyday life.

Bisbee was soon completely transformed. The former miner's homes were renovated and repainted in striking colors. Former mercantile stores were rebranded as art galleries and diners became gourmet restaurants. Many of the historic buildings in town, once the property of Phelps Dodge, or one of the other outfits, were given new life, like the Copper Queen's corporate headquarters, which is now the local history museum.

Looming above the museum, though, is a structure that has endured from the boomtown days of Bisbee and remains in operation today – the Copper Queen Hotel.

During the heyday of the town, the Phelps Dodge Company operated a massive mercantile store that catered to the needs of miners and their families. Each worker was given a credit account and purchases from the store were deducted from their monthly pay. It was an establishment designed to serve the needs of the working men, but the Copper Queen Hotel was just the opposite. Miners didn't sleep in the beds that were fitted with imported linens or eat the gourmet food in the restaurant. The hotel had been designed to serve the interests of management.

The 75-room hotel was built over an 18-month period at a price of around $75,000. It opened its doors on February 21, 1902, and newspapers called it "dazzling." Designed in the Italianate-style, the hotel's floor plan was considered the "most efficient that any architect could conjure" with all the ground floor leading away from the office. The interior was paneled with California redwood, and its kitchen was outfitted with all the latest appliances, including steam dishwashing machinery. The cooking appliances had been purchased and shipped from the Boston Street Range Company of Cincinnati. There were originally 44 guest rooms – 20 of which had private baths – and were "beautifully furnished with large brass and iron bedsteads with large box spring mattresses," heavy carpeting, and window drapery that was supplied by Marshall Field and Company of Chicago at a cost of $25,000.

The ladies' parlor, which was downstairs and to the right of the office, was "tastefully arranged in mahogany with rich green silk plush and satins." This was an important room because it was here that the wives of executives who traveled with their husbands were to be entertained during their stay. Beyond the parlor was the men's billiard room, a barber shop, washrooms, and bathrooms. To the left of the office was the large dining room, which was "the most cheerful and attractive to be seen anywhere." It was beautifully -lighted and had a seating capacity of 78 people. In the rear of the dining room were two smaller rooms for intimate family gatherings or business meetings. All of the china used bore the hotel monogram and each piece of glass was etched with the letters "CQ."

Next to the mines and administrative buildings of the Copper Queen Mine, the hotel was the most visible symbol of the company's power in Bisbee. Thanks to this, it had the best management money could buy. The hotel opened under the direction of Charles Rouser, who had previously run the high-class Indianapolis resort, the

Columbia Club. With a membership of more than 1,200 men, it was the most powerful in the city. Among its members were former President William Henry Harrison, General Lew Wallace, James Whitcomb Riley, and many others. Rouser seemed to be the perfect man to steer the new Copper Queen Hotel, but he didn't stay in Bisbee for long. He returned to Indianapolis to manage another hotel, so in January 1903, the Copper Queen was taken over by Tom Whitehead, a former Tombstone hotelier and the owner of the English Kitchen, Bisbee's finest restaurant. One of the first things he did was to convert the dining room into a café-style restaurant that served meals around the clock.

Within six months, Whitehead had turned the Copper Queen into the finest hotel in Arizona, excelling hotels in cities with three times the population of the small mining community. But later that summer, Whitehead gave up his lease to devote his time to ranching. His position was taken over by Edward Rouser, son of Charles Rouser, the hotel's original manager. Edward managed the Copper Queen until the spring of 1906, when he married and went on a honeymoon to Monterey, California. On the morning of April 18, the San Francisco Earthquake rocked the hotel where the Rousers were staying, and Edward and his new bride were killed.

The hotel weathered the changes in Bisbee, economical and otherwise. It survived the devastating fire of 1908 and the labor strikes in the 1910s. During the worst of it, the Bell telephone office at the Copper Queen became the communications center for the mustering force of strikebreakers who deported the men they claimed were a danger to safety in Bisbee. After the mines closed, the Cooper Queen was one of the historic buildings embraced by the preservationists, artists, and "hippies" who helped the town survive.

In the 1970s, a swimming pool was added, making it the only hotel in town with both an elevator and a pool. There are many famous guests who have stayed at the Copper Queen over the years, including John Wayne, who allegedly threw actor Lee Marvin through a saloon window. Others include Theodore Roosevelt, General John Pershing, Charlie Chaplin, Roscoe "Fatty" Arbuckle, Harry Houdini, Julia Roberts, Johnny Depp, and Senator John McCain.

Today, the Copper Queen is the oldest continuously operating hotel in Arizona, and I recommend it to anyone who wants a true taste of the past when they visit Bisbee. You'll see the town's history come to life, and if you're lucky – and are searching for ghosts – it might happen in more ways than one.

According to my friend Renee Gardner – who hosts an excellent ghost tour in Bisbee that you're going to want to take when you visit – there are at least 16 ghosts lingering behind at the Copper Queen. You don't find that hard to believe when you walk through the front doors and experience the place. There is certainly history here.

One of the ghosts is said to be that of an older man with a beard who wears a top hat and cape. He has often been seen in the Roosevelt Room, or in the hallway outside of it. He leaves no clue as to his identity, although its likely that he was a mining executive or some other wealthy visitor to the hotel from its early days.

A spectral little girl is often seen on the second floor, near the entrance to the pool. She has been spotted by former managers and some of the guests, although she seems to be very shy. A psychic who visited the Copper Queen believed that she was the spirit of a girl who was unable to find her parent's room and became lost.

Another ghost, dubbed the "Smoking Man," is frequently encountered, usually on the third and fourth floors, where the smoking gallery of the hotel used to be. He is sometimes seen – a gray-haired man in a suit and top hat – but more often, guests are overwhelmed by his pungent cigar smoke, despite the fact that smoking is not allowed in the building. Regardless, this phantom smoke will waft down hallways and into the rooms without explanation.

One of the most popular ghosts of the Copper Queen is Julia Lowell, a former lady of the evening who is believed to have possibly lived at the hotel during the Depression, when management rented out some of the rooms on a long-term basis to help with the overhead. Legend claims that Julia fell in love with one of her regular customers, a married man who had no intention of leaving his wife for a prostitute. In despair, Julia took her own life, hanging herself in Room 315. It has since been named in her honor. The stories say that Julia loves to taunt the men who stay in her room. She pulls blankets from the bed while they sleep, tickles their toes, and whispers in their ears. There are some who say they have seen her on the main staircase, wearing lingerie and carrying a wine bottle. When encountered, she is accompanied by the smell of old lilac perfume.

Julia may be the most popular lingering resident of the hotel, but Billy is the most active. He was a little boy who died by drowning in the San Pedro River. His spirit ended up at the hotel to be near his mother, who was working there at the time. She eventually passed on, but Bill has remained behind to become the Copper Queen's most playful ghost. He has been seen jumping up and down on the leather couch in the lobby and has been heard laughing in the hallways, followed by the pounding of a child's small feet as he runs away. He loves to pick up small, shiny objects but he never steals them – he simply moves them somewhere else. The only thing that he takes that never returns is candy that is left on a table unattended.

Billy is occasionally seen by the hotel's youngest guests. There is a story that has circulated about a little girl who was eating with her family in the hotel's restaurant. During the meal, she kept looking under the table. When asked what she was looking at, she replied that there was a boy beneath the table. Of course, when her parents looked for themselves, the boy was gone.

Once, a family with three children were staying at the Copper Queen and Billy did everything that he could to get their attention. They were preoccupied watching television, so Billy raised the volume up and down. When they didn't seem to notice, he tried turning the set off and on. Finally, he unplugged it from the wall. That was what finally did the trick.

Over the years, guests and Copper Queen staff have encountered many other ghosts or have had experiences they cannot explain. There is also a shadowy figure that has been seen walking back and forth at the entrance to the restaurant. He usually appears after the place has closed for the night. There is also a spectral man in rough, cowboy-like clothing who has been spotted sitting in a chair in the restaurant. Everyone who has seen him says that he is smoking a cigar, although they have never smelled the smoke. After a few moments, he disappears.

There is also a story about a woman in black mourning clothes, descending the main staircase, that has circulated in Bisbee for many years. Several employees say that they have seen her, standing on the first set of stairs leading up to the second floor. She is not the only specter that appears there. Employees have also seen another woman, who only descends the stairs to the point where she can be seen from the waist down from the desk. She is always wearing a dark beige skirt and a white blouse. One staff member saw her reflected in a mirror one day. Thinking that it was another employee, he turned around but there was no one there.

One night, an employee was working on the night audit in the front office when he heard loud footsteps coming from the second-floor mezzanine. Since it was very late at night, he wanted to make sure that no one was running around the building. When he got to the second floor, there was no one there.

The hotel's saloon has its own set of ghosts. During the early days of the hotel's operation, this was a much smaller space. The back half of the room was the offices for the Chamber of Commerce and Western Union. It was enlarged in the 1970s and now plays host to guests, musicians, and several ghosts.

One employee was sitting at a table in the back of the barroom one night and felt a presence standing next to him. He could see the person out of the side of his eye and could see a white shirt and tan pants. When he turned to speak to the person, though, he discovered that no one was there. This happened to him again a short time later, except this time, he felt an icy cold hand on his shoulder. When he turned, though, the figure had vanished and his cold hand went with him.

Female bartenders often sense the ghost of a man watching them from the liquor closet. When one of them mentioned the sensation to another bartender, she confessed to feeling it, too. It later turned out that even some of the female customers felt the same way. One of the women said that she once heard the voice of a man make a sexist comment when she passed by the closet and heard a knocking sound on the wall. Lights often turn on and off by themselves and tapping sounds are sometimes heard on the front window glass. There is never anyone standing by the window when it happens.

If you want to visit one of America's most interesting small towns – as well as one of its most haunted ones – be sure to go to Bisbee, Arizona. And when you do, make a reservation at the Copper Queen. Your nights may not always be peaceful ones, but I can promise you won't be sorry you made the trip.

18. THE ORIGINAL SPRINGS HOTEL
OKAWVILLE, ILLINOIS

Tucked away among the cornfields of Southwestern Illinois is the small town of Okawville. The quiet streets of the town these days offer little proof that it was once one of the most bustling towns in the region. However, from the late nineteenth to the middle part of the twentieth century, people from all over the country came to Okawville to take in the waters of a seemingly magical mineral spring that still exists beneath the town. During its heyday, a number of hotels and health resorts existed in town, offering healing baths to those who suffered from rheumatism, digestive ailments, and all matter of illnesses. Today, however, only one of those hotels remains today.

The Original Springs Hotel still stands on North Hanover Street and it is the only continuously operating mineral spring in the state of Illinois. It is a place of both history and mystery that still draws people from the surrounding area and beyond. They continue to come to the old hotel hoping to experience not only the rejuvenating waters of the old spring, but the strange and powerful aura of the hotel itself.

There are many secrets hidden away in the old place and many ghosts, as well. Many of the visitors that come here – along with staff members, many of whom have worked here for decades -- are unable to explain the odd attraction that they have for this place. There is also the mystery of why so many spirits have chosen to remain here, too. Is it merely the history that had taken place behind these walls or could it be the water that is hidden away beneath the building and the weird, magnetic qualities that it seems to have?

The mysterious waters of Okawville were first discovered in 1867. Rudolph Plegge was the owner of a harness and saddle shop in Okawville. After digging a well to supply water for his business, he discovered that the water was eating its way through his tin and copper buckets and kettles. When he heard about the problem with the water, a local doctor, Dr. James McIlwain, decided to test the water and found that it had a high mineral content. More tests were done in St. Louis and more minerals were discovered, comparing the water to the famous mineral baths in Hot Springs, Arkansas.

When Dr. McIlwain heard about the tests in St. Louis, he made arrangements to have one of his rheumatic patients, who was not responding to any other treatments, bathe in the water in Okawville. The man was almost immediately cured. Within a short time, Rudolph Plegge and a local German farmer, who had worked at mineral baths in his home country, opened a small bathhouse. The business prospered locally and was enlarged several times.

At first, the waters were not advertised outside of the immediate area. Okawville, known as Bridgeport until 1871, was not able to handle many visitors. The small town had few places to eat and only a handful of rooms in local boarding houses. They were better suited for overnight stays by traveling salesmen than for visitors making extended visits. It was also hard to reach the town by the rough area roads, but all of that was soon to change.

In 1871, the St. Louis & Southeastern Railroad came to town, followed by several small hotels, a general store, and a saloon. The Okawville House, a boarding house and saloon, opened on North Hanover Street in 1873. Rudolph Plegge dreamed of building a hotel to go along with his bathhouse, but it never got off the ground. It was not until the late 1880s that someone combined a hotel, restaurant, and bathhouse to change the face of the town forever.

In 1884, the wife of Reverend J.F. Schierbaum of Edwardsville, Illinois, came to Okawville to take in the waters. At that time, she was said to have been a hopeless invalid and had visited all the best doctors in St. Louis, who offered her no relief from her pains and ailments. She came to Okawville, bathed in the water, and was restored to perfect health. She was so overjoyed that she convinced her husband and several other ministers in the German Evangelical Church to buy Plegge's business and build a hotel on the site.

By September, plans were made to build the hotel. It was to be a grand structure made of brick that would hold dining rooms, a large kitchen, and 46 rooms. Work was started right away, but the brick design proved to be too costly and the hotel was built from wood instead. The new Mineral Wells Hotel was dedicated on May 28, 1885, with a large crowd of ministers, their congregations, and the general public in attendance. Things got off to a wonderful start and by 1886, business was so good that Reverend Schierbaum realized that he would have to enlarge the hotel before the next season. In those days, the hotel and baths were closed during the late fall and winter months. By the spring of 1887, the building was expanded to accommodate more guests and a new and luxurious bathhouse was also added.

The expansion also included a new engine house that would provide heat. Schierbaum purchased a used threshing machine engine for the engine house but, unfortunately, it exploded, scalding Reverend Schierbaum, C.L. Schulze, and a man named Meier. Schierbaum and Schulze recovered from their injuries, but Meier later died from his wounds. This was the first death to occur at the hotel, but it would not be the last.

As the hotel prospered, the town thrived with it. A new livery stable operated horse-drawn "buses" for many years, bringing passengers and their luggage from the train station to the Mineral Wells. By 1887, there were two separate companies providing this convenience. The new arrivals helped other businesses to also grow and expand. William Friedman, who operated a saloon and dance establishment called Apollo Hall, also opened a recreation area called City Park behind the nearby City Hotel. The park featured nightly band concerts in the summer and was said to be "patronized by best society, as well as the Mineral Wells guests."

In 1890, the Mineral Wells Hotel was sold to J.W. Schreiner of St. Paul, Minnesota. He had earlier journeyed to Illinois to take in the waters and was so relieved of his problems with rheumatism that he offered to buy the hotel and bathhouse. He and his brother, W.A. Schreiner, took over the operation and it began to grow. J.W. Schreiner became deeply involved in the local community and served as the fire chief and, later, as Okawville's mayor.

In 1891, the Schreiner brothers wanted to try and exceed the 9,000 baths they had given during the previous season and so they enlarged the bathhouse building to double its capacity. They had another hugely successful season but then, in November, after the closing of the hotel, disaster struck. During the early morning hours of November 8, a horrific fire swept through the building and reduced the place to a crumbling ruin. The reason for the fire was never discovered, but rumor had it that it was caused by arson. Apparently, someone had borne a grudge against the former owners of the hotel and, not realizing that it had been purchased by the Schreiner brothers, had broken in and had spread coals from the furnace across the wooden floors. No proof of this rumor was ever found, but the fire did not set back the Schreiner brothers for long.

That winter, they began to rebuild. The blackened remains of the old hotel were cleared in December and sand and brick was hauled in for the new foundation. Work was started on the bathhouse first and was mostly completed by February 12. The new structure was two-stories-high with an extra room across the center of the upper floor to contain large, hot and cold water reservoirs. The bathhouse contained 40 rooms, but the planned hotel was going to be much larger. By May, that building had also been raised and was expected to be ready for the June rush. They made it – but just barely. The hotel was completed by June 10 and opened, as one newspaper put it, "and none too soon either, for the irresistible flood of bathers is coming rapidly and taxing the capacity of hotels and boarding houses here."

A grand celebration was held in July that combined the Independence Day holiday and the re-opening of the Mineral Wells. The place was booked to capacity, as were other local hotels and private homes that seized on the popularity of the town's mineral baths to make some extra money renting out sleeping rooms.

In the spring of 1894, the Mineral Wells Hotel changed its name to a variation of the one that the place still has today – the Original Okawville Mineral Springs. It began to appear this way in all its advertising. With the new competition that was coming on the scene, the Schreiners wanted to make sure that everyone knew that their hotel and bathhouse had been the first in town. The ads continued to trumpet the healing benefits of the waters at the Original Springs, which was much better than the inferior qualities of its imitators – even though all the water came from the same source.

In 1898, the owners decided to start bottling the water from the springs. A small bottling operation was started and for many years, water was shipped by wagon and by train into St. Louis, where it was very popular as a medicinal tonic. Bottling continued on a small scale all of the way into the 1980s.

Although the exact date is unknown, at some point around 1900, the Schreiner brothers sold the hotel back to Reverend Schierbaum. There is no record as to why they sold the successful business, but it may have been because of the death of J.W. Schreiner. He vanished from the historical records at about this time, although his brother remained in Okawville for about a year after the sale and then moved to St. Louis in 1901.

Reverend Schierbaum continued the improvements at the Original Springs. In December 1900, he made arrangements with the village board to provide water to sprinkle the town's dirt streets with during the summer months and began enlarging the nearby Schulze Mill pond, which provided water for the boilers at the hotel. He also put in a larger electric generator plant and agreed to furnish Okawville with 40 streetlights over the next 10 years at a cost of $600 per year.

According to newspaper accounts, 1902 was a banner year for Okawville. The bathing season passed with the hotels filled to capacity, the bathhouses busy, and with local businesses profiting from the steady stream of visitors. "Okawville's fame is constantly growing," the newspapers stated, "and the growth of the village is steady and sure, while not in any sense a boom."

In May 1904, Reverend Schierbaum passed away at the hotel after a two-week illness. His death was a crushing blow to the family, but they were determined to keep the hotel running. Several family members pitched in with various aspects of the business, but Anna Schierbaum filled the role of general manager until her death seven years later. The family made sure that improvements continued. More rooms were added, the bathhouse was enlarged again, and an ice cream parlor and a theater operated in the building for a time. In 1910, the owners attempted to open a gambling room in the basement – which seems an odd choice for the family of a minister – but the license was denied by the village board.

Throughout the 1911 season, business at the Original Springs continued to be brisk, but in October of that year, Anna Schierbaum died at the hotel. She had been sick for some time, leaving her son, Ben, who had worked at the hotel as a clerk for years, to keep thing running. After his mother died, Ben officially became the manager.

Around the time that the hotel opened for the 1912 season in the spring, Ben married Alma Schulze, the daughter of family friend C.L. Schulze, who operated a store in the brick building across the street from the hotel. The marriage was apparently a troubled one from the start. While no details remain to explain what caused the issues between them, Alma left Ben in November 1916, soon after the hotel closed for the season. Not having any idea where she had gone, Ben spent several days searching for her, traveling as far away as Shelbyville, Illinois. After about three days, he returned home, dejected, and late one evening went to see her parents at their store across the street. They were unable, or unwilling, to help the young man and he returned to the empty hotel.

It was the last time that anyone saw Ben alive.

Five days later, a traveling salesman, who had been looking for the Ahring Hotel and was directed to the Original Springs by mistake, walked into the lobby of the place. Even though the hotel had been closed for the season, he found the front door unlocked and he called out to see if anyone was around. The front desk was deserted and so he started down the main hallway, past the desk, and the hotel office. After walking a short distance, he noticed a corridor that turned off to the left, which was then a passageway that led to the bathhouse. He took only a few steps when he saw the large pool of dried blood on the floor.

Startled, he looked to see a man, who would later be identified as Ben Schierbaum, slumped against the wall. Blood was sprayed all over the hallway and a good portion of his head was missing. In his lap was a double-barreled shotgun and next to it was a curtain rod that had been used to pull the trigger. Several letters and his wife's photograph were lying on the floor. Nearby, out of reach of the blood, was a letter that had been written to his father-in-law, Mr. Schulze, asking him to call the coroner and his brother, Dan, and then to "forget the whole matter." Ben had taken his own life in despair over losing his beloved Alma.

Sadly, Ben's body had been left unattended in the hotel for days. With Alma gone, no one realized that he was missing. Later, though, a strange story was told. According to a teamster named George Garbs, for days before Ben was discovered, his horses resisted going past the hotel for they apparently sensed that blood had been spilled inside.

Ben's funeral became the largest ever held in Okawville, with over 1,000 people in attendance. He was only 28-years-old at the time of his death. Whatever became of Alma is unknown, but there are some that believe that Ben is still lingering behind at the Original Springs.

The town of Okawville enjoyed another period of great prosperity in the early 1900s. A modern method of transportation for visitors from the train station to the hotels came about when the local livery man, Charles Mohr, purchased a new International truck chassis and had a wagon maker build a body that would carry 16 people. This sounded the death knell for the horse-drawn wagons that had been used in years past. But the event that occurred that really put Okawville on the map took place in 1919 and then was repeated again in 1924 and 1928. These years were the annual conventions of the "Egyptian Hustlers," which were held in various towns in southern Illinois every summer. The Egyptian Hustlers were an organization of traveling salesmen and businessmen. They took their name from "Egypt", the popular name for Southern Illinois and they "hustled" products for mostly St. Louis companies. When they came to town, hotels filled, there were dances and stage shows, carnivals and meetings, and something going on nearly every minute. Crowds and automobiles came from all over the region and nearly 30,000 people packed the town the first year. Later conventions brought a circus, a miniature world's fair, and even airplane rides to Okawville.

In November 1919, A. Sodini purchased the Original Springs from the Schierbaum heirs for $40,000. He planned to make a number of changes to the hotel and to begin operating the place year around, although that never took place. However, he did have the porch extended across the north end of the building and likely aligned the front steps with the front doors, as they appear today. Sodini owned the hotel for only two years.

The years that followed were times of declining business for the Original Springs. The owners struggled and sold out to a corporation that was formed in St. Louis, which also took over the Okawville Light & Ice Plant. The highlights of the next few years were the return of the Egyptian Hustlers in 1924 and a conference that was held in October of that year by Southern Illinois bankers. Business had been tapering off otherwise, though, and a hint of wistfulness emerged in a newspaper report about the July 4 festivities in 1925. The reporter commented that the weekend at the big hotels "looked like old times with the crowds."

In 1926, two St. Louis bank robbers were captured at the Original Springs. They were recognized by an off-duty Madison police officer who was staying there, and he called the St. Louis authorities.

But they would not be the only criminals to come to the Original Springs and were certainly not the most famous. In the middle part of the 1920s, the Original Springs was a frequent meeting place for infamous Southern Illinois gangsters Charlie Birger and the Shelton brothers, Carl, Earl, and Bernie. The men would later declare war on one another and engage in a series of bloody battles and assassinations in the region. However, in 1923, they had joined forces to oppose the Ku Klux Klan, who had moved into the area to crack down on bootleg liquor. It's likely that the hotel managers were customers of the Shelton brothers because it is believed that alcohol was available at the hotel throughout Prohibition. The current owners later discovered a trap door and a hidden room in the lower part of the hotel, where it is believed that liquor was hidden.

In 1928, the Egyptian Hustlers returned to Okawville for the last time, but the event now held little fanfare. The much smaller convention was held at Kugler's Park and while it did offer a carnival, contests, and other attractions, the crowds were certainly not as large as in years past. Interest in the mineral springs seemed to be waning, although the hotels still managed to fill up on weekends.

By late 1929, Community Estate, Inc., which was a St. Louis consortium that owned several hotels in the region, took over the Original Springs. Conrad Paeben, the attorney for the group, became closely affiliated with the hotel. Paeben announced a number of major changes for the hotel. A great deal of remodeling took place over the winter of 1929-1930, but many of the other changes that he proposed never occurred. The plans were created just as America was entering the Great Depression, which no one realized would be as lengthy or as severe as it turned out to be. One change that did take place, though, was the installation of a steam heating plant that would allow each room to be heated. The hotel could finally be open all year around, which had been talked about since its very beginning.

Even in the midst of the Depression, business continued to boom at the Original Springs. Paeben's shameless promotion of the hotel on radio and in print, using the phrase "Where Rheumatism Meets its Waterloo," brought in large crowds from St. Louis and the surrounding area. The hotel was constantly filled and over 3,000 baths were given during the 1930 season, using more than 225,000 gallons of the miraculous water.

Soon, however, the Depression began to take its toll. The Original Springs began trying to cater to the declining incomes of people in the region. An old bathhouse, long abandoned, was renovated into rooms for those who were unable to afford the regular rates at the hotel but who still wanted to take in the waters. Several cottages were also built with this same plan in mind and were located on the property for several years.

By 1933, things were very bleak in Okawville, but also became bleak for Conrad Paeben and Community Estate, Inc. It was discovered that he had embezzled about $14,000 (which was later found to be closer to $76,000) from the accounts of the Original Springs. In January 1933, he attempted suicide by drinking poison in his garage at 4950A Finkman Avenue in St. Louis. His wife found him unconscious in his car and rushed him to the hospital. He survived after several days of treatment – but not for long.

On April 10, 1933, he made another suicide attempt with poison and this time, he was successful. He was found unconscious in a room at the Belcher Hotel at 407 Lucas Avenue in St. Louis. He was rushed to City Hospital but did not survive.

He had become the fourth owner of the hotel to die and the second to die by suicide.

The management of the hotel was taken over by two of its employees, Tom Rogers and Louis Elardin. With the help of W.G. Frank, a local banker, they were able to keep the hotel open.

Tom Rogers, who had come from Chicago and had joined the staff of the hotel in 1931 as the chief clerk and auditor, was both community-minded and an astute businessman. He wrote editorials for the newspaper and gave lectures on improving business and tourism in Okawville. In February 1934, he began a series of Saturday night dances that were well-received by visitors and the community. The dances began at 9:00 p.m. and ended at 1:00 a.m. so that the hotel guests could "retire without disturbance." After the dance ended, the club rooms were opened for those who wanted to stay awhile longer. Beverages were also served and there was no specification as to what those beverages were, although advertising for the events assured everyone that "nothing will be permitted that would offend the most particular or be objectionable to any citizen of the community." Later that spring, the Original Springs Orchestra also began providing musical entertainment and beer was free for those who paid a 45-cent admission. A woman from St. Louis was hired to direct the orchestra and later, a floor show was also added. By July, the hotel was reporting record crowds on weekends.

Rogers continued to promote the hotel over the next several years and also became involved with the local Democratic Party. Meetings were frequently held at the Original Springs, as well as victory celebrations. In the spring of 1938, Rogers came up with another idea to drum up business at the hotel and opened the "Okaw Pleasureland" amusement park across the street. A dance floor was installed, and music was often provided by Gottleib and his German Band, the Dixie Blue Boys, the King City Wildcats, and others. Pleasureland also featured a horseshoe pit, ping pong tables, a croquet court, a softball and baseball diamond, pool tables, outdoor bowling, canoe rentals on Washington Lake, and more. Pleasureland lasted for exactly two seasons and then closed. The United States was still not out of the Depression, and even though things had started to look better in 1937, a recession had set in, making things even gloomier than they had been before. Rogers had given it a valiant effort, though, using radio and newspaper advertising to draw people to Okawville, but it met with only limited success.

In 1939, Rogers began diversifying his interests. He formed the Original Springs Dairy Co. and built a cheese factory. He encouraged local farmers to produce more Grade C milk, which was used in making cheese but not for bottling. It was not necessary for them to have expensive equipment for this type of milk and many of them even bought more cows to meet the demand at the new cheese factory. The company grew rapidly in its early years and expanded several times. It lasted until 1956.

Rogers also dabbled in farming and hog raising at his Original Springs Farms. Louis Elardin, who had once shared management duties with Rogers at the hotel, had gone into the tavern business, but lost all his money. He became an employee of the farm and Elardin and another permanent hotel resident and employee, Tony Hilleke, farmed with old equipment on Rogers' acreage and did routine tasks around the hotel. Both men managed to outlive Rogers and spent their lives at the hotel, even after a later change in management. In the 1940s, Rogers seemed to be more interested in his other business pursuits than in the hotel business and he did little to promote the Original Springs. He was content to develop his dairy and to raise hogs on his farm north of town.

Despite Rogers' waning interest, the hotel boasted record crowds on weekends. During the week, it was another story, though. World War II was the focus of most people's attention at that time and various shortages kept people close to home. Many of the rooms at the Original Springs were not opened and the corridors and dining room remained mostly empty.

As time went on, Tom Rogers became known for his increasingly strange and eccentric behavior. He lost interest in both the farm and the hotel. He seemed to be content with the few bathers who came each year and gave up on trying to promote the place. He took to wandering the empty corridors of the hotel each night, perhaps remembering the glory days of the past. Then, one morning in March 1962, he was discovered lying dead in one of the upstairs rooms. It is now Suite 350 at the hotel. A search for heirs was started, but none were ever found. His estate was settled in October of that year and the hotel was sold to Albert and Doris Krohne.

When the Krohne family took over the place, it had not been changed or updated in years. The only modern convenience in the rooms was a single light bulb that hung from a cord in the center of each room's ceiling. Communal bathrooms were located on each floor. With funds available for renovations, the Krohnes went to work. Some of the rooms were equipped with sinks and toilets, although usually just because a section of the room had been partitioned off. For several years, there were three categories of rooms to let at the hotel, good, better, and best. The good rooms had no facilities. The better rooms had a sink and a toilet, and the best rooms had showers. Tubs were later added to the "deluxe" rooms and priced accordingly.

Unfortunately, the renovations were slowed in the summer of 1963 when Albert Krohne was critically injured in a head-on collision with a truck. Having been a carpenter and building contractor before buying the hotel, he had been doing a lot of the work himself and underwent a lengthy recuperation. Among his injuries, he suffered a badly shattered knee, which had to have a metal pin inserted into it. He would later credit the mineral baths with helping him to regain his mobility.

In early 1965, the Boiler Room Lounge and Restaurant was opened to the general public. Before this, the kitchen had only been available to hotel guests. There were dances and live music on the weekends and it became a very popular nightspot. In 1972, an indoor swimming pool was installed.

The Krohne family remained at the Original Springs until the summer of 1974, when they sold out to Robert and John Schrage, who stayed for only two years. The Krohnes bought the hotel back from them in 1976. More additions were made to the Original Springs in the 1980s. A section of rooms, as well as banquet rooms, were added to the hotel in 1980. A recreation area was added around the pool, attracting more customers.

But then disaster occurred in 1988. On December 30, the hotel was closed for the Christmas holidays and only a small maintenance staff remained on the premises. A defective electrical outlet in the bar started a fire that burned through the walls and climbed all the way to the roof before it was noticed. Several older rooms were wiped out and many others were damaged. The fire department arrived quickly on the scene, but the firefighters were forced to cause more damage by cutting holes in the roof and knocking out windows in order to keep the fire from spreading. It took several weeks to clean up the damage and re-open the hotel. Renovations after the fire turned out to be beneficial to the business. Fire-damaged rooms were enlarged, walls were removed, and were remodeled to make room for larger beds, more furniture, and television sets, which would have never fit into the small rooms of the past.

The last change in ownership for the Original Springs occurred in May 1990 when the Krohnes sold the hotel to the present owners,

Don and Mary Rennegarbe. Mary had started working as a waitress at the hotel in 1978, never realizing that she would be the owner of the building someday.

After they took over the building, Don and Mary started working to restore the building to its former glory. That work continues today, keeping the hotel open and the bathing facilities open and welcoming to the public.

The Original Springs has weathered fires, the Great Depression, suicides, changes in management, two world wars, and the changing tastes of the American people. Through it all, the hotel stands as a monument to the past. Even today, people come from all over the region to take in the healing Okawville waters and to soak up some of the ambience of days gone by.

Healing waters and good food are not the only things that people come to the Original Springs for, though – many come looking for ghosts. And thanks to the unusual history of the hotel, and the colorful parade of characters who have passed through it, ghosts are something that many of them find.

Don and Mary heard the rumors and stories almost as soon as they took over the aging hotel. Staff members and desk clerks started to tell of strange noises that they heard in the building at night, including pacing footsteps in otherwise empty hallways, figures that were sometimes seen out of the corner of the eye, doors that opened and closed by themselves, the tinkling sound of old-time music that echoed in the corridors, and as one of the employees told me, the constant feeling "of someone watching you."

I have been visiting the Original Springs since the early 2000's and each trip is different from the last one. However, stories that I have collected from staff members and guests over that time have been eerily similar – or at least involve some of the same ghosts. One of them, a spectral woman in a white dress, has been spotted on a balcony that spans the pool area. Guests and employees alike describe the woman wearing a long, high-waisted dress and a hat from the early 1900s.

She has also been seen in other places in the building. One night, the front desk clerk heard a door open on the old main corridor. Glancing out, she saw a man in pajamas come out of the hotel's "Civil War Room," named for its décor. She recognized the man as having checked into the hotel with his wife a few hours before. The man stepped out into the hallway and looked around in bewilderment. Finally, with a puzzled look on his face, he walked up to the desk and asked if a woman had been seen in the hallway. When he was told that no one had been in the corridor, he explained that he had been lying in bed with his wife when he began to have the uncomfortable feeling that someone was watching him. He finally sat up and looked around the darkened room to see a woman standing near the end of the bed. She was wearing a long, white dress and had on a large hat that hid part of her face. She stood there for a moment, looking at him, and then she turned and walked toward the door. She never hesitated before passing right through it. The man refused to believe his eyes and he ran to the door and looked out into the corridor, believing that he would see a flesh and blood person walking down the hall – but it was empty.

It should perhaps be noted that this room – and the corridor outside of it – is located very close to the short hallway where Ben Schierbaum committed suicide in 1916. It has been suggested that perhaps the woman in white is Alma Schierbaum, the vanished wife of the unfortunate man. Has she returned to the Original Springs in death to atone for the guilt she feels over Ben's death?

Strange incidents and eerie sightings continue today. Many of the staff members at the hotel refuse to go upstairs and into the older wing at night. They have often heard strange noises in some of the locked rooms, as well as footsteps tapping in the hallways. One particular area that most find unsettling is a section off the second-floor corridor that is currently being converted from three small rooms into one large one. It was in one of the old rooms where a guest was staying one night and asked to be moved to another floor. He claimed that he heard whispering voices and felt uncomfortable cold spots moving into bed with him. Coincidence or not – one of these rooms was where former owner Tom Rogers was found dead back in March 1962.

Who haunts the Original Springs Hotel? Could the figures seen here, as well as the odd sounds that are heard, simply be memories from the past, repeating themselves over and over again? Or could there be conscious spirits from the glory days of the hotel, simply refusing to cross over to the other side? Might Ben Schierbaum, Tom Rogers, or other characters from the building's history still be lingering here?

Any of these things seem possible and perhaps all of them are. The Original Springs will continue to be a place that draws both the living and the dead to its door.

19. HOTEL DEL CORONADO
SAN DIEGO, CALIFORNIA

The Hotel Del Coronado in San Diego is one of the most beautiful hotels in the country – and some say, one of the most haunted. And I'd have to agree. It's long been one of my favorite spots with its elegant Victorian design, sandy beaches, and colorful history. The story of the resident ghost has long been an integral part of the hotel's past and it involves a young woman who checked in there on Thanksgiving Day, 1892 – and never checked out.

But that young woman does not haunt this hotel alone.

In the middle 1880s, all Southern California was in the middle of a real estate boom. To draw people to the San Diego area, railroad magnate Elisha Babcock and Hampton L. Story of the Story and Clark Piano Co. decided to build a luxury, seaside resort on Coronado Island, which was just offshore in San Diego Bay. The new hotel would be located on the island's southernmost point, along a wide sandy beach.

In those days, the island could only be reached by boat, so this added an air of exclusivity to the location.

Work on the hotel began on 28-acres of beachfront property in March 1887. The original plans called for just under 400 rooms so when it opened, it was the largest resort hotel in the world. Today, it's even bigger. With additions that have been made over the years, there are now 679 rooms, plus an additional 79 cottages and villas. It's now far beyond what the builders could have ever imagined.

The suites in the original structure, now known as the Victorian Building, were luxurious and the hotel was the first on the West Coast to be wired for electricity. There was a tea garden, tennis courts, and a saltwater pool, even though the ocean was just steps away. Perhaps the most outstanding feature of the hotel was the 23,500-square-foot main dining room, with its high, arched, pine-wood paneled ceiling. The entire exterior of the resort was painted pristine white and was capped by red roofs.

The cost of the construction far exceeded the initial estimates. It turned out that all the necessary materials had to be brought from outside the area, including lumber and the workers. Plus, fresh water had to be pumped over to the island from the city. The hotel was started with the best of intentions, but a real estate bust that occurred late in the construction threatened to sink the entire endeavor. At the last minute, though, sugar mogul John D. Speckels offered a welcome infusion of cash. By 1890, he had bought out all the other partners.

The hotel opened to great fanfare in February 1888 and its popularity was well-established before the 1920s. It already had hosted Presidents Harrison, McKinley, Taft, and Wilson. The hotel was later visited by Franklin D. Roosevelt, Dwight D. Eisenhower, John F. Kennedy, Lyndon B. Johnson, Richard Nixon, Gerald Ford, Jimmy Carter, Ronald Reagan, George H. W. Bush, Bill Clinton, George W. Bush, and Barack Obama.

By the 1920s Hollywood's stars and starlets discovered that "the Del," as it was often called, was the "in place" to stay. Many celebrities made their way south to party during the era of Prohibition and used the Hotel Del Coronado as their personal playground. Tom Mix, Tallulah Bankhead, Rudolph Valentino, Charlie Chaplin, Mary

Pickford, Mae West, and Ramón Navarro were a few of the many actors who stayed at the hotel during weekend getaways. Other notables have included Charles Lindbergh, Thomas Edison, Vincent Price, Babe Ruth, and L. Frank Baum, who is said to have used the Queen Anne-style turrets as inspiration for the description of the Emerald City of Oz. The hotel also became the backdrop for many films, most notably the 1959 Marilyn Monroe, Jack Lemmon, and Tony Curtis movie, *Some Like it Hot.*

During World War II, the hotel was used to house Navy pilots and the families of officers. By the end of the war, the neglected hotel had started to age, and while millions were spent to refurbish it, a new owner in 1963 planned to tear it down. But he changed his mind and remodeled and expanded it instead.

It remains today as one of the most beautiful resorts on the West Coast – and a one that is home to several ghosts. The iridescent eyes of a woman have startled many guests who stay in Room 3312. Many have awakened in the night to find those eyes staring at them from the end of the bed. Other visitors have experienced flickering lights, had the windows open and close by themselves, have seen the curtains move when there is no breeze blowing into the room, have heard unnatural sounds within the walls, or had the bed shake beneath them. Others have only felt a general restlessness and anxiety, but it's been bad enough that they have asked to switch rooms.

The room is so haunted that its strangeness even filters out into the corridor outside. Occasionally, passersby have seen unusual lights shining under the door. In the summer months, maintenance workers have found it almost impossible to keep the room's window screens from falling off. There is also something about the room that causes the lightbulb at the bottom of the nearest stairwell to burn out after only one or two days and, requiring its replacement.

It has been said that Room 3312 – which was once numbered 502 – was the room where original owner Elisha Babcock kept his mistress. Legend has it that she became pregnant and committed suicide soon after. Of course, this story is only a rumor that has never been confirmed because shortly before the police arrived to investigate the death, her body mysteriously disappeared.

Room 3502 is another haunted suite with a ghostly story that involved a VIP guest. During a visit to the hotel by Vice President George H.W. Bush in the 1980s, one of the agents from his Secret Service details was assigned to the room. During the course of a single evening, the agent experienced moving drapes, cold spots, and a strange light that manifested in the room. At one point, he called down to the front desk to complain about the loud talking and the incessant stomping about by guests on the floor above him – only to be told there was no one in the room. When he later awoke to see an apparition in the room, he finally asked to be moved somewhere else.

The staff was happy to do so because so many of them have had their own encounters with phantom guests. One of the hotel's first caretakers has been seen in the dining room, apparently testing the floor with his cane. A Victorian-era woman has been seen dancing in the ballroom. The ghost of a very sick young girl who was rushed to the hospital in 1950 has returned to roam the hallways, looking for the doll she left behind. There are also the ghosts of a little boy and girl – their identities unknown – who have been seen throughout the property. They are spotted in period clothing, laughing and playing or running up and down the stairs.

Many employees have spied a dark form moving behind the locked doors of lobby shops after hours. One shop manager arrived to discover that all the books on a lower shelf near the cash register had been moved around. Some were on their sides, while others had been scattered on the floor and were lying open and facedown. Staff members had even seen souvenirs fly off the shelves in some of the stores.

There are many spirits at the Hotel Del Coronado, but none of them are as famous as the ghost of Kate Morgan. She arrived at the hotel in 1892 and she has never left. Hotel guests and employees believe that the majority of the paranormal events that occur at the hotel can be connected to Kate. Witnesses report flickering lights, dramatic shifts in room temperatures, odd scents, unexplained voices, the sound of strange footsteps, and objects that move about by themselves. Some have even seen Kate Morgan herself.

Who was this mysterious woman and how did she end up spending eternity at the Hotel Del Coronado?

On November 24, 1892 – Thanksgiving evening – a pale, pretty women in her mid-20's walked into the luxuriously furnished lobby of the Hotel Del Coronado and asked for a room. She was later described by the coroner as being five-foot, six-inches, with a fair complexion, two moles on her left cheek, black hair, and brown eyes. During her stay, hotel employees – many of whom had frequent interactions with Kate – reported that she had appeared ill and very unhappy.

A woman traveling alone in those days, especially with no luggage, was frowned upon and viewed with suspicion, but the young woman told the desk clerk that she'd been traveling with her brother, Dr. M.C. Anderson. He had gotten off the train in Orange but would be arriving soon. She had no suitcases because he had been holding the claim tickets.

The sympathetic clerk believed her and registered her under the name Mrs. Lottie A. Bernard of Detroit. She was shown to Room 302 on the north side of the building. Over the course of the next few days, she frequently asked the staff about her brother's arrival, but he had not checked in and had left no message for her.

Meanwhile, it had become clear to the staff that the woman was ill. Several employees, including the pharmacist who ran the hotel's drugstore, suggested that she visit the hotel physician. But she assured them that she knew what was wrong with her – she suffered from neuralgia, a sharp, shooting pain that follows the path of a nerve. It's frequently due to irritation or damage to the nerve, such as the pain that continues after a case of shingles. She explained that her brother would treat her as soon as he arrived.

Later, though, when the hotel manager pressed her further, she confessed that she had stomach cancer. That, she said, was the source of her pain. The manager also discreetly asked her how she planned to pay for her stay, and she told him to wire G.L. Allen in Hamburg, Iowa. Whoever that person was, he did send the money. In fact, it arrived by wire on the morning that her body was discovered.

Despite her poor health, "Lottie" took a trip to downtown San Diego on November 28, where she purchased a handgun and some ammunition. That night, she was seen by other guests on the hotel veranda, looking out across the bay.

It was the last time she was seen alive.

Five days after she had checked in, a hotel electrician found her body on a small set of stone steps leading down to the beach. She had a gunshot wound to her head, which the San Diego County Coroner later determined was self-inflicted.

A search of her hotel room revealed no personal belongings. In fact, there was nothing to identify "the beautiful stranger," except the name she used when she registered: Lottie A. Bernard, from Detroit. After her death, police sent a sketch of her face and information about her death to newspapers and police stations around the country, in the hope that someone could shed light on "the dark mystery surrounding the suicide of the unknown girl at the Coronado Hotel."

Eventually, "Lottie Bernard" was identified as Kate Morgan, originally from Iowa. She had been born there as Kate Farmer in 1865 and on December 30, 1885, she had married a man named Tom Morgan. Reportedly, Morgan was a gambler, who may have made his living gambling on the railroad.

At the time of her death, Kate was employed as a maid by the L.A. Grant family of Los Angeles, working under the name of Kate Logan. She had told the Grants and her co-workers that she had fled from her husband, who was a degenerate gambler. Other than that, she never talked about her past.

On November 23, she had told the Grants that she was going to take a one-day trip to San Diego. When she didn't return, they contacted the police, who in turn connected her disappearance with the newspaper reports about the "beautiful stranger" at the Hotel Del Coronado.

Why had Kate gone to San Diego? And what was the true story of her illness? No autopsy was ever performed. Some answers may have been in the large stack of papers that Kate burned in the fireplace in her hotel room before she killed herself, but we'll never known. It turned out that there were no unclaimed suitcases at the train station, so there were no clues there.

As to the source of her illness, an anonymous "prominent physician" suggested in the *San Diego Union* that the early symptoms of pregnancy were almost identical to stomach cancer. His conclusion was that Kate had come to the hotel to use medications found in her room – including camphor and quinine pills – to try and induce a miscarriage. There may have been something to this suggestion. After the inquest, a gentleman came forward to say that he had seen Kate arguing with a man on a train en route to San Diego. The witness said that the man disembarked before reaching San Diego, and Kate continued to the Hotel Del Coronado by herself, where she eventually took her own life. Could this mysterious man have been the person who had gotten her pregnant, and then, after a final quarrel, abandoned her?

Given the national notoriety of the case and with no family to object, Kate's body was placed on display at the local mortuary, Johnson and Company, where is was kept while officials decided what to do with her remains. Eventually, Kate was buried in Mount Hope Cemetery, just east of downtown San Diego.

But her spirit has never left the Hotel Del Coronado.

Since her death, paranormal activity has been reported in the room Kate stayed in during her 1892 visit – Room 3327 --- and in other areas of the hotel. She has been encountered literally hundreds of times over the years, by a wide variety of guests and staff members.

It is said that personal items will often go missing in the room and then turn up somewhere else. Guests have awakened in the morning to find the room has been ransacked, as if by intruders, with all their belongings picked up and tossed around – even though the room has been locked all night. They have heard the sounds of disembodied footsteps in the dark and smelled a flowery perfume that comes and goes with no explanation. Sudden drops in temperature are common, as is having the linens suddenly jerked off the bed. The television and ceiling fan turn on and off by themselves and occasionally, guests will return to the room after dinner to find the faucets have been turned on in the sink and bathtub.

And sometimes, Kate herself is seen. A pretty, dark-haired woman in late nineteenth century clothing will sometimes be spotted in the middle of the night. Or if not seen, she still visits anyway. Guests will enter the room and find an impression of a person was left behind on the bed. During one particularly active period a few years ago, the housekeeping staff would only clean the room if they did so in pairs.

Kate doesn't always stay in her room. During her time at the hotel in 1892, she made liberal use of the lobby, veranda, and dining hall. Her ghost continues to follow that same route. She has been encountered in the third-floor hallway, in the garden, on the beach, and on the stone staircase where she ended her life.

Even when she does not appear, some guests seem able to sense her. They will occasionally say that they feel as though someone is watching them. Others report feeling overwhelmed by hopelessness and despair when they walk down the stairs where Kate's body was found.

Kate Morgan is, without a doubt, the most enduring spirit of this grand hotel and she continues to leave behind an impression on this place more than 125 years after her tragic death.

20. THE STANLEY HOTEL
ESTES PARK, COLORADO

There are few towns as beautiful as Estes Park, Colorado. Located in Northern Colorado, just outside the glorious Rocky Mountain National Park, the town offers breathtaking scenery, every kind of outdoor activity that you could ever want, and, of course, the Stanley Hotel, the inspiration for Stephen King's bestseller, *The Shining*.

The hotel was built in the mountains of Colorado in 1909 as a grand summer resort that catered to wealthy visitors from the East Coast. It had a storied history even before Stephen King set foot on the property, once hosting guests like "Unsinkable" Molly Brown and Theodore Roosevelt. Today, tourists flock to the hotel to take a tour, have a drink in the lounge, have a fantastic dinner, or spend the night in one of the hotel's historic rooms.

And, naturally, there are those of us who come for the ghosts.

The Georgian-style hotel in Estes Park opened its doors on July 4, 1909, the brainchild of American inventor and businessman Freelan Oscar Stanley who, with his twin brother, Francis, was the inventor of the steam-powered automobile, the Stanley Steamer.

Freelan and Francis had been born in Kingfield, Maine, on June 1, 1849, two of seven children of farmer Solomon Stanley, and his wife, Apphia. At the age of nine, the boys started their first business together, refining and selling maple sugar. They had wanted to buy wool for new school suits and books. At eleven, their great-uncle, Liberty Stanley, who had raised their father as his own son, taught them the art of violin-making. By the age of 16, Freelan had completed three instruments. He continued making them as a hobby for the rest of his life.

In 1870, the brothers started their college careers, intent on becoming teachers, but Francis dropped out and left to pursue work as a photographer. Freelan continued his schooling at Hebron Academy and then at Bowdoin College. After that, he accepted a position as the headmaster of a high school in Mechanic Falls, Maine, where he met Flora Jane Tileston, a teacher and skilled pianist.

Freelan's life might never have changed if something terrible had not occurred in 1881 – he contracted tuberculosis. He soon came to believe that his survival depended upon having a more active life, and he left teaching to start his own business, opening the Stanley Practical Drawing Set factory. Unfortunately, his new business was ruined in a fire which destroyed the whole of his investment only a year later, in 1882.

After leaving school, Francis had married Augusta May Walker and had opened a portrait studio. He had started experimenting with new techniques and quickly became passionate about the field. Following the fire at his brother's factory, Francis suggested that the two work together to create a new photographic product. By 1885, the brothers had established the Stanley Dry Plate Company in Lewiston, Maine. They changed the industry by convincing photographers to change to their system and leave the wet-plate process for developing behind. The brothers quickly amassed a small fortune and, in 1890, they moved their business to Watertown, Massachusetts, and bought homes in nearby Newton. They later sold the company to George Eastman of Eastman Kodak.

Located next door to the Stanley dry-plate factory in Watertown was a bicycle factory owned by Sterling Elliott. Francis quickly became fascinated with the new bicycle craze and tried to get his wife to try it out. But when Augusta fell off the bicycle that he bought for her she swore she'd never ride again. He promised her that he would build something safer that the two of them could ride together. Francis began building an automobile out of a wagon and bicycle parts from the factory next door. After considering several ideas, he came to believe that steam power for the automobile was the most practical option. In 1897, the brothers took the new car to the Boston Auto Show, so impressing the crowds that they were soon producing autos as the Stanley Motor Carriage Company. From that moment on, Freelan Stanley was also committed to his brother's passion for motor cars. In 1899, they sold the company for $250,000 in cash, but the new owners later separated, and the company fell apart.

The Stanley brothers had not lost interest in automobiles, however. They took part in a number of publicity stunts for which Stanley automobiles received much notoriety. In August 1899, Freelan and Flora Stanley became the first of many motorists to reach the top of Mt. Washington, the tallest peak in New England. In November of the same year, Freelan gave William McKinley a tour of Washington D.C. in a Stanley automobile, marking the first time a sitting U.S. President had ridden in a car.

Disappointed that their original company no longer existed, they decided to start over again from scratch. They improved on their old designs and resumed production of the new, improved Stanley Motor Carriage.

Then, in 1903, at the age of 54, Freelan's tuberculosis returned. His prognosis was so bad that his doctor told him that he'd likely be dead within a year. The most highly recommended treatment of the day was fresh, dry air with lots of sunlight and a hearty diet. He decided to go west in hopes that the climate might prolong his life.

He and Flora arrived in Denver, Colorado, in March and after a stay at the famous Brown Palace Hotel, Freelan arranged a consultation with Dr. Charles Bonney, the preeminent American expert on tuberculosis. He recommended that the couple rent a house in the city and look for improvement. But Freelan didn't get better. Dr. Bonney then suggested a summer in the mountains, so Freelan and

Flora left for Estes Park, where they rented a cabin. Over the course of the warm season, Stanley's health improved dramatically. Impressed by the beauty of the valley and grateful for his recovery, he decided to buy some land there and build a summer home.

In late summer 1903, he acquired property and with the help of an English architect, work was started on a cottage with four bedrooms, gracious living areas and a modern kitchen, so that Flora could entertain summer guests. Freelan, whose primary leisure activities involved billiards, violins, and steam cars, designed a basement with space for a billiard table and a detached garage with a violin workshop and a turntable, so that the steam car could exit frontwise rather than in reverse. The front door opened onto a veranda facing south with a view across the Estes Valley towards Long's Peak, which Dr. Bonney pronounced as the perfect place to take in the fresh mountain air.

By 1907, Freelan had recovered from his illness, but he and Flora had become so enamored with Colorado that they decided to stay. But not content with the rustic accommodations, lazy pastimes, and relaxed social scene of their new home, Stanley resolved to turn Estes Park into a resort town. He purchased land that had once been part of a private hunting reserve and began construction on the Stanley Hotel.

Many thought his dream to build a resort hotel in the mountains was foolhardy. At that time, there was no railroad linking Denver and Estes Park, and it was a difficult journey on unpaved roads. To prove that guests would have no problem reaching the hotel, Freelan made one of his publicity stunt trips by motorcar up to the resort.

Freelan designed the hotel himself and paid for the construction with cash. To power the new hotel, Stanley constructed the Fall River Hydro-Plant which, consequentially, brought electricity to Estes Park for the first time. Upon opening, the hotel had 48 guest rooms, each pair sharing one bathroom. It had a fully electric kitchen and steam laundry, a hydraulic elevator, and running water, electric lights, and telephones throughout. Built only for seasonal use, though, heat wasn't installed at the hotel until 1979.

Near the main structure, Freelan built a Concert Hall complete with a Steinway Grand Piano as a gift for Flora. During the day, guests at the Stanley enjoyed golf, bowling, horseback-riding, and motor excursions. At night, guests enjoyed formal dinners, concerts, and lighter entertainment such as billiards. The steam car played a pivotal role in the operation of the Stanley Hotel. To transport visitors to and from the hotel, Freelan created a 12-seat model, which was thereafter marketed as the "Mountain Wagon," and it became popular at other resorts in the West.

Freelan's presence – along with the construction of the hotel – encouraged the town of Estes Park to incorporate in 1917. In the years that followed, Freelan organized and partially funded the paving of local roads, gifted property to the community, helped establish schools and hockey rinks, and played a large role in the creation of the Rocky Mountains National Park.

By 1926, Flora's eyesight had deteriorated to the point that she was no longer comfortable with traveling back east to Massachusetts. Freelan decided that it was time to retire and to sell the hotel. He sold it to the Stanley Corporation, a private company established to manage Freelan's assets in Estes Park. Without Stanley's fortune to pad the annual budget, though, the corporation soon filed for bankruptcy. Stanley purchased the hotel back at a low price and passed it off again in 1930 to fellow auto and hotel magnate Roe Emery of Denver, who remained the owner until 1947.

In 1939, Flora suffered a stroke and died in their Estes Park home. Without his wife – and his beloved hotel – Freelan didn't seem to have anything left to live for. He left Colorado and returned to Massachusetts, where he died from heart failure on October 2, 1940.

It was the end of an era in Estes Park and the loss of a man who had changed everything about the community and created a hotel that would become a legend.

From the day the hotel opened, Freelan Stanley planned to cater to the rich and famous. Even during the Depression, when business was slow, Stanley did not allow guests who didn't meet his standards. As a result of its exclusivity, the hotel became a popular spot for celebrities, millionaires, and industrialists. Among the first visitors were Harvey Firestone, J.C. Penney, John Phillip Sousa, "Unsinkable" Molly Brown, and Theodore Roosevelt. As standards loosened up, the Hollywood crowd also dropped in. Stars like Cary Grant, Doris Day, Bob Dylan, and others came for the weekend.

And then on October 30, 1974, the hotel was visited by a then little-known writer named Stephen King, who truly put the Stanley Hotel on the map.

At that time, King had just started to enjoy his first success with his book, *Carrie*. He had written another *'Salem's Lot*, but was looking for ideas for his next title. His publisher was concerned that he would be pigeonholed in the horror genre, but that didn't worry King. The stories in his first two books had taken place in his native Maine, so he planned to set his next book somewhere else. He spread a map out on the table, put down his finger, and found himself pointing at Colorado. So, he and his wife, Tabitha, gathered up their two kids and moved to Boulder. After being there for about six months, they wanted to have a weekend without the kids and drove to Estes Park and the Stanley Hotel.

They arrived at the hotel on the night before Halloween, unaware that the hotel was going to close for the winter season the next day. They were the only two guests in the place and spent the night in Room 217. They had dinner that night in the Cascades Restaurant and were the only patrons. Their table was the only one that was set, and there was only one dish available on the menu.

After dinner, Tabitha went back to the room, but Stephen wandered the hallways of the sprawling hotel. With no other guests and no activities going on, he must have heard every creak, groan, and imaginary whisper that the old resort had to offer.

But it was the dream that really inspired the story to come.

Soon after falling asleep, Stephen had an unsettling nightmare about this three-year-old son, Joe, being chased down the hotel corridor by a fire hose. After he woke up, he got out of bed, lit a cigarette, sat down in a chair by the window, and looked out at the mountains. By the time he had finished with his cigarette, he had the bare bones of an idea about a haunted hotel that closed for the winter – a book that would become *The Shining*.

Probably every reader of this book knows the story, but if you don't, you may want to skip the next paragraph.

A former teacher turned writer and recovering alcoholic with anger issues named Jack Torrance takes the position of winter caretaker at the Overlook Hotel. He brings along his wife, Wendy, and his son, Danny, to the hotel, which is completely cut off from civilization after the first snow. Danny is no ordinary little boy. He has a psychic ability that Dick Halloran, the cook at the Overlook who meets Danny just as the hotel is closing for the winter, calls "the shining." The hotel turns out to be infested with sinister spirits and when they are unable to take control of Danny, they possess Jack, who then attempts to kill his wife and son. Danny uses his abilities to call for help and Dick Halloran returns to save them. They narrowly escape just as the hotel is destroyed in a boiler explosion.

The book became a tremendous bestseller and is still considered a favorite by many King fans (including myself). In 1980, the book was adapted into a film by Stanley Kubrick, starring Jack Nicholson, but it was not filmed at the Stanley. Years later, in 1997, though, the Stanley was transformed into the Overlook for the filming of the 1997 television mini-series version of *The Shining* – and we'll come back to that in a bit.

It was *The Shining* that truly made the Stanley famous, but it turns out that literary and cinematic ghosts are not the only kind that haunt the hallways of the hotel – there are real spirits here, too. However, none of them are as sinister as the ones created by the mind of Stephen King.

The most frequently seen ghost is that of Freelan Stanley. He often makes appearances in the lobby or in the billiards parlor, which was his favorite room in the hotel. Some of the bartenders have reported seeing him pass through the lounge, but any attempt to catch up with him as he walks across the room ends in failure. He simply disappears.

In the ballroom, staff members and guests alike have heard phantom music or have seen the piano in the room play by itself. Even with no one sitting on the bench, the keys have been seen to clearly move, accompanied by musical notes. Usually, though, the music is heard from the corridor and it stops when someone enters the room. The spectral pianist has never been seen but its assumed that the spirit is that of Flora Stanley, who loved to play for guests at the hotel. The grand piano had been a gift from her adoring husband and its thought that she still continues to play for both Freelan and the guests in the afterlife.

The ballroom also features another haunting that is straight out of the pages of *The Shining*. Security personnel, as well as workers in the adjoining kitchen, have reported hearing the noise of a party in full swing when the room is actually empty. There is, however, no reports of a phantom bartender named "Lloyd."

Unexplained noises and footsteps have been heard throughout the building. They occur most often on the fourth floor. When the hotel first opened, adult guests stayed on the first three floors of the building, while children and their nannies stayed on the fourth floor. Today, guests who stay on this floor are often disturbed by the sound of children laughing and playing in the hallway. There have been many reports of guests who have called down to the front desk to complain, only to be told there are no children on that floor. When they look out into the corridor for themselves, they find the hall to be empty and silent.

In some of the rooms on the fourth floor, children's handprints sometimes appear on the mirrors. Guests have returned to their rooms and discovered that their belongings have been moved around. Some rooms are more active than others – like 401, where children have been heard eerily singing in the closet. The windows in that room sometimes open by themselves. In Room 407, lights turn on and off and the toilet has a habit of flushing on its own.

The most active room on the fourth floor is 418. Guests who attempt to sleep in that room are often awakened by the sound of children in the middle of the night. Some have heard children in the room from outside, even when the room is empty. Housekeepers have entered the room and found the imprint of bodies on the bed, as if someone had been sitting or lying on it, even though the door was locked.

The apparition of a man has been seen in rooms all over the hotel at night and sometimes guests claim they have awakened to find him looking down at them. When discovered, the ghost rushes to the closet and vanishes.

The most famous haunted room in the hotel, though, is Room 217, where Stephen and Tabitha King stayed during their visit. In his book, King created a Room 217 in which a malevolent ghost lingered in the bathtub and tried to injure Danny. In real life, the room is haunted by a much more benevolent spirit. She has been dubbed "Miss Wilson," and legend states that she was a maid working in this room during the early years of the hotel when a gas explosion occurred. She survived but was badly injured. After her recovery, she was given a job at the Stanley for life. She remained in the hotel's service until she died of an aneurism 40 years later – in Room 217.

Apparently, she has never left this room. Guests will often find their covers turned down on the bed or their luggage unpacked and suitcases put away, even though housekeeping has never entered the room. Sometimes, Miss Wilson feels mischievous and hides things or pulls the blankets off the bed in the middle of the night.

Occasionally, skeptics who stay at the Stanley Hotel are turned into believers, which is exactly what happened during the filming of the 1997 mini-series version of *The Shining*, which took place at the Stanley.

Stephen King, who had never been happy with the Kubrick adaptation of his book, wrote the screenplay for the mini-series and director Mick Garris, who had enjoyed earlier success with King with the 1994 mini-series of *The Stand*, was hired to direct. A decision was made to film on location at the hotel that had initially inspired the book, so ABC-Television took over the Stanley for six months in January 1996.

The mini-series starred Steven Webber as Jack Torrance and Rebecca De Mornay as his long-suffering wife, Wendy. Courtland Mead, who was 9-years-old at the time of the filming, played Danny.

Stephen King made a cameo appearance as one of the ghosts--the leader of an undead orchestra.

During the filming, the entire cast and crew stayed at the hotel, and they soon discovered that the spooks were not only in the series. "We had people moving out of the rooms," producer Mark Carliner later said. "We had to relocate a number of our crew. The hotel makes sounds. It creaks. The hotel is alive."

Steven Weber frequently heard the stories and it became the source of gossip with the crew, although everyone did their best to downplay the haunting around Courtland Mead.

"I did hear several macho, butch grip-types come downstairs shaken after a night's sleep," Weber said, "saying, 'Hey, man! Something went through me last night.'" He laughed about how those "beefy members of the crew whined like babies."

Even in the fictional world of Stephen King, real-life spirits managed to intrude and became a lot scarier than what could be found in the pages of a book. It proves once again that truth is stranger than fiction.

BIBLIOGRAPHY

Bailey, Lynn R. – *Bisbee: Queen of the Copper Camps*, Westernlore Press, Tucson, AZ; 2002

Boardman, Mark – "Bullock: The True Story Behind the Deadwood Legend, *True West*, Cave Creek, Arizona; June 2019

Bradley, Mickey and Dan Gordon – *Field of Screams*, Globe Pequot Press, Guilford, CT, 2010

Chicago American
Chicago Tribune

Gardner, Renee – *Southern Arizona's Most Haunted* – Schiffer, Atglen, PA; 2010

Guiley, Rosemary Ellen – *Haunted Salem*, Stackpole Books, Mechanicsburg, PA; 2011

Kuhn, Laura – *Kings and Pawns*, Bourbon Orleans Hotel, New Orleans; 2012

Mayo, Matthew – *Haunted Old West*, Globe Pequot Press, Guilford, CT; 2012

Murphy, Michael – *Fear Dat*, Countryman Press, New York; 2015

Nashville Journal, Illinois

Norman, Michael and Beth Scott – *Haunted America*, Tor Books, New York; 1994

Ogden, Tom – *Haunted Chicago*, Globe Pequot Press, Guilford, CT; 2014

– *Haunted Hotels*, Globe Pequot Press, Guilford, CT; 2010

Okawville Times, Illinois

Owen, Craig – *Haunted by History*, Bizarre Los Angeles, Walnut, CA; 2017

Parker, Robert – *Haunted Louisville*, Whitechapel Press, Decatur, IL; 2007

Pisterman, Lisa – "Who is the Real "Lady in Blue" of the Seelbach Hotel?, *Leo Weekly*, Louisville, Kentucky; October 2018

Scales, Keith – *House of a Hundred Rooms*, 2017

Schaefer, Susan – *The Crescent Hotel*; 2015

Selzer, Adam – *The Ghosts of Chicago*, Llewellyn Publications, Woodbury, MN; 2017

Stieg, Warren – *Where Rheumatism Meets Its Waterloo*, Okawville, IL; 2003

Taylor, Troy – *Big Book of Illinois Ghost Stories*, Stackpole, Mechanicsburg, PA; 2009

– *Bloody Hollywood*, Whitechapel Press, Decatur, IL; 2008

– *Dead Men Do Tell Tales*, Whitechapel Press, Decatur, IL; 2008
– *Haunted New Orleans*, History Press, Charleston, SC, 2010

– *Haunting of America*, Whitechapel Press, Chicago, IL; 2010

– *Weird Chicago*, Whitechapel Press, Chicago, IL; 2009

– *Wicked New Orleans*, History Press, Charleston, SC; 2010

Whitmer, Jamie Davis and Robert Whitmer – *America's Most Haunted Hotels*, Llewellyn Publications, Woodbury, MN; 2016

Williams, Docia Schultz – *History and Mystery of the Menger Hotel*, Republic of Texas Press, Dallas, TX; 2000

Winer, Richard and Nancy Osborn – *Haunted Houses*, Bantam Books, New York; 1979

Witzel, Michael Karl – *Strange 66*, Voyageur Press, Quarto Publishing Group; 2018

And Personal Interviews and Correspondence

Special Thanks to:
April Slaughter: Cover Design and Artwork
Lois Taylor: Editing and Proofreading
Lisa Taylor Horton and Lux
Orrin Taylor
Rene Kruse
Rachael Horath
Elyse and Thomas Reihner
Bethany Horath
John Winterbauer

Kaylan Schardan
Maggie Walsh
Cody Beck
Becky Ray
Tom and Michelle Bonadurer
Susan Kelly and Amy Bouyear
And the entire crew of American Hauntings

ABOUT THE AUTHOR

Troy Taylor is the author of nearly 130 books on ghosts, hauntings, true crime, the unexplained, and the supernatural in America. He is also the founder of American Hauntings Ink, which offers books, ghost tours, events, and weekend excursions. He was born and raised in the Midwest and currently divides his time between Illinois and the far-flung reaches of America.

www.ingramcontent.com/pod-product-compliance
Lightning Source LLC
Chambersburg PA
CBHW062047080426
42734CB00012B/2577